Making a Difference

Sat. 5:00

Cambridge

① at Club
St is 1st left
Devon Downs
Trail last house
11770
stucco w/
green
shutters

4:45

Making a Difference

*Selected Writings
of Dorothy Watson*

edited by
Sandra Wilde

Heinemann
Portsmouth, NH

HEINEMANN
A division of Reed Elsevier Inc.
361 Hanover Street
Portsmouth, NH 03803-3912

Offices and agents throughout the world

Library of Congress Cataloging-in-Publication Data
Watson, Dorothy J. (Dorothy Jo)
  Making a difference : selected writings of Dorothy Watson / edited
    by Sandra Wilde.
      p. cm.
    Includes bibliographical references (p.   ).
    ISBN 0–435–08873–4
    1. Watson, Dorothy J. (Dorothy Jo).   2. Reading.
    3. Reading—Language experience approach.   4. Miscue analysis.
    I. Wilde, Sandra.   II. Title.
    LB1050.W365 1996   96-11839
    428.4–dc20   CIP

A portion of Dorothy Watson's royalties from this book are being donated to the Whole Language Umbrella.

A portion of Sandra Wilde's royalties are bing donated to Sitton Elementary School in the St. John's neighborhood of Portland, Oregon, to be used for books selected by a committee of teachers and children.

Editor: Toby Gordon
Cover Designer: Jenny Jensen Greenleaf
Manufacturing: Louise Richardson

Printed in the United States of America on acid-free paper.
00 99 98 97 96   DA   1 2 3 4 5

I've heard that by our fortieth year we have the faces we deserve. Not only has my fortieth birthday come and gone, but my fortieth year of teaching has also passed. I hope I deserve what I see in the mirror, for it is a face surrounded by dozens of other faces. This book is dedicated to all those friends, colleagues, and family who are reflected in the mirror, those who never fail to encourage, inform, and make me smile.

Dorothy Watson

Contents

Preface

In selecting work for this anthology from scores of published articles and book chapters, our guiding principle was to choose work that is of historical importance, that is central to Dorothy's body of work, that is not widely available, and/or that is of ongoing relevance to teachers. (Dorothy is also the author or coauthor of several books, and we have included the most important of these in a brief curriculum vitae.)

We have grouped the articles to reflect major themes, arranged roughly in the order of their emergence in Dorothy's writing; the articles within each section are arranged chronologically. Dorothy has written brief introductions to each article to place them in the context of her thinking today.

Minor changes from the form in which the articles were originally published represent corrections, clarifications, and the elimination of repetition.

For their help on this book, we would like to thank Jan Allen, at Portland State University, Helen Shaw at Colophon, and Toby Gordon, Alan Huisman, Mike Gibbons and his staff, Renée Le Verrier, and Melissa Inglis, at Heinemann.

Acknowledgments

Discovering myself as a learner and as a teacher has never been a matter of singular introspection; I've always depended on the conversations of others to bring my own thinking to light. The creation of this work is no exception.

My first acknowledgment must be to Sandra Wilde, who surprised me with the idea of this project in the first place and who continues to amaze me with her creative energy and thoughtful insights on everything from metaphors to auto mechanics.

My sincere thanks to inspired and inspiring teachers who may at one time have been my students but who are always and forever my teachers. I am grateful to remarkably generous colleagues who share their beliefs and their practices with me. Mid-Missouri TAWL (Teachers Applying Whole Language), the Whole Language Umbrella, and CELT (Center for Expansion of Language and Thinking) are the groups of educators that never fail to give me support whenever I need it and are kind enough to listen to my opinions and ideas.

Colleagues and friends in the College of Education at Mizzou, particularly those teachers of teachers in the Department of Curriculum and Instruction, have provided me with valuable critiques, questions, and encouragement. I am grateful for their influence on my inquiry.

A special thanks to Ruth Davenport, Nancy Browning, and Marilyn Richardson for their thoughtful suggestions, opinions, and sleuthing for very "seasoned" references. I also owe a debt of gratitude to Donna Hale and Beverly Vaughn for their unfailing patience and kindness to every student, faculty member, and greenhorn department chair who crossed the threshold of 212 Townsend Hall.

Finally, I must thank Marie Harper, who may have taught me more about teaching and learning than all others. Thanks, Mother, for a life filled with lessons about love.

Dorothy Watson

Making a Difference

Introduction

Dorothy Watson:
A Life of Teaching and Learning

In July 1995, Dorothy Watson and I sat down for an hour at the Whole Language Umbrella conference in Windsor, Ontario, and she talked with me about her life as a teacher, from her childhood days teaching neighborhood children after school to her current work with the Whole Language Umbrella. That interview is a fitting introduction to this book, since the writing that Dorothy has done over the years grows so much out of her personality and her history as a teacher.

Sandra Wilde

What led you to be a teacher, and what was your first year of teaching like?

From childhood, I knew I wanted to be a teacher. I would get the kids in the neighborhood rounded up and have "after-school school."

How old were you when you were doing that?

I think I started that in about fourth grade. This was during the Depression; nobody had any money. We didn't have anyplace much to play, so the kids, instead of being bored or getting into trouble, would come over for my brand of skill and drill. I'd give them pieces of paper and tell them what to write and draw. Could it be I invented worksheets?! We played school a lot, and I would never let anybody else be the teacher.

After I finished high school I went to a small Presbyterian liberal arts college, Park College, in Parkville, Missouri, on a scholarship.

They didn't have an elementary education department, so I majored in psychology. When I moved to Kansas City, teachers were scarce and I got a temporary certification. I substituted in all areas of Kansas City, and found that I loved teaching in the inner-city schools. I don't know why. I liked all the places I went, but there was something special about the inner-city kids.

That November I got an offer to teach in the Italian district in Kansas City, a combination fourth and fifth grade. At that time I thought a combination class was the worst thing that could happen. I remember walking into that classroom and finding that the desks were not bolted down but on sliders, so that you had to put them together in rows.

They could slide back and forth on tracks?

Yes. Nobody ever moved them, though. I remember deciding—I can't believe this, this was the first or second day of school—that I was going to move those things. But what I didn't realize was that you had to match up the seat of one with the top of another one on a different slider. The kids were moving those desks and it was bedlam. George climbed on top of a desk and shouted, "What were Tarzan's last wo-o-o-rds?" Then he jumped off the desk and wailed, "He-e-e-lp!" For some reason, it struck me funny. At that moment the principal walked into the room. Fortunately, she was wonderful, took it in stride. Her name was Marietta Hockaday. I knew she didn't like this, but she had a good sense of humor and was always supportive of young, inexperienced teachers. I was blessed with three great principals. I don't know what I would have done otherwise.

That first year I worked hard at keeping the fourth and fifth graders separated and all of their work separate. The second year Miss Hockaday was going to reward me by giving me the fifth grade, and I heard myself saying, "No, I wouldn't mind taking the split grade again."

I was at Gladstone School for three years. I loved the families there. I remember them, I remember the kids. It was a magical time for me, because I got to teach without being constrained by someone else's curriculum. I was also beginning to read things. I remember discovering John Dewey and talking about his work in a master's seminar with the dean of the education school in Kansas City, Hugh Spear, and a marvelous teacher named Gil Rees. It was a wonderfully enlightening time.

I was asked to go to Nelson School, the university's lab school. On my first day I saw a woman standing at the side door with a very big shaggy dog. The woman said, "Oh, Princess," patted the dog on the head, opened the door, and let the dog into the school. I thought,

Who is this person breaking the rules? I should report her. It was the principal, Mary Elizabeth Thomson.

Mary Liz was—and continues to be—influential in my life. She was the first school-based educator I knew who was genuinely child centered. She was an advocate for all children no matter their social or economic condition. Everything she did stemmed from what was best for the learner. She was a superlative mentor teacher. While I was at Nelson School I met another woman who became a lifelong friend. Lolly Haskell started the first school library in Kansas City. Mary Liz and Lolly to this day continue to be supporters of children and of education.

The last school I taught at in Kansas City was Garrison School. It was located between two government housing projects. Conrad Miner was the principal. I had taken a year's sabbatical leave to finish my master's program, and when I returned to the classroom I wanted it to be in the inner city. I learned a great deal at Garrison School; most important, I learned not to make assumptions about what kids were or were not capable of doing.

What was the population of that school like, what kinds of kids?

They lived in the housing projects, mostly white kids, but maybe about ten percent African American, all poor, but all bright! My first year there I taught sixth grade. There was a group of five rough boys in the class, all bigger than I was. The other kids were coming along fine, and we were doing great things and having fun. But these boys were just—they hated school, and, frankly, I didn't know what to do. So I told them that if they would stop disrupting the class, I would do something with the five of them every other Friday after school. They could decide what it was going to be, within reason.

The first place they wanted to go was a big ultramodern carwash. "Everything's up-to-date in Kansas City!" The carwash was a hit. We went twice, five boys crammed into my car. That was the year I had to give up my VW bug and get a bigger car.

The university student teacher supervisor was "intrigued" with our class because it was "very different." He said, "You're the first class I've seen that doesn't do traditional spelling lessons." One Friday the boys wanted to see where the supervisor lived, in a subdivision south of town. (The school was in the north part of town, by the river.) As we drove into this rather ritzy housing complex, Marvin McKenney said, "My God! Dr. C's projects are sure better than ours!" Right, Marvin, housing projects are not all the same!

This was the class that taught me about standardized tests. After the kids had taken the Metropolitan Reading Test, I said, "Okay, how did you do?" They groaned and agreed that it was bad. Bobby Evans, one of the group of five, said, "One of those questions didn't have the right answer." Then he went up to the board and wrote *project*. I said, "Oh well, that can be a verb or it can be a noun." And he said, "No, no, no. You don't understand. It's like they didn't have the *right* answer." And I said, "Well, like what?" He said, "Well, like we *live* in the projects." At the time, we were beginning to be concerned about the inequality of standardized tests for different cultural groups. That's the first time it hit home.

That school was a wonderful experience for me. I left Garrison to direct the Cooperative Urban Teacher Education program, in which undergraduates volunteered to student-teach in inner-city schools. After a year, I became the director of the Teacher Corps for the university and the Kansas City school district. That's when I met David Allen. Talk about changing your life around! Dave said, "Dorothy, you've got to get out of here. You're directing a program with a focus in reading education, and you don't believe in the things you're having the interns do." I kept saying, "Dave, I don't know what I believe." He said, "You have to go work with Brooks Smith and Ken Goodman." That's when I went to Wayne State.

And after you completed your doctorate, you went to the University of Missouri?

No, I first taught at the University of Houston in Victoria for three years. When Steryl Artley retired at Mizzou, he called Ken, who recommended me.

In terms of people you've read and people you've worked with, who have been the biggest influences? You've mentioned Dewey and Dave Allen and Ken Goodman. Anyone else that stands out?

Brooks Smith. His class in curriculum was eye-opening. When I was at Gladstone School, I kept thinking, There are very rich things happening in this neighborhood, but these kids need to see the rest of Kansas City. So I wrote a grant proposal, and got a few hundred dollars. We went all over Kansas City. One day I took the kids to a dress rehearsal at the Lyric Opera. They usually laughed and talked on the bus trip back from our jaunts, but this time they were absolutely quiet. John Madrid was sitting two seats in front of me. I said, "John, how'd it go?" He turned around in his seat, and he said, "Well, Mrs. Watson, I hate to tell you this, but I think we ain't ready for opera yet." Brooks Smith and the Gladstone kids taught me about valuing what we really are ready for.

Who else? Maxine Greene, Louise Rosenblatt, Yetta [Goodman].

Who would you tell teachers are the two or three most important people they should be reading?

It's hard to choose only three important educators. I just finished teaching a class in which we investigate whole language theory and theorists. The theorists we study vary somewhat from class to class, but some are always included. I feel so strongly that we need to understand John Dewey's theories that I present his work throughout the semester, tying it to the theories and assumptions of other researchers and educators. Experienced teachers who take this class find it important to study Lev Vygotsky, because his beliefs about the social nature of learning undergird learning experiences in whole language classrooms. This past semester, the students also studied Mikhail Bakhtin, Don Graves, Don Murray, Ralph Peterson, Yetta Goodman, and of course Frank Smith and Ken.

You do a lot of work with graduate students and teachers in the field. What are the principles that guide how you help them learn?

That we're both learners. I don't use the term *mentor*, there's something about it that's hierarchical. I don't use *novice/expert* either. I mean, who's the novice, who's the expert? It's just not the right metaphor for me. We're partners. Maybe it's selfish on my part, but I go into classrooms or workshops, any teaching situation, to learn. For example, the students in my undergraduate methods of teaching reading class become pen pals with Caroline Dye's first graders; it's a partnership. That has to be a guiding principle for everyone, that we're *all* going to come out of this learning.

Do you do that with your preservice classes too?

Absolutely. We focus on inquiry, and I tell them my own current inquiry question, whether it's short term or long term. I'm always working on one.

Give me an example.

One year my undergraduate students complained we were spending too much time on administrivia. So I said, I'm going to set up an inquiry. Let's institute an advisory committee in this class. How do we go about it? How do we make it effective? My inquiry is usually curricular. The topic is always one that nags at me, something I must find out about.

When you research something, do you read what other people have done or do you do action research?

Well, a lot of times I don't know of anyone who has formally grappled with the problem. I didn't know anybody who had tried an advisory committee, for example.

In the area of literacy, what do you think are the most important things that today's teachers need to know and do?

We need to know about the reading process. We need to let miscue analysis inform us. Many educators are still unaware of this important investigative tool. Even teachers who are doing very good things in their reading program are not sure why they are doing them. For example, we need to know why we invite students into literature study, why we use big books, why strategy lessons are a part of our program. We need to gather evidence through kidwatching (Yetta's term) and miscue analysis and use that information to direct and support our curriculum. But I need to be careful here. When my stance was "wholier than thou" (Ken's term), I said that teachers shouldn't "do activities" unless they knew all the theory behind them. I don't say that anymore. This may sound as if I'm contradicting what I said earlier, but I don't think I am. Doing something without knowing why may be a way to *begin* a whole language program, but it is only a way of getting started. For example, a teacher may see another teacher doing something exciting with her students, ask the teacher about the experience, and start doing it in his own classroom. That teacher has borrowed a practice and now must explore its effect on his students and on himself, must investigate the theoretical underpinnings. Many teachers enter whole language through the practice door, but the wise teachers know they can't stop there.

And what do you think teachers should be doing in the classroom?

They must put themselves as well as their students at its heart. It's not a matter of turning everything over to the kids; it's the partnership that's so powerful. Whole language teachers don't give up teaching in order to include students in the teaching-learning experience.

What are you working on now in terms of your thinking, your writing, your own growth?

The notion of community. Given my interest and the nature of the smart people I'm working with, the sense of community in my graduate classes evolves in all kinds of quirky, wonderful ways. But I haven't found that to be true with undergraduates.

You mean you have to work harder at it?

Yes. I work at things that you think you shouldn't have to work at, like talking with students. I make an effort to get to class ten minutes beforehand so I'm there when the early birds arrive. I make sure that nobody else is scheduled to use our classroom for thirty minutes after class is over, so that if students want to talk with each other or with me, they can. I try not to get uptight if the kids aren't smiling at me all the time or if I say something I think is really funny and they groan, "Oh, no!" Barbara Bell did a study on community in one of my classes and found that the kids thought I had a good sense of humor. I said, "What! Well, you'd never know it."

Anyway, I'm studying how you build community, especially in an undergraduate class. We're also redoing our undergraduate program, totally revamping it. We're trying to break down the barriers between the disciplines, do a true kind of integration. I'm not sure what that means yet or where it will lead us.

When you think back to the very beginning of your career in relation to where you are now, what's the same, what's different?

The students are very much the same. I started teaching in the mid-fifties, but I still think there are just so many gut things that are the same with learners. They're so creative and inventive and open—until we shut them down.

What's different is the explosion of knowledge related to literacy education, literacy learning. There were so many things we didn't understand when I started teaching. And I think that's true for math, art, music, and science, too. I hear myself saying, If I'd only known then what I know now. I have always been a learner, that's the thing that's kept me going, kept me from burning out. I have always begun every day knowing that I'm going to learn something.

Also, I have always had support groups. As a kid, I had the Girl Scouts, the bird-watchers club, the vegetable-garden club. Everything in my life was a "club." I felt a need to be with like-minded people.

I'm noticing your hand motions as you talk about this, a gathering-in gesture.

Exactly! We always had to gather in. It was the same with the family; we had the rituals, rites, and celebrations that Ralph Peterson talks about. Those are the things that have sustained me: knowing that there's always something new to learn today and that it's going to be fun. And then knowing that there are people who care so deeply about you and you for them. That's remarkable.

Is there anything else you'd like to talk about?

The Whole Language Umbrella, I suppose, because it has to do with the opportunity to learn and to be nourished and renewed by others.

Tell me about your role in getting it going.

Officially, we first met in 1989, but there was a lot of preliminary work before that. A group of people had met with Ken [Goodman] in

Tucson the summer before, fifteen teachers who drafted a constitution. They were educators from all over the United States and Canada. They asked me to be the first Whole Language Umbrella president. After talking by phone with all fifteen members of that planning group, I said I would do it. We just rolled up our sleeves. There were groups meeting all across North America, and one of our first intentions was to pull these groups together, to find out who we were. We had dozens of lists of whole language teachers that we sorted through. We got ten thousand dollars from the CEL group in Winnipeg. That was the seed money for WLU.

At that first Whole Language Umbrella conference in St. Louis, we could only accommodate two thousand people. We had to turn people away. This year [1995] at Windsor is the conference's sixth year. We know this is where we get renewed and where we build information. I want to work hard to continue the Whole Language Umbrella. We've got an excellent president, and we've got to support her in any way we can. We've got to nourish this organization that we've built. It's important in substantial and symbolic ways. WLU is our life-support line.

I was so pleased to hear that you're planning to donate your first year's royalties from this book to the Umbrella.

It's the least I could do to pay back all they've done for me and for the profession over the last several years. And I hope others will think about supporting the Umbrella by becoming individual members and through donations. Supporting the Whole Language Umbrella is an unparalleled investment in our future.

Part One

Miscue Analysis and Other Forms of Evaluation (1980–1992)

Miscues We Have Known and Loved

(with John C. Stansell)

John Stansell and I had a wonderful time deliberating dozens of miscues given to us by students, colleagues, and friends. We chose the ones in this piece for two reasons: they showed the reading process in action, and most of them made us laugh. If you accept our invitation to collect and study favorite miscues, you'll have fun rethinking the role that off-the-page information in union with the text has on readers who are constructing meaning. Have a good time with this one, and share your beloved miscues with your colleagues—that includes me! I've got some interesting ones I can send in return. For instance, five-year-old Monica read the following sign to her mom, who wanted to stop for a "fast cup of coffee" before continuing shopping:

Catch Coffee Quick
Cajun Cafe Grill

Considering the currently popular view that literacy is on the decline, probably no one would be surprised if a middle-aged woman in search of a powder room were to walk through a door clearly marked *Power*

Originally published in *Reading Psychology* 1 (1980), 127–32. Copyright 1980 by Taylor & Francis, Inc., Washington, DC. Reprinted with permission. All rights reserved.

Room. Indeed, such an incident might be accepted as another example of the sorry state of literacy in this country and cause feelings of real pity for the poor woman who was seemingly unable to discriminate between *powder* and *power*. It may also be seen as indicative of a need for greater emphasis on word-attack skills in school reading programs.

There may, however, be second thoughts upon discovering this incident actually occurred and the reader in question was the late Dr. Nila Banton Smith, former president of the International Reading Association, who delighted in telling this story on herself. Not wishing to question Dr. Smith's word-attack skills, one would perhaps be led to the question of why a proficient reader would perform as she did in this situation.

The miscues (Allen & Watson 1976) we have known and loved are those, like Dr. Smith's, that both raise this question and lead us to an answer. Occasionally startling and often amusing, these miscues allow us to see contributions of the reader to the understanding of written messages. Looking at them, we cannot doubt that comprehension of text is always at least partially a function of what the reader brings to it—prior knowledge, the organization of that knowledge, and, in Dr. Smith's case, expectations based on such knowledge.

The knowledge of the world and of language a reader brings to print is itself organized and further serves to organize and direct perception. Some theorists (Adams & Collins 1977; Anderson et al. 1977) have used the term *schema* to refer to organized human knowledge. A schema may be thought of as a network of interrelated concepts; for example, one's schema for *dog* may include such notions as *four-legged, tail, wet nose,* and *friendly*. We would expect a dog to have these attributes (and perhaps others as well) and would therefore tend to perceive any animal having these attributes as a dog. If we were to encounter a doglike creature— one that had perhaps some of the right attributes but not all of them, or one that had additional features that were not part of our schema—one of two things would probably result. We may create a new schema (or modify the existing one) to accommodate this new creature. Or we may "force" this creature to fit our existing schema, ignoring some of its characteristics. On the basis of our *existing* knowledge structure (schema), we would perceive it to be a dog.

This notion of schema is closely related to the concept of cognitive *scripts,* as described by Pearson and Nicholson (1976) and by theorists in the field of artificial intelligence. The term *script* refers to the organized information a computer must have in order to approximate human problem-solving behavior and, metaphorically, to the organized information human beings bring to bear upon such problems as making sense of print.

The miscue examples that follow illustrate how the various schemata or scripts that a reader may bring to the act of reading interact with those of the author. The internalized organization of prior knowledge of the world and of language (i.e., schema) enables a reader to predict what lies ahead in written messages, while relying on a relatively small amount of visual information (Goodman 1967; Smith 1978). If a reader's predictions can be confirmed—if they make sense and sound like language—then they become the message for that reader, even though it may be somewhat at odds with the message constructed by the author. These miscues, then, show us that for readers of all ages and backgrounds, comprehension is not a process of coming to know exactly what the author said, but one of constructing a message that reflects perhaps as much of their psycholinguistic background as the author's.

In the following examples we see the effect that developing, perhaps tentative, schemata have on readers.

An adult reader, having just completed a careful perusal of her Mutual of Omaha insurance policy, read from an education text "The teacher and the student had a mutual trust for each other" and remarked, "Oh, they have the same insurance company." A young reader who had not eaten for several hours and very clearly considered her next meal well overdue produced this response:[1]

$scamburger

Jack pulled the rifle out of his scabbard.

The power of hunger to influence a reader is shown again in the example below from another young reader whose lunch hour had been encroached upon:

breakfast was served

He knew the baskets would sell well at their summer camp.

Like an overdue lunch, a delayed recess can manifest itself in the oral reading of young children, as illustrated by the following:

play

Mr. Diaz said, "Miguel, will you help me before you go ^ outside?"

playtime was

. . . and his parents talked in English.

the recess

But she didn't relax, always being aware of her responsibility. . . .

---

[1] Substitution miscues written directly above the relevant text and the symbol $ used to designate a substitution that is not a real word. Omitted items are circled, and insertions (including inserted punctuation) are written above a caret (^).

An applicant for a teaching job encountered a shoe polish machine shortly before his interview and produced this response:

apples
Polish applied.

Four graduate students in reading encountered their friend in the lobby of a movie theater; the friend, who was the projectionist at the theater, was busily reading a book, and the students noted its title. On their way into the movie, one of the students remarked, "Why was Mike reading a book about reading?" Another answered, "I don't know; I noticed that too." After the film, they sought out their friend to ask him about his sudden interest in their chosen field. They then discovered that he had been reading a book in his own field, one entitled *Reeling.* And we have no doubt that the cinema student above could easily reveal his knowledge of moviemaking as he reads, just as the younger reader below showed her knowledge of a popular rock group, Gladys Knight and the Pips:

the Pips
King Arthur and his knights . . .

Some of the miscues that we know and love, like Dr. Smith's and the others above, serve to illustrate the influence of schemata linked to the reader's immediate situation upon the reading process. Others reveal the influence of schemata involving things less immediate but nonetheless powerful. An adult reader we know often reads *taxes* for *Texas* as April 15 approaches. In a town where a large toymaking firm has a plant, children produced this miscue:

Mattel
There are baseballs, bats, marionette dolls, and big balloons.

The next miscue comes from the South Texas ranch country, as might be expected.

Charolais
"Uncle Charles?" asked Mr. Miller. "No." "Then it must be Uncle
Angus
August."

Then there was the ardent Democrat who read the text below as follows, shortly after November elections:

Vice President, elect Mondale!
Vice President-Elect Mondale was the author of. . . .

A young reader showed his acquaintance with a particular beverage with the following miscue:

Las Cervezas
Juby is my oldest friend. He lives in Los Cordovas.

People can even reveal their vocations as they respond to print. During a recent controversy over the busing of school children, some households displayed signs in their windows to protest the decision to bus their children. A priest couldn't understand why so many people had signs up that said, "This family will not be blessed."

Another South Texas reader revealed his culinary knowledge with the miscue below.

Sancho stood beside the table and watched Rosita mix cornmeal for
tamales
tortillas.

In South Texas, people use cornmeal for tamales and *masa harina* for tortillas; almost no one uses cornmeal for tortillas, as they may do elsewhere.

Other miscues reveal concern for persistent problems people must live with. The adult reader below had the fuel crisis on her mind when she read:

coveted
Texas gas is converted. . . .

One persuasive and powerful force in any individual's life that shows up often in reading is an organizing schema for one's first language or dialect. When American adults read a short story written by a British author, involving characters who speak British English, no one is surprised to see them translate the printed dialect to more familiar American forms, as shown below:

headlights
I switched off the headlamps of the car . . .

minute
Stop. Wait a moment, Timber.

Nor is anyone likely to be too upset when teenagers, reading the same story, do some translating into their own terms, as this college freshman did:

I carried the ice pack to the bedroom and laid it across Harry's fore-
your
head. "Keep you cool."

Sometimes, however, there is concern when young readers produce language forms that differ from what may be called, broadly,

Standard English, as the following readers did.

"I haven't been bitten," he whispered.

sheeps
The sheep were in the bedding ground.

sung
He was no longer shy as he sang his song.

throwed
He threw the ball to third base.

he
The baby ^ said some new words.

was
He stopped as if he were frozen.

The point these miscues help us make is that all these readers, whose responses to print show the influence of their dialects, are doing good things. Their preferred language schemata lead them to generate meaningful predictions and they are processing print for sense rather than for the sake of oral accuracy.

Another more general point to be made about the miscues we have thus far presented is they come from readers of all ages and thereby suggest that the influence of schemata in reading (i.e., the constructive nature of comprehension) is independent of age or educational attainment; thus if we can be amused by what happened to Dr. Smith and to other adults, then there is no cause for alarm when young readers do the same things.

It should also be mentioned that readers reflect the influence of their background knowledge when they engage in retelling a selection. This influence may be manifested in a number of ways: through addition of information not given in the story, reordering of the sequence of events described by the author, omission of events regarded as impossible or irrelevant, or, more generally, producing an interpretation that reflects the reader's personal knowledge of the world.

Recently a proficient ninth-grade reader retold a story set in Colonial India with two Englishmen and a Hindu physician as major characters. Her retelling described "these two frontiersmen" living in a "log cabin" (referred to in the text as a "bungalow"), and their experience with the "tribal witch doctor." Rather than deciding this reader is not very proficient, we would suggest that her knowledge of Colonial India is not extensive while her knowledge of frontier America is, and her understanding of the story occurs as a function of this knowledge.

Paying attention to retellings is important in two ways: first, the retelling a reader gives can often confirm indications of the influence of reader schemata that surface during reading as miscues; second, it is not always possible to observe miscues (e.g., when the reader is engaged in silent reading) and in such situations a retelling may be the only available source of data.

Finally, we would like to point out we are not indiscriminate lovers of miscues. There are those we have known but not loved, and they are the ones that show the unfortunate effects of instruction that focuses a reader's attention almost exclusively on fragments of language (i.e., letters and words) and neglects meaning structures produced by author and reader. In such instruction, the reader's goal is to rigorously reconstruct an author's message. It is believed that a precise reconstruction can be achieved only if the reader is willing and able to attempt an exact oral rendition of print, even though making such an attempt disregards the role of the reader's previously acquired and organized knowledge in reading and results in a high tolerance for nonsense. A final set of examples will suffice to show how a young reader's instruction-based schema for reading is manifested in his strong concern for total accuracy, reflected in the graphophonemic similarity between miscues and text words, and which causes him to greatly corrupt meaning.

> *$genly*
> *$gerly*
> *gen + ly he cried*
> *g-g-grn cried*
> . . . untied the dogcart that generally carried loads of wood. . . .

>   *pound*   *though*
> "Not grandfather's precious ax, that he was so proud of," thought
> *Summer*
> Suzanne.

>   *$conted*
>   *cont-t-t*
>   *con-ten*
> Rain could not wash him away and he was contented.

>   *horses*
>   *horse*   *of*
> These he made in blocks for building houses and roads.

>   *$discomfortaly*   *cities*
> Men were shouting directions to his father and the cries of many
> *gales of ice through his nose*
> gulls added to the noise.

Many readers, both old and young, share this youngster's apparent conviction that reading requires an accurate rendition of all the author's words in order to reconstruct precisely the author's exact meaning (Harste & Burke 1977; Stansell, Harste & De Santi 1978). These readers need to discover that only when they make use of their own organized knowledge in reading can they expect to make sense of print and that the sense they make—the message they construct— must necessarily reflect their knowledge as well as that of the author.

References

Adams, Marilyn J. & Collins, Allen. 1977. *A schema-theoretic view of reading* (Technical Report No. 32). Urbana, IL: Center for the Study of Reading.

Allen, P. David & Watson, Dorothy (Eds.). 1976. *Findings of research in miscue analysis*. Urbana, IL: National Council of Teachers of English.

Anderson, Richard C., Reynolds, R. E., Schallert, Diane L. & Goetz, E. T. 1977. Frameworks for comprehending discourse. *American Educational Research Journal, 14,* 367–81.

Goodman, Kenneth S. 1967. Reading: A psycholinguistic guessing game. *Journal of the Reading Specialist, 6,* 126–35.

Harste, Jerome & Burke, Carolyn. 1977. A new hypothesis for reading teacher research: Both the *teaching* and *learning* of reading are theoretically based. In P. David Pearson (Ed.), *Reading: Theory, research, and practice* (Twenty-sixth yearbook of the National Reading Conference), pp. 32–40. Clemson, SC: National Reading Conference.

Pearson, P. David & Nicholson, Tom. 1976, December. *Scripts, texts, and questions*. Paper presented at the annual meeting of the National Reading Conference, Atlanta.

Smith, Frank. 1978. *Understanding reading: A psycholinguistic analysis of reading and learning to read* (2nd ed.). New York: Holt, Rinehart & Winston.

Stansell, John C., Harste, Jerome C. & de Santi, R. J. 1978. The effect of differing materials on the reading process. In P. David Pearson (Ed.), *Reading: Disciplined inquiry in process and practice* (Twenty-seventh yearbook of the National Reading Conference), pp. 27–35. Clemson, SC: National Reading Conference.

Watching and Listening to Children Read

I wish this piece were titled "Kidwatching, Miscue Analysis, and Several Other Assessment Strategies That Give Information About Students' Reading—Along with a Few Experiences That Help Readers." Admittedly, that's a rather long title, but it's closer to the content of the chapter than the original one. I hope this article will help renew belief in the power of the informed teacher's observations, especially since, for example, eighth graders and their parents are still told things like "John is reading on a third-grade level."

In late September, a nine-year-old friend dropped by for a chat. Our conversation drifted to school work and, predictably, I asked Janey what she was reading. After telling me about the books she was reading at home, including ones she had written herself, she volunteered, "But I guess you want to know what I'm reading at school. You know," she continued with all the assurance gained from four years and four weeks of schooling, "we can't really read until we finish our tests. After that we can get into our groups; we can go to the library then, too. After the tests." Janey explained that all this made perfectly good sense because "the teacher doesn't know how we read until the scores come back." I stifled a rebuttal and pinned Janey's two-page story on my bulletin board.

The purpose of this article is to help teachers use observations rather than formal testing to find out (from the first day of school to the last)

Originally published in *Observing the Language Learner,* edited by Angela Jaggar and Trika Smith-Burke (Urbana, IL & Newark, DL: National Council of Teachers of English & International Reading Association, 1985, pp. 115–28). Reprinted with permission.

how their students handle text in a variety of forms and in a variety of situations. By using information gained from these observations, teachers not only have reliable data for assessment but have a realistic base on which to plan curriculum and instructional procedures. But before turning to the what, when, and how of observing students, teachers need to consider what they believe about language and how children learn language; that is, they need to be aware of their own theoretical position concerning the reading process. When beliefs are clear, teachers have a better understanding about their expectations of readers, as well as a guide for making instructional decisions.

A View of Reading

The suggestions in this article are consistent with a view of reading that holds to the idea that readers construct meaning as they bring information that is already in their heads to the messages authors have encoded in text. The information readers use has many dimensions, including background experiences, knowledge of language, expectations about the text, perceptions of themselves as readers, and information gained from everyone and everything in the context of the situation in which they are reading. The works of Goodman (1982), Smith (1978), and Rosenblatt (1978) support the view that reading is a transactive process that involves both the potential of the reader and the potential of the text. For example, when proficient readers are presented with interesting, well-written text, they look like what they are—good readers reading good discourse. If these same readers are presented text that is unpredictable, lacks cohesion, is conceptually inappropriate, and holds no interest, the students will appear to be poor readers—their potential diminished by poor text. Readers who do not have requisite background knowledge or appropriate linguistic experiences may cause a well-written text to appear poorly composed. When we observe changes in students' behavior as they meet different texts, we must be aware of both text and reader potential and look for the dimensions of influence each has on the other. A transactional view of reading forces us to become textwatchers as well as kidwatchers.

Watching the Reader: When to Observe

This text-contributing/child-contributing view of reading demands that we observe the reader before reading, while reading, and after reading (Robinson 1980). Let's consider how each phase is important.

Before the book is opened, students have experienced life and language and they have formed opinions of themselves as learners and readers. They have also formed opinions about the content and the format of the text they are to read. Proficient readers use appropriate information from their own background knowledge, as well as signals from the context of situation (setting, participants, purpose) to anticipate meaning (Halliday 1978). Proficient readers expect to find certain kinds of messages couched in certain forms depending on the circumstances. Math books, Judy Blume stories, cereal boxes, and public bathroom walls signal specific concepts, language, and conventions. Good readers know this and use such knowledge to construct meaning, even before their eyes are on the print.

Teachers can get an idea about children's willingness to bring their own off-the-page information to the reading act by asking students what they expect to find in different texts: a warranty for a toy, instructions for a video game, a gum wrapper, *Time* magazine, the science book. The specific information children have in their heads (before reading a particular text) can be tapped by the teacher's invitation: tell me everything you know about the subject. For example, before inviting her students to read a biography of Benjamin Franklin (Fritz 1976), one fifth-grade teacher asked her students to tell everything they knew about Franklin. The children offered information in many forms (words, phrases, titles, even a picture of a kite). The teacher listed all contributions, accurate and inaccurate, on the board. She asked the students to look for patterns, ways to categorize the information. Labels emerged for some categories, and questions arose about the accuracy of some of the information. The teacher used the students' responses to assess how much background information they had or were willing to present to the class that would aid in reading the text. More personal comments about the activity were revealing: "If it's like the story of Samuel Adams, it will be great!" "I have trouble reading anything in that book. Can I work with Ned?" This before-the-book-is-opened activity provides information on which to make decisions about classroom organization and reveals students' judgments of their own abilities to handle the assignment. By listening to children the teacher can immediately encourage some students to begin reading with no further delay, and can invite other children to read a conceptually related but far "friendlier" text or suggest that reading partners join efforts or that a child pursue another activity that is of equal or perhaps more worth.

While reading, proficient readers use both off-the-page information (prior experiences and situational circumstances) and on-the-page information to direct their strategies—sampling print, predicting

emerging structures and meanings, confirming or rejecting their predictions, correcting if necessary, and constructing meaning. By observing Jonathan and Leroy as they were reading silently, a second-grade
teacher learned a great deal about their strategies for comprehending
text. When Jonathan didn't know a word, he interrupted his friend to
ask the pronunciation. Leroy, on the other hand, made pencil marks
in the margin of his book when he came to something he didn't know,
but always continued to read. Leroy knew he would probably be able
to figure out meanings on his own as he gathered more information
from the author. Observing these two boys, the teacher made a point
of helping Jonathan find more productive and self-reliant strategies in
order to construct meaning, and she made a point of asking Leroy if
his strategy was paying off and of encouraging him to continue its use
if it proved helpful.

Following reading, students have options. They can share their
new information and feelings with others; they can use the new experience as a basis for further readings; they can store the experience
for later use; or they can never consciously consider the information
again. After Donald, a third grader, read a story from *In the Magic Listening Cap* (Uchida 1955), he combined an episode in "Three Tests for
a Prince" with his abiding interest in the movie *Raiders of the Lost Ark*
and wrote the following in his journal:

> Indiana Jones was a holot worst off than the prince. Indiana didn't
> have a beautful blue scarv to wave over his head three times to make
> the snakes disapear. Indiana had to use his branes to get away from
> the terible snakes. The prinse had the scarf to help him get away
> from the crul and shelfish king.
>
> > Goodluck Indiana!!!!

By watching Donald's after-the-book-is-closed activity it was not difficult to see that this reader/writer enjoyed and understood "Three
Tests for a Prince"; no need for a quiz or book report. By comparing
his new journal story with earlier attempts, both Donald and his
teacher agreed that he was developing a real knack for writing very
good beginnings and endings—they caught the reader's interest. They
also saw that Donald was taking more risks with spelling; his attempts
always made sense, and his spelling was moving slowly but surely toward more and more standard forms. But most important of all, they
found that Donald wanted to continue working on this piece, possibly comparing the prince's other tests with more of Indiana Jones's
adventures. Donald's next book was in the making!

Watching Readers: What to Look For

The transactional view of reading helps us know what to look for as we observe children interacting with texts. We must focus our attention on certain aspects of readers' behaviors and texts, but at the same time we should be flexible about what we observe. Here are some possible questions to consider when watching readers.

Concepts About Print and Print Settings

1. To what extent does the student attend to print? For example, does the student focus on the print as someone else is reading?

2. How does the student handle books? For example, does the student hold the book right side up, turn pages one at a time, and point to the place where one should begin reading?

3. Does the student expect the print to make sense and have personal meaning? For example, does the student seek out text that will satisfy her need for information about feeding hamsters?

4. How does the student use information from the print setting (e.g., where the print is found, its format, who asked that it be read, why it is being read)?

Use of Background Knowledge

1. How does the reader bring background knowledge and linguistic information to the reading situation?

2. How does the reader approach text? Is there an effort made to appreciate and live the written experiences by relating the text to his own life?

3. How does the reader use memory as a reading aid? For example, when asked to read a familiar song, riddle, or self-authored story, does the reader use memory (i.e., familiarity with the material) as a basis for predicting and making inferences?

Use of Strategies

1. How does the student handle the information-giving systems of language? Does the reader use a flexible strategy that encompasses all language cues (i.e., semantic, grammatical, sound/symbol) to construct meaning or does the reader rely on a single cueing system (e.g., sound/symbol)?

2. Does the reader proficiently sample, predict, and construct meaning from text?
3. Does the student monitor her reading by asking, "Am I making sense of what I am reading?"
4. Does the reader self-correct when the flow of language and meaning are interrupted?
5. Is there a dialect or first-language influence on the student's reading and how does the student handle this influence?
6. What strategies does the reader use to approach suitable but unfamiliar text?

View of Self as Reader

1. What does the student think of himself as a reader?
2. In what circumstances and how often does the student make the decision to read?
3. What risks are taken by the student as she reads?
4. How realistic is the student's judgment of his knowledge of concepts and discourse forms needed to read various texts (e.g., science or history materials, poems, or drama)?

The answers to these questions will provide information that is immediately applicable in building a reading program. However, if long lists bore you, perhaps Smith's advice (1973) will give you ample guidance: "Find out what a child is trying to do and then help him do it" (p.195). Good kidwatchers make it a point to see the student's strengths first. This does not mean that problems are ignored. It simply indicates that teachers need to build their reading programs on what students are doing right, not on what they are doing wrong.

Informal Kidwatching: Observing Spontaneous Activities

Kidwatching is an ongoing process that begins the minute children enter the classroom and continues throughout the day. It involves informal assessment of student use of language in real situations. Let's look at what happened in a first grade on the first day of school:

The teacher welcomes the children as they enter the room and invites them to sit with her to chat and get better acquainted. On the board there is a nametag for every child. Within three minutes, Robin notices his nametag and points it out to the group. The teacher asks if others can find their names. Almost immediately Mary, Jimmy, and Rose find their tags. As the names are removed from the board, Mike, Peggy, and Marty feel more confident and find their tags. Ricky chooses Robert's tag and the teacher praises Ricky for making a good guess and urges him to try again. Ricky is hesitant, and the teacher asks the class to read aloud with her the remaining names. As the children read their names they get their tags. The teacher talks with the children about why they have nametags and then she asks each child to stand and read his or her tag to the other children. She asks every child to read one other nametag of someone they know, and then she asks if anyone wants to read the nametag of someone they don't know. Robin, Jimmy, Mary, and Marty read two names each. Steve reads his name and the nametags of the two other Steves in class.

The teacher tells the children that she has written each of them a letter; they discuss their experiences with receiving letters and what might be in their teacher's letter to them. Clara and Jimmy tell about the letters and cards they get from their grandmother. Bill, Joe, and Ricky say they have never gotten a letter, but their parents have.

The children go by twos to the mailboxes and locate their letters by finding their names under their boxes. Most of the children find their names immediately, a few get help from their partners. Six children, including Joe, Nancy, and Bill, read the remaining names with the teacher in order to find their letters.

Again the children discuss what they might find in their teacher's letter to them. Several children say that the letter will begin with "Dear _____" and end with "I love you." The children open their letters; all of them hold the paper right side up and read, "Dear _____. " Rose slowly reads aloud the entire letter with support from Marty and Gwen. As Rose reads, Clara and Carol begin to mumble along, pointing to the print. Delbert announces that he can't read and his teacher recommends that he pretend to read. Joe makes a telescope of his paper and peeps at Nancy, who discovers that letters make dandy fans. However, both Nancy and Joe tell what was in their teacher's letter after it is read aloud. The teacher and the children read the letter, which has been copied on a large piece of chart paper. Children wearing blue read it, and volunteers read it. Rose, Mike, and Robin read the letter as a trio, Robin looking at the print and Mike and Rose looking at their audiences.

The teacher then invites the children to write a letter to her. They discuss what they might write about, discuss not being able to write (pretending is okay), choose either lined or unlined "stationery," and begin to write their letters by using scribbles, pictures, letters, words, sentences, and always—meaning. The teacher becomes a "talking sec-

retary" for Nancy, Robert, Janis, Becky, and Delbert. More than half
the children read their letters to either their partner or their teacher.

The teacher watched and listened, and learned that three of her students could read unfamiliar predictable print (Rhodes 1981). She
found out that her students knew a great deal about the functions of
a letter (e.g., it tells you something about what's happening and asks
questions), and the form of a letter (e.g., it begins with Dear——
and ends with I love you). She discovered that all the students could
reply to a letter. Some wanted to dictate their messages and have her
write, while others scribbled, drew, and used some standard lettering
to create their messages. She learned that Janice, Becky, and Delbert
needed a great deal of encouragement, support, and confidence building. As the teacher was learning about her students on this first morning, the twenty-five first graders were finding out something about
themselves—they could read and write, and, in the words of one six-
year-old, "that is what I came to school to do."

Within the first few days of school, teachers can learn about their
students' reading behavior by inviting them to (1) listen to stories and
predict ideas, sentences, and words; (2) read the repetitive phrases or
last lines of stories (e.g.,"and Drummer Hoff fired it off") written on
the board or read from an oversized big book (Holdaway 1979); (3)
read silently something of their own choosing; (4) read notes that arrive from the nurse or principal and compose a reply; (5) read their
own and group compositions; and (6) read signs and notices around
the school and neighborhood.

More Formal Observational Techniques

In most cases, informal observation and listening results in solid information on which to build a reading program. More-formal techniques, however, help us confirm hypotheses.

The Burke Reading Interview (1980) provides data for understanding how students perceive reading and themselves as readers.
This straightforward interview takes about five minutes to administer
and consists of the following questions that can be modified depending on the students:

1. When you are reading and you come to something you don't
   know, what do you do? Do you ever do anything else?
2. Who is a good reader?
3. Why is _____ a good reader?

4. Do you think _____ ever comes to something s/he doesn't know when s/he is reading?

5. If _____ did come to something s/he didn't know, what would s/he do?

6. If you knew that someone was having trouble reading, how would you help that person?

7. How would a teacher help that person?

8. How did you learn to read?

9. What would you like to do better as a reader?

10. Do you think you are a good reader?

From the answers to these few questions a teacher can determine a student's personal model of reading. Students reveal in their answers what they believe reading is all about ("sounding out syllables," "knowing the words," "getting meaning") and how they think reading should be taught ("learn the sounds of the letters," "learn every word and get them right," "understand what you know and what the author knows"). Such information lets the teacher know if the child's personal model of reading is consistent with the teacher's and provides a realistic basis on which to develop appropriate reading strategies.

Another technique that can help the teacher is miscue analysis (Goodman & Burke 1972), an investigation into how students handle the information cueing systems of language (semantic, syntactic, graphic, and phonemic) as well as how they use information in their heads and in the text to construct meaning. For example, Mike's miscues are marked on the story below. (Substitutions are written above the text, omissions circled, insertions marked with a caret (^), repetitions underlined and marked ®, corrections underlined and marked ©, and pauses longer than five seconds marked with a large *P*).

Arnie's
_An-_
Andre's Secret

P (Splash!)

Arnie   © *when*   © *ov-*
Before Andre knew | what was happening, his boat (had) turned | upside

                                                              slipped
down. The big load of wood he had worked so hard to cut (had) spilled

© *out of*   _Andy_
into the water all around him. Frightened, Andre cried out for help.

              worried about   *hearing*
At the same time he wondered if anyone (could hear) him.

It might appear that Mike is a poor reader who needs more word-attack skills. However, from a transactional perspective Mike is using the cueing systems of language to sample, predict, correct, and construct meaning. His miscues are high-level ones that help him maintain consistent meaning. Let's consider Mike's reading.

1. Substitution of *Arnie* and *Andy* for *Andre.*
   Mike is unfamiliar with the name *Andre* and attempts to make a reasonable substitution. When he decides on Andy he stays with it for the remainder of the story.

2. Omission of *Splash!*
   Mike is not willing to take a risk without more redundancy in the text. He might be urged to fill in the omission after reading further. This omission did not detract from the story. Also, in Mike's retelling (below) he says, "Andy splashed into the water."

3. The omission of *had,* the substitution of *slipped* for *spilled,* and the substitution of *worried about anyone hearing* for *wondered if anyone could hear.*
   These miscues show Mike's attention to grammatical, semantic, and graphic cues.

4. The correction of *when* for *what, ov-* (over) for *upside down, out of* for *into.*
   These miscues show Mike's ability to correct in order to gain grammatical acceptability.

After reading the entire story Mike was asked to tell everything he could remember. He began with:

> Well, that was a good story because Andy found his granddad's ax. But it started out bad when Arnie put too much wood in a little boat and, well, it turned over and Andy splashed into the water and he was scared that no one would hear him yellin'. He was also froze when they pulled him out.

Even from this small portion of Mike's retelling it is apparent that he was monitoring for meaning. Although he made many miscues, they did not disrupt the reading process. Mike constructed meaning, and he expressed that meaning in the retelling—using his own preferred language.

Miscue analysis may be carried out in a formal manner by tape-recording a student's reading, marking the miscues as above, and coding the information (see Goodman & Burke 1972). It can also be done informally as teachers listen to children read different material. Children can be instructed to make note of their own miscues and discuss them later with the teacher or the class (Watson 1978). Once teachers add miscue analysis to their assessment procedures, they never again listen to children read in the same way. Miscue analysis helps teachers look at what children are doing "right" while becoming aware of their problems in reading.

Another technique for gathering information in a natural setting is ERRQ (Estimate, Read, Respond, and Question). ERRQ combines the retelling procedure of miscue analysis with the questioning procedure of ReQuest developed by Manzo (1968, 1969). The technique can be used with student and teacher, student partners, and in small and large groups. The basic procedure is this:

Estimate: The student quickly looks over the text and estimates the amount of text she can read with understanding. This estimate should be based on the student's background experience with the concepts involved, the author's organizing structure and style, as well as the student's past successes or failures with similar discourse. After the student estimates how far she can read with understanding, she pencils in a ✓ in the margin.

Read: The student reads aloud or silently. In rare instances the teacher and the student may read together. Usually the teacher decides how the reading is to be done, but the student might make this decision.

Respond: The student responds both by giving her reaction to the message and by retelling the text.

Question: The student asks the teacher one or more questions followed by the teacher asking the student one or more questions about the selection read.

The ERRQ procedure can be followed step by step, or it may be modified by the teacher or the readers. For example, readers may estimate a "reading distance," discover that they are monitoring for meaning, and decide to read farther before responding. On the other hand, readers may overestimate and decide to respond before the full distance is reached. In either case, students have the opportunity to gain control, to have a say about their own reading. Once readers make an estimation, they seldom ignore their commitment. Another modification involves the questioning procedure. Although students always are encouraged to ask a question, it may not always be productive for the teacher to ask a question.

The ERRQ procedure provides a format for students to reveal their ability to size up a passage, judge their own proficiency, talk about themselves as readers of a particular passage, read silently and aloud, explore their own minds and the mind of the author in order to respond to the text, and finally, to develop their own ideas and seek further information through questioning.

Summary

No two snowflakes, popcorn kernels, or children are exactly alike. Therefore, to watch, enjoy, and describe snowflakes, popcorn kernels, and kids, we need a variety of devices that can be used flexibly and, in the case of snowflakes and kids, fast! Standardized measurements for nonstandardized kids fall short of helping teachers watch, enjoy, and describe. Scores don't sharpen our vision or insight. They don't bring a smile or knowing nod. A score of 3.2 doesn't begin to describe a child's ability to use language.

Classroom observation offers a natural, positive, and professional way of gathering information about the reading process. Kidwatching teachers believe that curriculum must be based on the strengths of children, that making a mistake is not the end but rather an indication of what readers are trying to do. These teachers continue to broaden their own knowledge about language, about learning, and about the reading process. They do this because they realize it will help them know better what to look for when they observe children. The techniques suggested in this article are only a few methods that allow teachers to discover their students' proficiencies and problems while encouraging the natural process of learning to read.

References

Fritz, Jean. 1976. *What's the big idea, Ben Franklin?* New York: Coward, McCann & Geoghegan.

Goodman, Kenneth S. 1982. *Language and literacy: The selected writings of Kenneth S. Goodman* (Vol. 1). Boston: Routledge & Kegan Paul.

Goodman, Yetta M. & Burke, Carolyn L. 1972. *Reading Miscue Inventory manual: Procedures for diagnosis and evaluation.* New York: Macmillan.

Halliday, M. A. K. 1978. *Language as social semiotic: The social interpretation of language and meaning.* Baltimore: University Park Press.

Harste, Jerome & Burke, Carolyn L. 1980. Understanding the hypothesis: It's the teacher that makes the difference. In B. P. Farr & D. J. Strickler (Eds.), *Reading comprehension: Resource guide* (pp. 111–24). Bloomington, IN: School of Education, Indiana University.

Holdaway, Don. 1979. *The foundations of literacy*. New York: Scholastic.

Manzo, Anthony V. 1968. Improving reading comprehension through reciprocal questioning (Doctoral dissertation, Syracuse University, 1969). *Dissertation Abstracts International, 30*, 5344A.

Manzo, Anthony V. 1969. The ReQuest procedure. *Journal of Reading, 13*, 123–36, 163.

Rhodes, Lynn K. 1981. I can read! Predictable books as resources for reading and writing instruction. *The Reading Teacher, 34*, 511–18.

Robinson, H. A. 1980, February. *Reading and writing strategies throughout the curriculum*. Paper presented at the Annual Conference on Reading, University of Missouri at Columbia.

Rosenblatt, Louise. 1978. *The reader, the text, the poem: The transactional theory of the literary work*. Carbondale, IL: Southern Illinois University Press.

Smith, Frank. 1973. Twelve easy ways to make reading hard. In Frank Smith (Ed.), *Psycholinguistics and reading*. New York: Holt, Rinehart & Winston.

Smith, Frank. 1978. *Understanding reading: A psycholinguistic analysis of reading and learning to read* (2nd ed.). New York: Holt, Rinehart & Winston.

Uchida, Y. 1955. *In the magic listening cap: More folktales from Japan*. New York: Harcourt Brace Jovanovich.

Watson, Dorothy J. 1978. Reader selected miscues: Getting more from sustained silent reading. *English Education, 10*, 75–85.

Miscue Analysis for Teachers
(with Janice Henson)

*Here is a refresher on miscue analysis procedure, from the selection
of the student to the application of the information. We hope it will
remind you of the sort of reading research that provides important
and usable information about the reading process, about the
reader, and about the reading program. For me, the heart of this
piece is in the stories Janice Henson tells about Tim, Jimmy, and
other readers. Through her use of miscue analysis, this caring
teacher discovers her students' giftedness*

Ted has me puzzled. He's in the fourth grade and can't even read a
first-grade book. He's been tested and tested—the ITBS, an IRI, the
state test—but the scores don't tell me much. I am desperate and
ready for suggestions anyone has to offer.

To educators who have voiced similar concerns, we suggest a form of
whole language evaluation that includes its most formal technique—
reading miscue analysis.

In this chapter, we offer a rationale for the use of miscue analysis,
tell a bit about the background of the instrument, present one form of
the Reading Miscue Inventory (RMI), and perhaps most important,

Adapted from *Assessment and Evaluation for Student Centered Learning*, (2nd ed.), edited
by Bill Harp (Norwood, MA: Christopher-Gordon), pp. 67–96, where it appeared under the title "Reading Evaluation—Miscue Analysis" in a substantially different and
expanded form.

show how miscue analysis can lead to specific strategies within a whole language curriculum.

Why Are They Called Miscues?

The term *miscue* is used in billiards when the cue stick slips off the ball; in the theater it refers to an actor's answering a wrong cue or missing one. Ken Goodman saw some parallels to reading and made use of the term in his 1964 research and later in 1973 when he developed the Goodman taxonomy of reading miscues (Goodman 1982). Goodman rejected the idea that teachers can really understand reading by looking at paper-and-pencil test scores, so he proposed an interesting alternative. He asked children to read aloud a story that they had never read before and then to tell what they remembered of it. As students read, they deviated from the text; Goodman called these unexpected responses "miscues." It's important that he didn't call them errors or mistakes; to do so would have meant that the reader was totally responsible (if not guilty) for the deviation. As Goodman investigated children's miscues, he realized that the miscues were not equal in terms of how they changed the text. In fact, some miscues didn't cause any change in meaning or in syntax, while others destroyed both.

What Can Reading Miscue Analysis Do for the Teacher?

Ted's teacher presents a problem that we feel only miscue analysis as part of whole language evaluation can address. It can help in at least three ways.

First, miscue analysis provides information about language and about the reading process. Without such information, Ted's teacher is vulnerable: "I'm desperate and ready for suggestions anyone has to offer." The feeling of desperation may stem from her feeling that she doesn't know much about the reading process or about the role of linguistic knowledge in readers' construction of meaning. With information about the natural reading strategies of sampling from text and from background experience, predicting what is coming up in the text, confirming when the reading makes sense and sounds okay, and integrating new information with old, the teacher can knowledgeably study Ted's reading. She can also evaluate materials and methods of reading instruction and make decisions consistent with solid information about how language and the reading process work together.

Second, miscue analysis provides information about Ted's reading as it is going on, his beliefs about reading and reading instruction, and his comprehension. Through marking and coding the reading, teachers can judge the proficiency and efficiency with which readers are handling text. The Burke reading interview, and reflection on reading (self-evaluation) are two parts of the inventory that let the teacher in on what students think about (1) themselves as readers, (2) reading instruction, and (3) their performance on the material they have just read. The student's retelling reflects the reader's comprehension of the text.

Third, miscue analysis enables the teacher to create a curriculum where students' strengths are valued and used while their needs are clearly addressed. Miscue analysis points the way to strategies and suggests materials that will help students become more proficient readers.

Alternative Ways to Conduct Miscue Analysis

Over the years, many educators helped themselves to Kenneth Goodman's work, adapting it to their own settings. In 1987, Yetta Goodman, Carolyn Burke, and Dorothy Watson built on Goodman and Burke's original *Reading Miscue Inventory* (1972) in order to provide four different miscue analysis procedures. Their work, *Reading Miscue Inventory: Alternative Procedures* (1987), is the basis for the suggestions given in this article.

There are four miscue analysis procedures. Procedure III is introduced in this chapter. Procedure I is the most complex and time-consuming option; it offers intensive information about a reader's individual miscues in relationship to all other miscues. Procedure I is recommended for teacher education courses in which there is a focus on miscue analysis and for some research studies. Procedure II assesses miscues within the structure of the sentence. This option is often used by reading teachers or special education teachers who need numbers, profiles, and forms for student records. Procedures II and III provide in-depth information about a student's reading and are similar in their focus. Procedure IV is an informal analysis to be used with students during individual reading conferences.

No matter which procedure is chosen, after doing even one miscue analysis, teachers say they never again listen to students read in the same way. We agree with their assessment and invite you to investigate this whole language evaluation procedure.

An intensive study of miscue analysis requires more information than can be provided in a single chapter; therefore we suggest that teachers read *Reading Miscue Analysis: Alternative Procedures.*

Preparing for Miscue Analysis

Selecting Students

Select a student who presents a challenge to you—one who is a real puzzle. Ted is a prime candidate. He is not the least proficient reader in class, but he is the most baffling: "I don't know what to do with or for Ted." (However, don't choose your most troubled reader, who may produce a discouraging number of complex miscues and therefore be overwhelming for anyone using the procedure for the first time. Save that reader for a time when you have gained more experience.)

Selecting the Story

Although the length of the story used for miscue analysis depends to some extent on the age of the reader, there must be a complete text with a beginning, middle, and end. The story should be new to the reader, although the concepts should be familiar. It must be written in a way that supports readers in their attempt to make meaning and should therefore be "reader-friendly" rather than complicated. Since a minimum of twenty-five miscues is needed to give a description of a reader's strategies, the story must be slightly difficult for the student. Teachers usually collect two or three stories that are, in conventional terms, one or two years beyond the grade level indicated by the student's reading test scores. Some teachers use the best stories out of basal readers; this provides a grade-level designation that is understood by skills-oriented educators and parents. Reading time usually takes fifteen to twenty minutes, depending on the age and proficiency of the reader.

Preparing the Typescript

The student reads directly from the original source or from a very good copy. If a copy is used, the passage should look as much like the original text as possible. Specifically, the length of lines and pages, the spelling, and any special tables, charts, or pictures must be identical to the original text. This gives the teacher information about the influence of the physical text and format on the reader.

The teacher needs a typed version of the text, triple-spaced to allow room to record miscues; a wide right margin allows space for coding miscues and jotting brief notations. The last line of each original page is indicated on the typescript by a solid horizontal line. This format helps the teacher determine if turning the page influences the reader. The line and page number of the original text are typed along the left margin of the typescript; for example, line 4 of page 1 of the original text is typed *0104,* line 16 of page 12 is typed *1216.*

Taping the Reading Session

In addition to collecting all the materials and having the tape recorder in good working order, the teacher arranges suitable tables and chairs, proper lighting, and a reasonably quiet location. If only the tape-recorder's built-in microphone is available, be sure to choose a setting where background noise is minimal and test the recording level before beginning.

The reader and the teacher sit either side by side or across from each other. As the student reads, the teacher marks as many miscues as possible on the typescript. If the student is bothered by the marking, the teacher should discontinue marking until the pupil becomes absorbed in the reading. Since the session is audio- or videotaped, the teacher need not worry about getting all the information on the typescript. Marking the miscues is easier if the teacher is familiar with the story.

Instructions for Reading

Teachers briefly explain to students that they are taping them in order to learn more about their reading. Before a severely nonproficient student sees the story, the teacher might say, I'd like you to read this story called "Space Pet," or, This story is about something you might be doing this summer—camping.

Students are asked to read the story aloud and to read as if they were by themselves. They are told they won't receive any help and that when they are finished the teacher will take the book and ask them to retell the story in their own words. To assure readers that the procedure won't last all day, teachers let students see exactly how long the story is. Ted's teacher gave the following instructions:

> Ted, thanks for agreeing to read this morning. I think we can find out a lot about your reading. Have you ever read this story or heard it before? [Ted looks at the story and shakes his head no.] It's six pages long. [Ted checks the number of pages.] Please read aloud; I'm going to record your reading. When you come to something you don't know, do whatever you would do if you were reading all by yourself. I won't interrupt you. [This lets Ted know that he isn't going to receive help.] When you're finished, I'll take the book and then ask you to tell me the story in your own words. Any questions?

Reading Miscue Inventory: Procedure III

The remainder of this article introduces Procedure III, the option that is used most often by classroom teachers.

The components of the RMI should not be viewed as parts of a formula. Teachers and researchers must decide the focus of their evaluation and use the components accordingly. We believe, however, that the following will provide abundant information for the teacher who is faced with a problem reader:

1. Initial interview
2. Oral reading
3. Retelling: unaided, aided, cued
4. Reflection on reading
5. Analyzing the miscues: marking, coding, profile
6. Curriculum planning

Initial Interview

The instrument most often used to initiate the RMI is the Burke Reading Interview, but teachers may want to devise their own set of interview questions. No matter what form it takes, the purpose of the interview is to find out how students feel about themselves as readers and about the reading process. The first question of the interview helps teachers learn how students handle difficult text. This example from Karen, a third grader, illustrates the kind of information obtainable:[1]

Teacher: When you're reading and you come to something you don't know, what do you do? (Burke Q1)

Karen: It's pretty fun to me when you read and you say *blank* or *something* and you go back and you try to figure out what the word is. It's like a mystery to me.

No interview should be seen as a script to be followed slavishly. Many times, follow-up questions need to be asked:

Teacher: When you're reading and you have some trouble, or you come to something that gives you a problem, what do you do? (Burke Q1)

Connie: Tell the teacher.

Teacher: What do you tell her?

Connie: I tell her I have a problem with my reading.

---

[1] Excerpts are from interviews that were done as part of a Weldon Spring Grant, University of Missouri, 1987–88.

Teacher: Let's say the teacher wasn't there and you had a problem with reading. What would you do?

Connie: I'd go find her and tell her what I need.

Teacher: Do you ever do anything else when you have a problem?

Connie: When I'm at home I tell my parents. And when my dad and mom's—my sister—I ask her about it.

These answers to follow-up questions suggest that Connie has one major strategy to fall back on when she has trouble reading: she usually relies on help from others. It is important to find out if Connie realizes the teacher will not give her such help during the miscue process.

Questions may be added to any interview. Carol's views of reading practices are revealed in these interview questions:

Teacher: Would you like it if your mom [still] read to you?

Carol: Yeah, to bring good memories back.

Teacher: What kind of good memories?

Carol: How fun it was when she read to me. . . .

Teacher: What do you like about how reading is taught?

Carol: Teacher reading to you.

Teacher: How do you feel about that?

Carol: It reminds me of when my mom read to me, when I was a kid.

Carol has less positive response to another instructional method:

Teacher: Which do you like best, silent reading or oral reading?

Carol: Silent reading.

Teacher: Why is that?

Carol: Because I like reading to myself—because—I'm embarrassed to read books.

Teacher: You're embarrassed to read books out loud?

Carol: Most of the time.

Teacher: Why is that?

Carol: 'Cause I miss words and the class laughs at me.

This question about family literacy provided information about Mike, a fifth-grade boy in a remedial reading class:

Teacher: Who reads at your house, Mike?

Mike: No one, hardly.

Teacher: Nobody.

Mike: Just my uncle.

Teacher: Does he live with you?

Mike: Yeah.

Teacher: What does he read?

Mike: Car books or something, you know, how to fix your engine or something . . . and like getting parts for his motorcycle or something, just reading.

The influence of reading in this family became evident when Mike was asked about the kind of things he liked to read:

Mike: Like, I don't like stories that much, but I like, like how to build things or something, or 'struction, how to take things apart or something.

Oral Reading

Unaided oral reading provides a "window on the reading process." The reader is allowed to work through the text without help or interference. This not only reveals in-process comprehending (see below), but it provides information about the student's view of instruction. When third grader Sarah read "Zoo Doctor," she kept hesitating, waiting for her teacher to supply unknown words. When she wasn't given the expected help, she said, "My teacher last year said to skip it. Do you want me to skip it?" Sarah didn't trust the strategies she had been taught and needed confirmation that they were okay. When she found out that she could rely on strategies that moved her along in the text, she began to read the story with relative ease and with comprehension. If the teacher had supplied unknown words or corrected Sarah's miscues, none of this information would have come to light.

Checking oral reading against the retelling of the story helps teachers evaluate alternative approaches to instruction. Mitch, a fifth grader, remembered very little of the story "First Kill." Without the oral reading, his teacher might conclude that Mitch had problems reading the words in the text. This wasn't the case. Listening to Mitch read orally revealed that he was excellent at *recoding*, going from print to sound. What he didn't do well was to invest himself in the reading, which became evident when he was unable to retell the story. Without that commitment to the text, Mitch was unable to monitor his meaning construction process. Mitch actually skipped entire paragraphs without changing his speed or without correcting himself.

Retelling

Comprehension or lack of it can never be based solely on observing reading performance as it occurs; therefore, retelling is a vital part of miscue analysis.

Unaided retelling consists of readers' retelling the story in whatever way they prefer. Unaided retelling is introduced simply with, Tell me all you remember about the story. With this prompt, some students willingly recreate the story, often including plot, characters, and underlying theme. If encouragement is needed, the teacher can provide open-ended prompts such as "Tell me more" or "What else do you remember?"

In aided retelling, the teacher picks up on anything the reader has mentioned during the unaided retelling. Here the teacher must be careful not to put words in the student's mouth. Sam, a third grader, said during the unaided retelling, "And he saw something bad. And he, he saw something coming out of Mrs. Miller's window, and the fire truck came, and it took the house somewhere . . . that's all I know of." The teacher aided but didn't redirect the retelling with "You say the fire truck came and took the house. Tell me more about that."

Misconceptions can be cleared up during aided retelling, as when Sherry, a fifth grader, read "Zoo Doctor" and substituted the word *indigestion* for *injection*. On the second encounter with the word she substituted a nonword. She never said *injection*. During the retelling, however, she discussed the elephant getting a shot and the danger of the needle breaking off if the elephant moved. Sherry obviously understood the author's intended meaning.

Cued retelling is a way of helping readers realize that there is more in the story to be told; for example, in one story, five animals helped a princess escape an evil knight. Sally told in great detail what three of the animals did. When it was obvious that she was not going to tell more, the teacher said, "Sally, you mentioned how the dog, the kangaroo, and the cat helped the princess. Were there any other animals that helped her?" Such a question obviously cues the reader that there were other animals and that it is important to report that information.

Reflection on Reading

This procedure involves self-evaluation and self-reporting. Students often have reading problems that are difficult to pinpoint and to understand. When teachers need more information or need to confirm what they learned from the miscue analysis and retelling, it makes sense that the students themselves should be consulted. After the cued retelling, the teacher asks the student to reflect on the reading by posing questions such as:

How do you think you did with your reading?

How do you think you did when you talked about the story?

When did the reading go well? (Return the book to the student.)

Where did you have trouble? (Student may point to a specific word or mention a confusing concept.)

Why did you leave out this word?

Do you remember what you said for this word? What do you think it means?

Did the pictures help or bother you?

To help Kate reflect on her reading, Kate's teacher asked her about specific miscues. Kate, a third grader, liked to read, but her oral reading was not very fluent. She often made miscues that seriously affected the meaning of the story. Kate's teacher expected her to have just as much trouble with the retelling, but this was not the case. In her retelling, Kate included most of the major elements of the story and was correct on many of the details. To help understand this apparent discrepancy, Kate's teacher asked her to comment on some of her miscues. Here a more complete picture emerged. Below we see how Kate attempted to bring her knowledge of language into the meaning-making process in order to work through an unfamilar concept. She actively tried to construct meaning even though she didn't know the words. Kate read a sentence about filling a water *trough*, for which she substituted the word *through*. She was asked to respond to her miscue:

Teacher: What does that mean, "I filled the water *through* twice?"

Kate: That, well, I don't know if that's the true word, but like, *through twice,* I thought that was because he poured it in, but now I just noticed that, 'cause when it [goes] through when you, like, when you go through a hoop it just goin' straight through, but I know you don't pour water through it.

Teacher: So what do think about that?

Kate: That maybe that it could be a different word, or that maybe there's a word like it, like homophones, or there's another one, but it's the opposite of homophones, maybe it's one of those, like the word's the same, if they're spelled the same but they mean different.

At other times, Kate was able to come up with the author's intended meaning, even though it wasn't apparent from her oral reading:

Teacher: Would you read this paragraph?

Kate: While they *whipped* the medicine and water from their faces, the [inaudible] were figured out what to do next. (Text word is *wiped*.)

Teacher: What does it mean, "They whipped the medicine"?

Kate: Like they, I was thinking that maybe they shoved it in, or they gave it to her really fast and then, she threw it out, the water really fast, too. And then she wipe, they wiped their faces from it. They wiped their faces from the, see, from their face, they wiped the medicine and water from their faces.

When information from the student's reflection on reading is added to the other RMI information, a more complete picture of the reader is constructed. In Kate's case, she did far better on retelling than anyone expected considering the large number of miscues she made. This would indicate that her active approach to constructing meaning was paying off.

Analysis: Marking the Miscues

Understanding any cognitive process is difficult. We can't see into the mind and can only rely on the observable information available. Reliable evidence for understanding the reading process comes from an analysis of a reader's miscues. In this analysis the teacher looks for patterns that tell something about readers' use of the diverse cues of language and the strategies they use to process written material.

The first step in analysis is to mark the typescript. Some marking can be done as the reading takes place, but even so it is necessary to listen to the recording to confirm exactly what the student did. Tapes of readings can also be used to show the longitudinal development of students.

Most of the RMI marking is very straightforward. Substitutions are written above the word in the text:

fresh
Something was wrong inside those four tons of flesh and bones.

Read: Something was wrong inside those four tons of fresh and bones.

Omissions are circled:

He reached through the bars to lay a hand on (the) elephant's trunk.

Read: He reached through the bars to lay a hand on elephant's trunk.

Repetitions of a word are marked with a circled R and a line under the repeated text:

As | Jim left the hospital with a box . . .

Read: As Jim Jim left the hospital with a box . . .

The same notation is used when a miscue is repeated:

six
About | sixteen million units of penicillin . . .

Read: About six six million units of penicillin . . .

Multiple repetitions are indicated with lines below the repeated text. Each line represents a repetition:

When there was no more smoke ‖the firemen . . .

Read: When there was no more smoke the the the firemen . . .

Insertions are marked with a caret:

said
What's the matter, old girl? ∧ the zoo doctor asked.

Read: What's the matter old girl? said the zoo doctor asked.

Corrections are marked with a circled C and a line under the text that was read. The line should stop at the end of the last word spoken before the correction.

those
He reached | through the bars to lay. . .

Read: He reached those the bars, through the bars to lay. . .

said
And | she ∧ isn't going to like it.

Read: And she said isn't going to like, she isn't going to like it.

Don't talk to her, Doc, ‖the keeper |said.|

Read: Don't talk to her, Doc, said the keeper, the keeper said.

Unsuccessful attempts to correct are marked with UC, nonwords are marked with a $.

(UC) *through*
water
I filled her | trough twice.

Read: I filled her water twice, through twice.

UC *$scisee*
$ sooks
The zoo has no scale big enough to weigh Sudana.

Read: The zoo had no sooks scisee big enough to weigh Sudana.

Occasionally a reader will say the correct word and then replace it with a miscue. This is called abandoning the correct response and is labeled AC.

(AC) *what do we*
They figured out│what to do next.

Read: They figured out what to, what do we do next.

Some miscues are complex and difficult to mark. If you are unsure of a marking, it is best to write out in the margin what the reader said and number each attempt. In all cases, the criteria to use when marking are accuracy, clarity, and efficiency. In other words, your marking must accurately reflect what the reader did, should be possible for others to interpret, and should be relatively easy to record.

Analysis: Coding Miscues and Creating a Profile

The purpose of coding is to facilitate the analyzing of miscues. An important assumption of miscue analysis, based on extensive research, is that not all miscues are equal. A simple counting of errors does not provide usable information, but through an analysis of miscues teachers can learn how the student handled the cues of language and what strategies were used.

At the most basic level, miscues are analyzed in terms of their syntactic and semantic acceptability. In other words, if a miscue is made, does the sentence result in something that sounds like English (syntax check), does it make sense (semantics check), and does the miscue change the meaning of the story? An additional question gives information about the graphic (letter) similarity between any substitution and the text item for which the word is substituted. Four questions are asked in this RMI procedure:

Is the sentence, as finally read by the student, syntactically acceptable in the reader's dialect and within the context of the story?

Is the sentence, as finally read by the student, semantically acceptable in the reader's dialect and within the context of the entire story?

Does the sentence, as finally read by the student, change the meaning of the story? (Question 3 is coded only if Questions 1 and 2 are coded yes [Y]).

How much does the miscue look like the text item?

The questions are answered by reading the sentence as the reader left it. Consider Kate's sentence:

$suffle   weight   where
Her sulfa would have to be weighed out; sixty grams(of sulfa) were
    of very
used for every thousand pounds of elephant.

Read: Her suffle would have to be weight out; sixty grams where
used of very thousand pounds of elephant.

The answers to the RMI questions:

1. Is the sentence syntactically acceptable?   No
2. Is the sentence semantically acceptable?   No

Not all miscues result in such a dramatic change in syntax and semantics. The highest-level miscue is one that does not substantially
change either syntax or semantics:

    Susan
Sudana was sick.

The sentence is coded as both syntactically and semantically acceptable. The substitution of *Susan* for *Sudana* does not change either the
grammar or the meaning of the sentence. This sentence would be coded:
Y for syntax and Y for semantics. In this case, the reader read *Susan* for
Sudana throughout the story; therefore there was no change of meaning either at the sentence or story level and the miscue is marked N
(no meaning change).

The following sentence is very different.

                                fresh
Something was wrong inside those four tons of flesh and bones.

This sentence is coded N for syntax and N for semantics because it is
not grammatically acceptable to say, "four tons of fresh," and the resulting sentence does not make sense.

A sentence can be syntactically acceptable but not be a meaningful sentence. This most often happens when there is a substitution of
a nonword (marked with a $):

                                    and through her
            ears   her $thrit ____|____
He slipped his hand under her ear, down the length of her rough leg
and back along her body.

Read: He slipped his hand under her ears, down her thrit and
through her leg and back along her body.

The nonword *thrit* has the characteristics of an English noun,
making it an acceptable placeholder in the sentence. Despite the many
miscues, Kate followed the rules of English syntax.

Occasionally miscues will only partially change the meaning of either the sentence or the story, as in this example:

> *said*   *came*
> He saw Mrs. Miller come home from the store.
>
> Read: He said Mrs. Miller came home from the store.

The right margin of the typescript serves as a coding form for the first three questions (e.g., 5. Y Y N placed in the margin near the fifth sentence shows that the reader produced a syntactically and semantically acceptable sentence with no meaning change).

To code graphic similarity, the marking of H (for high similarity), S (for some similarity), and N (for no letter similarity) is placed on the typescript in a circle directly above the word-level substitutions. High similarity means 2/3 or more of the text word and miscues are the same, such as *whipped* for *wiped*, while some similarity is about 1/3, such as *those* for *through*.

After the sentences and substitutions are coded, they should be summarized, as in the following hypothetical example:

Syntactic Acceptability	41 Y	82 %	9 N	18 %			
Semantic Acceptability	35 Y	70 %	15 N	30 %			
Meaning Change	2 Y	6%	8 P	23 %	25 N	71 %	
Graphic Similarity	27 H	45 %	12 S	20 %	21 N	35%	

The percentages for the first three questions are based on the number of sentences coded, while those of graphic similarity are based on the number of coded word-level substitutions.

Finding Time for Miscue Analysis

Although miscue analysis is time-consuming, it can be incorporated into the whole language classroom. It is interesting but unnecessary to analyze the reading of students who are progressing and enjoying their literacy. Select for miscue analysis the students whose strengths and weakness are a puzzlement to you and possibly to themselves, students such as Ted.

Scheduling the data collection does not require a major revamping of the class schedule. One thirty-minute block for the reading and retelling, fifteen minutes for the Burke reading interview, and possibly a fifteen-minute follow-up interview will be needed. Teachers might ask a student teacher or aide to take on class responsibilities while they work with a reader. Perhaps colleagues can take turns taking both classes to free up time for each other to do miscues.

The reading interview and any follow-up needed to clarify a student's answers might be worked in during regular conferences. If conference time isn't available, search your schedule for those times when students can manage without your supervision.

The analysis of the data must be done when the teacher has time to study the reading phenomena. It isn't possible to say how long it will take to mark and code the miscues and analyze the retelling and reflection on reading; it depends largely on the reader's responses. However, with experience, and if the retelling is listened to carefully but not transcribed, an hour or two will often suffice.

Application to Curriculum Planning

The major purpose of reading evaluation is curriculum planning. Miscue analysis is especially suited for classroom application because it provides a great deal of in-depth information; this information must be analyzed before it can shape the curriculum for Ted or any other reader. One method of analysis is to look for trends or patterns that reflect the complete reader. These patterns often emerge as questions like the following, which should be answered in light of all available data.

1. How does the reader feel about herself as a reader? How does she feel about reading?
2. What strategies does she see as legitimate? Does she know when a strategy is not working? Does she have alternatives?
3. How well do her strategies work? How compatible is her meaning construction with the original text? What conditions facilitate meaning construction? Which ones hinder it?
4. How does the reader define literacy? What does she see as the main purposes of reading and writing?
5. What is the role of literacy in the family?
6. What instructional procedures does the reader perceive as facilitating learning? Which ones have an adverse effect?

The following questions are informed by looking at miscues:

1. What percentage of sentences make sense within the context of the story?

2. Does the reader correct miscues? What types of miscues are usually corrected? What types of miscues are usually left uncorrected?

3. Does she substitute words that look or sound like the words in the text?

4. If she substitutes *blank* or nonwords, how are they used?

5. What kinds of words are most often miscued on? Are they usually function words or content words?

6. Does she have many regressions? Do the regressions result in corrections?

7. Does she attempt to sound out words? Are there multiple attempts at a word? Is she usually able to produce the intended word?

8. Does she omit sections of the text? Are these omissions noted by her?

9. Does she change the punctuation? Do these changes result in meaningful sentences or nonsense?

10. For all of the above, were there trends? Did the trends change as the reading progressed?

Discovering the Giftedness in Each Student

The best reason for learning miscue analysis is to discover students' hidden abilities. Miscue analysis can reveal remarkable abilities in students who, according to test results and performance with basal readers, have serious reading problems. That's because tests are designed to reveal weaknesses. Miscue analysis, in contrast, enables teachers to see past weakness to discover strengths.

Jim

For example, speaking a nonstandard dialect is often seen as an academic weakness. A dialect that includes sentences such as *Wait till her baby be born* may cause problems on typical reading tests. However, an informed teacher can look at miscues with an eye to distinguishing between reading problems and dialect differences.

For instance, a seven-year-old rural Missouri boy named Jim, while reading a story about secrets being whispered into animals' ears, substituted a word that sounded like *our* every time he came to *ear*. He never changed or corrected this substitution or hesitated before the word. During the retelling, when he talked about *ears*, he pronounced them *ours*. This is evidence of a phonological dialect difference rather than a reading problem. As far as Jim knew, *ear* was pronounced *our*.

Joseph

One of the main reasons typical assessment procedures don't reveal student strengths is that they do not capitalize on student interests. With miscue analysis, student interests can become part of the assessment. Taking student interests into account can sometimes result in dramatic revelations, as happened with Joseph, a student I [Janice Henson, here and in the rest of this section] was tutoring. He was nine when we first met.

I was told that he could not read a word and didn't even know the alphabet. I saw him for about six hours, scattered over the span of a semester. Throughout that first year, it appeared that the only words he could read were his name and the names of some family members. I saw Joseph a few more times during the second year. During Black History Month, I wore a button bearing a picture of Martin Luther King, Jr., along with a quote by him. Joseph was interested in the button so I gave it to him.

He wanted to know what the quote said. I read it to him and then wrote the words on a piece of paper. I read the quote again, pointing to each word as I read. I then asked Joseph to read it to me. He gave his customary I-can't-read response. I asked him to point to any words he knew and read them. The quote and Joseph's response follow:

> We must ⟨learn⟩ to ⟨live⟩ together as brothers or we are going to ⟨perish⟩ *go*
> together as ⟨fools⟩.

After the first attempt, I asked him to try again and he read every word except *must* and *perish*.

Joseph's teachers at school didn't know that he had learned to read because he had never gotten the chance to initiate reading based on his own interests. As a result, at school during reading group, he did as he had always done: when he came to a word he made a feeble attempt at sounding it out and then waited for the teacher or another student to tell him the word. By having him attempt to read something that he'd chosen himself without assistance, I discovered that he was on his way to becoming an independent reader.

Bill

Bill, a fourteen-year-old boy who says he isn't a good reader because he reads slowly and stumbles over words, reads a newspaper article about a local basketball star. Just as he said he would, he reads slowly and stumbles over words. He makes many miscues. When he is asked to retell what he has read, he asks, "Do you want it told back in the order it happened or the order it was in the newspaper?"

Bill then proceeds to retell every detail of the story, including addresses, times and dates, and number of points scored. During the reading he omits the word *heckle,* but during the retelling, he explains that the crowd at the game was making nasty remarks about a player. Bill does indeed "sound like" a poor reader, but through miscue analysis, it is possible to discover his remarkable abilities to comprehend detailed information.

Gordon

Gordon, a fifth grader, lives on a Navaho reservation and is in the Chapter 1 program in his school. He has little confidence in his abilities and seems more interested in joking than in learning.

One morning, I read the book *Buffalo Woman* by Paul Goble to a group of four boys, including Gordon. When I had finished reading, Gordon asked me a question about something in the book, so I told him to read the page to find out. He immediately started reading out loud until he came to the sentence: "My Grandfather is chief of the Buffalo Nation." At the word *chief* he stopped and looked up at me. When I didn't tell him the word, he asked me what it was. I told him that I wasn't going to tell him the words, so he would have to skip it or put in something that made sense.

He skipped the word and finished the sentence and then asked me again what the word was. I told him, "Put in a word that makes sense." He substituted the word *chicken.* I said, "Does that make sense?" He laughed and said no. "So why did you say *chicken?*" I asked. He said it was because they both started with a *c.* I said, "Forget about the *c,*" and I took the book away from him. "Now," I said, "tell me a word that makes sense." "Leader," he said.

Gordon and I learned a lot from this encounter. He learned that "making sense" is what is most important. I learned that he tended to rely too much on sound/symbol cues, but that he was capable of using meaning to help him figure out words. I would never have discovered this if I had told him the word or if I was not aware of the different cueing systems of language that are part of miscue analysis.

Carla

Carla, a fourth grader who likes to read and says she is a good reader, makes few miscues as she reads a difficult story, but she substitutes the word *shouldered* for *shuddered* and does not correct it or use the word *shuddered* in retelling. She is asked how she figures out the meaning of an unknown word. She says that she uses the meaning of the sentence to figure out the word and explains the process in this way:

> Well, if the sentence read, There is poverty on Main Street, I would know that means the people were poor because Main Street might be a trashy street and then it might say there is poverty on Main Street. [It's] like hide-and-go-seek!

From her description of the reading process, coupled with her success as a reader, it is possible to conclude that Carla's miscue was not significant enough to be considered a problem.

Jim, the seven-year-old with the rural Missouri dialect, sometimes skips "little" words and sometimes transposes letters in words, as he did in this example (the circled d's indicate dialect miscues):

    tell   *trigger*   (d) *scket*
First I have to bell my tiger, said Oliver. Oliver whispered the secret
   (d) *our*
into his tiger's ear.

A teacher trained in miscue analysis would not consider any of Jim's problems significant because the omissions didn't cause a loss of meaning during the retelling and because he corrected *trigger* to *tiger* in the second sentence.

Roger, age nine, produced the following miscue:

    wished
I waited and waited and waited at the cellar door.

It appears, to miscue-trained ears, that Roger was using his knowledge of story and of syntax to jazz up an otherwise boring sentence.

Supporting Readers' Problem Areas

Once teachers are trained in miscue analysis, they not only become aware of strengths but can also spot potential reading problems. For example, when first grader Susan tries over and over again to sound out every single word she sees without making any attempt to make meaningful substitutions, it could be a sign that she is relying too much on a single cueing system. Or the same could be true when Sean "correctly" sounds out the word *mischief* as *mis-chief* without ever trying to combine the two syllables into a recognizable word.

The Burke interview (Goodman, Watson & Burke 1987) can be a source of information about many potential problems. Finding out that students do not like to read or that they think they are bad readers can help teachers adjust curriculum to their needs. It is also important to find out what student interests are. John, a fifth grader, said he didn't like to read in school because the emphasis was so much on fiction. John wanted to read about things like *'struction* (construction) instead of having to read stories.

In a secondary reading class, according to tests, Alan was classified as borderline mentally retarded, reading on a second-grade level. He expressed interest in books about horses and dogs and asked if he could read *The Red Pony*, by John Steinbeck. I told him he could, but the book might cause him some trouble. I went about my teaching duties and occasionally glanced at Alan.

He sat for almost an hour, slowly turning pages, all the time paying rapt attention to the book. Finally, he came to me and said he was confused about the pony, it seemed to disappear after the first chapter. I had many other things to do at that moment, so I told him to reread the last two pages of the first chapter. In a few minutes he came up to me with a look of complete satisfaction. He said, "Now it makes sense. The pony died." I confirmed that revelation and told him to reread Chapter 2 with that information in mind. I spent, at the most, five minutes with Alan, but in that five minutes I learned more about his reading ability than I could from any test.

By viewing Alan as someone who could use all of the cueing systems of language to make meaning from print, I allowed him to attempt reading that should have been far too difficult for him. By regarding reading as a process of making meaning, I was able to get a great deal of information about Alan's abilities to get meaning from print as he reads.

I saw the attention of a normally restless boy held by the act of reading; I saw him struggle to make meaning from the text, without asking for assistance until he was unable to make sense of the story; I saw him reread the text and correct his misinterpretations. I saw all of this as I went about the business of teaching. At the time, I jotted a few words down in my ever-present notebook (I call mine "What I Noticed"). At the end of the day, I took a minute or two to transfer the information to his folder.

Once teachers view reading through the lens of miscue analysis, it becomes the basis of all their reading assessment. This doesn't mean that these teachers are doing miscue analysis on all of their students all of the time. That would be far too time-consuming. Instead, as they go about their teaching duties, they keep their eyes and ears open for examples of students using language. The earlier example, where Godon substituted *leader* for *chief,* occurred as part of a reading lesson. When it happened, I made a note of it and later transferred that information to Gordon's folder. The whole procedure took about sixty seconds.

Conclusion

This chapter is an introduction to a reading miscue analysis procedure that provides teachers with immediate and accessible information about the reading abilities and needs of students. The authors encourage teachers to pursue the study of this whole language evaluation instrument by delving into the references and resources listed below. We hope, too, that teachers will investigate the informative qualities of the Reading Miscue Inventory—by using the inventory, along with the reading interview and other suggestions given above, to gather information about a student who poses curricular questions and uncertainties. We feel such a comprehensive study will provide an abundance of data on which a strong and appropriate reading program can be built.

References

Goodman, Kenneth S. 1982. *Language and literacy: The selected writings of Kenneth S. Goodman* (2 vols.). Boston: Routledge & Kegan Paul.

Goodman, Yetta M. & Burke, Carolyn L. 1972. *Reading Miscue Inventory manual: Procedures for diagnosis and evaluation.* New York: Macmillan.

Goodman, Yetta M., Watson, Dorothy J. & Burke, Carolyn L. 1987. *Reading Miscue Inventory: Alternative procedures.* New York: Richard C. Owen.

What Exactly Do You Mean by the Term *Kidwatching*?

When Yetta Goodman invited teachers to become kidwatchers, authentic assessment became attainable. I'm convinced that kidwatching was the beginning of the phenomenon of teacher as researcher. Teachers took Yetta's idea and made it their own, in brilliant and exciting ways. They discovered genuine settings that revealed a learner's strengths and problems. They created expeditious means of collecting rich information, and they devised ways of recording, analyzing, and reporting their data. Based on genuine evidence about learners they then developed learner-centered curriculum.

Dear Dorothy Watson:
Okay. I understand the *importance* of "kidwatching." Now, can you tell me the why, what, and how of kidwatching? Is it a formal observation or a casual one? What do I do with the information I gather? How can I become a good watcher? *What exactly do you mean by the term* kidwatching*?*
Thank you,
An Eager Observer

Originally published in *Questions and Answers About Whole Language,* edited by Orin Cochrane (Katonah, NY: Richard C. Owen, 1992), pp. 98–104. Copyright 1992 by Richard C. Owen. Reprinted with permission.

Dear Observer:

We all know teachers who appear to be scrutinizing their students, watching their every move, making mental notes of their problems and deficiencies for later remediation. With a glance at their well-organized gradebooks, such teachers can usually report their pupils' rankings, percentiles, and letter grades in every conceivable subdivision of the curriculum. Such is not the kind of *watching* Yetta Goodman advocated in her 1978 article "Kidwatching: An Alternative to Testing."

The whole language community was ready both for Goodman's concept of evaluation and for the label she gave it. Despite a few attempts to discredit the term, *kidwatching* captured the essence of real and natural evaluation and identified the kind of assessment missing in many conventional classrooms. Whole language teachers never viewed the term as flippant or casual, nor did they think of kidwatching as less important than other types of evaluation.

Now that the term is being used more and more in professional literature and is appearing as an evaluation strategy in school and district curriculum guides, closer definition is needed. I offer the following: *Kidwatching is enlightened observation of learners; it is a professional endeavor enacted by teachers who have done their homework on learners, learning, and language development.* With that as a working definition, further questions arise:

1. How do we become enlightened, knowledgeable observers?
2. What should we be watching?
3. How do we watch?
4. How do we respond to the things we've seen?
5. Should *learner*watching (including student and teacher) replace *kid*watching?
6. How do we know when we've been good watchers?

How do teachers become enlightened, knowledgeable observers? As are all whole language strategies, kidwatching is theoretically based, is demanding, and is exciting. Anyone can *look* at children writing an entry in their logs, see them scratching out, rewriting, conferring with a neighbor, sighing, and gazing into space. Anyone can *look* at a pen pal letter and respond as one preservice teacher did: "If this is the way first graders 'write,' I think I'll teach upper elementary!" This is *looking* at an activity and *looking* at a product, but not *understanding*, not kidwatching. A teacher who is enlightened about language in use, learning theory, the writing and reading processes, invented spelling, principles of working and communicating with others, and handwriting formation will understand that the scratching out, rewriting, conferring with a neighbor, even the sighing and gazing into space, are rich with information about a child's intention, progress, and meaning.

Kidwatchers are those teachers who have investigated the reading process through a study of miscue analysis, have developed "miscue ears," and can therefore evaluate the substitutions, omissions, and insertions made by readers. Kidwatchers are teachers who understand that reading is a *transaction* between text and reader. Watchers can therefore gauge the influence that the syntax and semantics of a story might have on a language user. Kidwatchers are teachers who observe learners in a literature study group sharing ideas they have never expressed before and can explain the phenomenon in terms of the social nature of language and language learning. Kidwatchers are teachers who observe students halfheartedly answering questions at the end of a social studies chapter and later observe those same students devouring the latest information about dinosaurs, and can then explain the different behavior in terms of student interest and language use. The first steps toward becoming a kidwatcher are clear—inquiry into language, literature, learning, and learners.

What should we be watching? Because whole language teachers have a background of information in language development, miscue analysis, process writing, invented spelling, and social interaction, they are prepared to expect certain behaviors in learners. These expectations are good guideposts along the observational path, but the expectations never limit the teacher's view. There must always be room for the unexpected, the idiosyncratic, the individualistic, the thing that has never been said or done before. Teachers watch for specifics in both meaning and form. In watching writers, teachers ask, Are ideas and content becoming richer and more fulfilling for the learner? Are students willing to share their own efforts and help others as well? Is spelling developing from invented to more conventional form? Is syntax becoming more standard? Is handwriting becoming more legible?

Because of their background knowledge, teachers can formulate questions and direct their kidwatching in very organized and systematic ways. In addition to specific behaviors within the process of language learning, teachers watch for the holistic orchestration of language learning—how kids are getting it all together. For example, when teachers see children using the inquiry techniques learned in researching a social studies concept in an interview with the school principal, the teacher knows that good orchestration of learning has taken place. Not only have students applied what they learned in one setting to another, but they have done so under their own steam; that is, without direct instruction, they made personally meaningful connections across curricular contexts.

Teachers watch not only for students' growth but for development in curriculum as well. They ask, In what curricular circumstance can limitless and exciting progress be observed? When they detect signs of restricted and narrow growth, they ask themselves if the curriculum is being controlled by texts, tests, and teachers. Such narrow curriculum is then compared to that in which students, along with their teachers, are in control.

How do we kidwatch? The watching teacher must believe that children have knowledge, information, skills, and abilities. If teachers don't accept this assumption, they will only look at, not understand, learners. The noticing teacher isn't blind to students' needs and problems, but he or she always sees learners' *strengths first.* Such a teacher values something within each pupil and makes a point of highlighting that accomplishment, no matter how minimal it might appear to those who are not kidwatchers.

Teachers observe as an anthropologist might, systematically and with purpose; they watch and watch again, never willing to let one glance tell all. Observant teachers are wary of drawing simple cause-and-effect conclusions, preferring to gather as much data from as many sources as possible before making curricular decisions. Whole language teachers understand that the learner's intentions and abilities can be masked by final overt behavior and by a finished project; therefore they study the process as well as the product. In studying the product, they are never misled by it, always judging the product in light of observations of the means taken to reach it.

Much kidwatching is not recorded, but more and more teachers see value in recording and reporting data gathered from such powerful evaluation. Some teachers jot down on each student's page in a loose-leaf notebook signs of learner development, questions that arise, and possible next steps. Because such personal data is rich with context and detail, it is valued by parents who are eager themselves to be kidwatchers. Although kidwatching requires an informed and energetic educator, it becomes second nature for teachers within a supportive and natural whole language classroom.

How do we respond to the information gained through kidwatching? By watching and understanding learners, teachers themselves become learners. They learn about *students* as individuals and as members of the classroom community; they learn about *themselves* as teachers and as members of the classroom community; they learn about the *curric-*

ulum and its appropriateness; and they learn about their own *theories* of literacy and learning. What is done with such rich information? Such knowledge is crucial to supporting each learner's growth and development within a whole language curriculum. Specifically, by referring to a historical record of kidwatching observations, a teacher can show learners, other educators, and parents the direction and depth of progress. A noticing teacher can remind students who "have nothing to write about" that in their journals they have mentioned some interesting topics that would make intriguing stories. Kidwatchers can suggest specific reading and writing strategies for pupils who are struggling with their literacy development. Teachers who have developed student sensitivity know when to make a suggestion, offer a resource, or issue an invitation, and when to back off.

Critical kidwatching provides a cross-check with other evaluation reports. For example, a student is described on a cumulative record as being disruptive and as having difficulty in sustaining attention. By observing that learner in a variety of classroom settings, the teacher finds that the description is accurate when the student is required to take part in activities for which he has no interest, background, or need. On the other hand, the description does not fit the student when he is involved in learning situations that intrigue, motivate, and serve a purpose. Through kidwatching, the curriculum as well as the student is observed, informed, and enriched by the information gained.

Whole language teachers are constantly testing their theory: kidwatching provides a beliefs-in-action evaluation. Observations made over time and in different curricular settings within the classroom confirm teachers' beliefs about learning and teaching such as:

1. The learner is indeed the informant; no one else can provide such powerful curricular information.

2. When learners gain control of the curriculum, they also gain control of themselves, both academically and in terms of behavior.

3. When learners are allowed to explore and share their explorations, they take on the appearance of scholars.

4. Language is deeply embedded and evident in real and functional contexts; that is, students read, write, listen, speak, and think authentically and with determination when their curricular endeavors make sense.

5. Learning is not linear; rather it is circular and doubles back on itself, hits plateaus and takes nose dives, but develops and deepens within the safe and rich environment of a whole language classroom.

6. Learners who are inquirers rather than collectors of facts are able to adapt what they learn in one situation to other situations.

7. Learners are able to correct themselves when they are in social settings in which conflicting information is allowed within a supportive environment.

8. When all voices are considered valuable, students realize that they are not expected to be silent about literature, life, and their own learning.

Should learnerwatching *(including student and teacher) replace* kidwatching? It makes sense that if kidwatching empowers teachers, it can also empower students. Whole language teachers believe that both teaching and learning are inquiry. Therefore, it makes good whole language sense to invite students into the observer's circle. Students should be encouraged to become aware of their own abilities to ask questions, solve problems, and look at the world in ever-expanding ways. As pupils become aware of themselves as respected and valued learners, they become aware of other learners around them. They, too, are enlightened observers not only of themselves and their peers but of their teachers and their curriculum as well. When this happens, kidwatching takes on creativity and power. When this happens, students realize that through the interpretation of their own learning and through their perceptions of how others learn, including their teacher, they are indeed able to take risks, to redefine the texts of their world, and to become creators of knowledge themselves.

How do we know when we've been good kidwatchers? This may be the easiest of all the questions to answer. Successful kidwatchers have no doubt that they are informed about their students' development. They have confirmed some of their expectations and they are totally surprised by other observations. Successful kidwatchers have a sense of being enabled because what they have learned enriches and gives strength not only to themselves but to their students and the curriculum as well.
Sincerely,
Dorothy J. Watson

Reference

Goodman, Yetta. 1978. Kidwatching: An alternative to testing. *National Elementary Principal, 57,* 41–45.

Part Two

Working
with Readers
(1973–1988)

Helping the Reader: From Miscue Analysis to Strategy Lessons

This piece is dedicated to all doctoral students who have been told by their committee members, Save that information and write it for publication after you finish your dissertation. Most doctoral students are convinced that they probably won't live through Chapter 5 and don't want to be told that if by some miracle they do finish, they are once again expected to sit in front of a blank page or empty screen. Dear colleagues, writing is possible after the dissertation, with, of course, relentless nudging on the part of your adviser.

This is the first piece I wrote after my dissertation. It was a taxing experience but nevertheless an honor to contribute to Ken Goodman's book, Miscue Analysis: Applications to Reading Instruction. *I was more than a little pleased to realize that more than two decades after I wrote this piece, the strategies suggested for Tim still seem right on the mark. I was also pleased that I've learned a few lessons since my dissertation days. That inflexible use of the MCP (male chauvinist pronoun)—"his pupils," "he can help students," "they did it for him"—is mighty grating and embarrassing in the nineties! When did I discover that there were female teachers and students? The gender-specific pronoun wasn't the only surprise: I write about readers interacting with the content of the story. After reading Louise Rosenblatt's work and after many conversations with Carolyn Burke and Jerry Harste, my*

Originally published in *Miscue Analysis: Applications to Reading Instruction,* edited by Kenneth S. Goodman (Urbana, IL: ERIC Clearinghouse on Reading and Communication Skills & National Council of Teachers of English, 1973), pp. 103–15. Reprinted with permission.

language choice today would not suggest that the reader and text come together and then part unchanged. Now, I would use the term transacting, *a word that suggests that both the reader and the text can be affected. You may groan as I did when I read about readers' habitual associations, implying that readers respond to one text item just as Pavlov's pup responded to that dinner bell. Finally, in 1973, even though I knew that reading was not, as Ron Wardaugh put it, "barking at print," I limited reading to "getting the author's message." Somewhere in the intervening two decades, learners (students and teachers) have taught me that proficient reading isn't limited to "getting the author's message" but entails constructing something that makes sense to the reader by using the author's text, the situational context, and the reader's background. (I'm living proof that whole language teachers live and, in doing so, learn.)*

Miscue analysis can be useful to the teacher in finding the reading strengths and weaknesses of his pupils. But a key question for teachers is whether this knowledge will suggest ways to help readers become more efficient. Further, can the procedures and findings of miscue analysis help the teacher build an instructional program on ground rules that are linguistically and psychologically sound? Can these findings help the teacher produce practical, specific, and relevant activities that pay off in the classroom? This article presents ways in which miscue analysis can lead to effective reading instruction.

Strategy Lessons

Within the reading process, there is an element of organization that requires readers to use specific strategies. These strategies are, in a sense, stored in the long-term memory of the reader and are energized when the reader interacts with print. The strategies involve predicting, confirming, correcting, and integrating meaning; they are available to the less proficient as well as to the accomplished reader. The accomplished reader, however, has sufficiently mastered these strategies so that he reads with ease; the inefficient reader is less able to take full advantage of the strategies and usually labors over the task.

To clarify the relationship of the reading strategies to the model of reading, Goodman and Burke (1972) have organized a paradigm that presents, within the subsystems of the language, an outline of the reading strategies that children control with varying degrees of proficiency. This paradigm is *not* a developmentally and hierarchically arranged catalog of skills that must be tested and drilled.

With this paradigm of strategies, the teacher has guidelines for obtaining information about the reader and his process of reading. With specific information (gained from miscue analysis) about the student's degree of facility with language, the teacher can now develop lessons that are directly significant and immediately applicable to the student's needs. Such lessons have been labeled *reading strategy lessons* by Goodman and Burke. Strategy lessons are developed as needed, but, because readers often have similar difficulties, the lessons can be used (perhaps with modification) with other students.

A relevant starting point for developing lessons that make use of the interrelated systems of the language is to study a profile of the reader's strengths and weaknesses. One instrument used for obtaining such information is the Reading Miscue Inventory.

To show how strategy lessons can grow out of miscue analysis, we will examine the data gathered from Tim, a fifth-grade student.

The graphic/sound profile (Figure 1)[1] illustrates Tim's use of visual and phonetic information. Such use of graphophonics appears to be an indisputable strength, but it must be viewed in relationship to the read-

Figure 1.
Tim's graphic/sound profile.

SOUND/GRAPHIC RELATIONSHIPS					
Sound			Graphic		
High	Some	None	High	Some	None
100	100	100	100	100	100
90	90	90	90	90	90
80	80	80	80	80	80
70	70	70	70	70	70
60	60	60	60	60	60
50	50	50	50	50	50
40	40	40	40	40	40
30	30	30	30	30	30
20	20	20	20	20	20
10	10	10	10	10	10

(handwritten annotations: Sound High 53%, Sound Some 20%, Sound None 27%; Graphic High 63%, Graphic Some 20%, Graphic None 17%)

[1] Although these tables are largely self-explanatory, a full explanation of how they are arrived at can be found in Goodman, Watson, and Burke (1987).

Figure 2.
Tim's comprehension score.

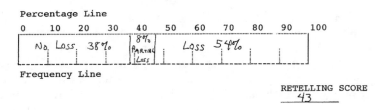

Percentage Line

Frequency Line

RETELLING SCORE
43

er's facility with syntactic information. Data must also be analyzed as it relates to the student's ability to make sense of his reading; therefore, it is essential that his comprehension score be considered (Figure 2).

After relating these elements, we see that this reader's syntactic and semantic strategies are not used sufficiently—partially as a result of overattention to the graphophonic cueing system. In other words, Tim often overuses phonics.

When the efficient reader begins the graphic selection process, he is guided by information provided by the three subsystems of the language as well as by his personal past experiences; consequently, the final perceptual image is a hybrid of what he expects to see and what he actually sees. The efficient reader samples just enough from print to confirm his conceptual predictions while an inefficient reader allows the print to mislead him or to impede his progress. The following examples indicate ways in which Tim relied heavily on graphic cues and made limited use of syntactic and semantic information:

1. "Not Grandfather's precious ax, that he was so proud of,"
    through summer
    thought Suzanne.

2. . . . on the family's small farm, and he looked tired.

3. I wouldn't lend it to anyone but you.

The grammatical function graph, as shown in Figure 3, indicates that the reader did not always substitute words that had the same grammatical function as the text word. However, occasionally Tim used syntactic cues along with graphic ones, making his reading sound like acceptable language even when he was unable to produce a sensible sentence. Note the following examples:

Figure 3.
Tim's grammatical/function graph.

GRAMMATICAL RELATIONSHIPS						
Function			Relationships			
Identical	Indeter-minate	Different	Strength	Partial Strength	Weakness	Over-correction
100	100	100	100	100	100	100
90	90	90	90	90	90	90
80	80	80	80	80	80	80
70	70	70	70	70	70	70
60	60	60	60	60	60	60
50	50	50	50	50	50	50
40	40	40	40	40	40	40
30	30	30	30	30	30	30
20	20	20	20	20	20	20
10	10	10	10	10	10	10

(Annotations: 49% Identical; 51% Different; 1% Strength; 14% Partial Strength; 70% Weakness)

                    $discomfortaly   cities
1. Men were shouting directions to his father, and the cries of
        gales of ice through his nose
    many gulls added to the noise.

                                         as   they
2. He went on snapping beans without a word, only now and then
    gathered   *eyes in*
    glancing out of the corner of his eye at Suzanne.

Tim's repeated miscues (Figure 4) show how he handled unknown words that were repeated throughout the text: he had persistent difficulty with words that had two or more lexical meanings or
grammatical functions, and he habitually associated one word with
the visual cues of another word (e.g., *tracks* for *traps*).

Tim was inordinately concerned with visual cues. When confronted
with unknown words, he either omitted the word or produced a word
or nonword that tended to match fairly well graphically but did not
necessarily fit syntactically or semantically. Some specific miscues help
us discover the strengths and weaknesses of his reading.

If we were concerned with the quantity rather than the quality of
miscues, we might be distressed by our reader's first miscue (*Andrea*
for *Andre*)—which he repeated sixteen times. (The name appeared in
the text twenty-eight times.) Tim first substituted *Andrea*; then, per-

Figure 4.
Repeated and multiple miscues.

Reader	Text	Frequency of Miscue Occurrence
the	a	2
[omission]	adventure	2
[omission]	all	2
as	and	4
An + dra	Andre	1
Andrea	Andre	16
Anly	Andre	1
[omission]	Andre	4
Andrea	Andre's	1
Andrea's	Andre's	2
and	as	1
is	as	1
in	at	1
is	at	1
carton	certain	1
[omission]	certain	1
gleam	glance	1
gathered	glanced	1
gathered	glancing	1
and	had	1
has	had	1
was	had	1
as	he	1
for	he	1
she	he	2
he	it	2
was	it	1
[omission]	it	2
is	its	1
he	of	2
[omission]	of	1
one	on	2
and	said	3
$Suma	Suzanne	1
$Sunda	Suzanne	1
Arumba	Suzanne	1
he	Suzanne	1
[omission]	Suzanne	2
as	that	1
[omission]	that	1
his	the	1
it	the	1
then	the	1
[omission]	the	2
tracks	traps	2

haps in an attempt to assign a boy's name to the male character, he substituted *An+dra* and *Anly*. Tim omitted the name four times, produced partial words three times, and finally settled for *Andrea*. These miscues did not result in problems with meaning because in his retelling of the story Tim said, "Andrea was just a regular boy who kept putting things off." Nevertheless, Tim might have had an easier time if he had decided earlier to accept *Andrea* for *Andre* and then had no further concern with getting a graphic-phonemic match.

Tim substituted the names *Suma, Sunda,* and *Arumba* for *Suzanne.* He omitted the name twice, substituted the pronoun "he" once, and on the seventh and all subsequent occurrences (ten), Tim pronounced the name correctly. *Suzanne* was a name Tim had heard prior to the reading.

Tim also had some problems with familiar words. *As* was substituted for *and* four times, although in fourteen occurrences the word *and* was read correctly. The substitution of *and* for *said* was made twice. There were thirteen other occurrences of *said,* which appeared in a variety of syntactical positions; these were all read correctly.

Most of Tim's repeated miscues involved function words (*as* for *and, and* for *an, as* for *that, the* for *a,* and the omission of *that* and *the*), which resulted in no particular loss of meaning and did not disrupt the flow of his reading. However, several of his substitutions (*then* for *the, it* for *the*) rendered the sentences grammatically unacceptable. An efficient reader would correct, either orally or silently, unacceptable structures. Rather than correct, Tim tended to accommodate by restructuring the phrase or clause, as follows:

1. Andre put one *(of)* his father's old ax*(es)* on the sled. "Yes," he said

    An—   on

    sandy
    a little sadly.

2. *as they gathered*
    . . . only now and then glancing out the corner of . . .

3. *we were*
    (UC) wer—   and Andrea was
    "I know \where there's just the right one," said Andre: "It's

    into   in
    growing in the woods across the bay."

Although Tim's accommodations frequently destroyed or modified meaning, they occasionally made sense:

1. *very   Andrea   felt very warm*
    The kitchen was ^warm and cozy, and *(adventure)* *(seemed)* far away.

2. *with   with*
    . . . when fishermen were *(repairing)* their nets . . .

Tim had several miscues involving pronoun substitution:

1. *she*
    . . . but somehow he didn't . . .

2. *her*
    . . . to get his cap

a   *she*
3. . . . make some rabbit traps," he said.

(c) *he*
4. . . . It would be dreadful if it was lost.

He
5. . . . Suzanne ran to get . . .

Tim corrected some of his pronoun substitutions, but the majority were left uncorrected. He might not be aware of a pronoun's antecedent, resulting in an inability to predict the correct pronoun. The uncorrected substitutions reflect the reader's lack of proficiency with confirming and correcting strategies. Tim's retelling of the story indicates that he knew "Andrea" was a boy and the main character. However, he was confused about Suzanne's relationship to Andre, even though the brother-sister relationship was referred to four times in the story. When asked who Suzanne was, Tim replied, "Just a—sorta like a girl. Probably one of his relatives or something."

There are several word omissions on Tim's repeated miscue list. He omitted the word *adventure* twice. He also had single omissions of *repairing, shivering, generally, precious, sharpen, pretended,* and *juniper.* He omitted *certain* once and substituted *carton* for *certain* one time.

In his retelling, Tim recalled all the individuals in the story—but only significantly developed the character of Andre. He hinted at both the plot and theme, although he was far from specific. He recalled six major incidents in the story but was confused about the setting and background.

Strategy Lessons for Tim

From a careful examination of the reading profile graphs, the list of repeated miscues, and the retelling of the story, we can draw some conclusions about Tim's reading and make some specific suggestions concerning his reading instruction.

Except for proper names, Tim's repeated miscues for the most part involved the substitution of function words, usually replaced within grammatical boundaries (e.g., noun marker for noun marker). Tim was able to read all of these function words, correctly in a different context. There was no evidence of ignorance or confusion of letter-sound combinations; therefore, flashcard drill of "sight words" would be inappropriate. Also, there was no evidence to indicate that Tim needed drill on sounds. In fact, his overattention to graphophonic cues proved to be a handicap to some degree when he became overly concerned with matching letters to sounds and with meaningless accommodation of the substituted words. Not only must Tim make his reading sound like language, but he must attend to the meaning as well. Tim could begin to understand the importance of gaining the author's message by reading stories to younger children. He should also be encouraged to talk about and to retell stories to others.

Tim occasionally substituted nonwords for unknown words (*happing* for *hopping*, *discomfortaly* for *direction*, *greenwuck* for *evergreen*); but, for the most part, he simply omitted the unknown words without making a stab at them. Goodman and Burke have made the following suggestions for dealing with such omissions: "The reader should be encouraged to move from (1) omitting unknown words to (2) producing nonwords with appropriate grammatical inflections to (3) producing words that have some related meaning to (4) producing words with close meaning similarity" (p.101).

Tim should attempt to substitute words that are real and grammatically suitable for unknown words. To strengthen predicting strategies on the basis of grammatical function and meaning, the teacher might read aloud from Tim's own book, pausing frequently and allowing him to fill in the pauses. Following success with this, the teacher could place a transparent sheet of paper over Tim's book, black out various words that are highly predictable, and have Tim guess at the blacked-out words on the basis of sentence structure and meaning. The following story could also be used with Tim:

Alexander's Adventure

There once was a little black kitten named Alexander. Alexander was not treated very well by the boy who owned him. The boy sometimes _____ his tail. He often forgot to give him _____ and water and he didn't _____ with him very much, either. Alexander felt very _____ and thought he would _____ away. He would start a new life. He would have an adventure. He would go to Colorado.

So Alexander _____ out of the window and started on his long walk to Colorado. Sometimes he was lonely and tired. His adventure wasn't too much fun, especially when he got chased by a _____ or when there was no food and he was very _____ .

Then one day Alexander saw a boy sitting on the front steps of a little house. Alexander just couldn't help himself. He _____ to the boy and rubbed his back against his arm. It was love at first sight! The boy, whose name was Walter, gave Alexander food to _____ and then scratched his neck until the tired Alexander fell _____ . Walter and _____ played together every day and they were both very happy.

Maybe someday Alexander and Walter will go to Colorado together.

Readers are often pleasantly surprised to discover that they can easily manage this activity. They begin to gain confidence when they realize that their substitutions sound right and that they make sense as well. As readers improve their skills, the exercises can be made more difficult. Other cloze procedures (omitting words with specific grammatical functions for which meaning can be easily ascribed, or omitting words at random) could be useful in helping readers antici-pate grammatical structure and in developing awareness of grammat-ical function.

We discussed earlier Tim's trouble with pronoun antecedents. The following story presents two characters, brother and sister; their mas-culine and feminine pronouns appear later in the story—after the brother-sister relationship is established. The names of the brother and sister are introduced, without explanation, near the end of the passage. The teacher may want to discuss with Tim the relationships involved.

My Little Brother and My Big Sister

Sometimes I get so mad at my little brother and my older sister! They bug me to death! Last night my brother took his crayons and scribbled all over my homework paper. Because he messed it up, I had to do the whole thing over again. He is always getting into my things. My big sister is just as bad. She thinks the whole house be-longs to her. She washes out her clothes and hangs them all over the bathroom.

Between the two of them I think I'm going nuts. Sometimes I wish I had never heard of brothers and sisters. Look! She's been in my room again. I can tell because my sweater isn't on the floor where I left it. What nerve! What's this? She left me a note.

Hi,
Billy and I have gone for a walk. He cried all morning be-cause he thought you were mad at him about the home-work paper. He is really sorry.
We made some cookies and left them for you in the kitchen.
We love you.
Helen

Gosh, I have a nice brother and a neat sister.

The teacher must proceed carefully when helping children correct their miscues. Overemphasis on correcting miscues could lead stu-dents to believe that reading is an exact process and that word-by-word perfection is desirable. Tim must believe that reading is not just "barking at print"—rather, it is getting the author's message.

Sometimes it is necessary to reread in order to correct misconceptions or simply to make a fresh start when meaning is slipping away. Tim rarely did this. The following story is designed to encourage him to reread when it is desirable to do so. When Tim is given the story, it should be made clear that during the reading it will be necessary to backtrack in order to clarify certain points. This passage also might be used to illustrate how an author develops the major plot question.

Jim's Adventure

There were three ways of getting from the Robinson farm to Sam's cabin. Sam was the Robinson's nearest neighbor and it was two miles to his place if you took the path that went safely along the edge of the forest. Jim's father always made him take this path to Sam's if he was going alone.

The other two ways to Sam's were by river.

The quickest route was by turning off the main stream about half a mile from the landing, shooting twenty feet of narrow rapids, then proceeding on the river's branch until you landed almost at Sam's back door. This was the quickest route, but the most dangerous, and Jim's father had forbidden him to take it.

The third way to Sam's was also by river and was quite safe, especially with two people handling the canoe. This river route simply involved staying to the right bank of the river all the way from the landing to Sam's waterfront dock.

Jim's heart was pounding as he guided the canoe into the icy water. As he paddled along the dark right bank of the river, his arms began to ache but he did not slow his pace. At the first sound of the rapids, Jim slowly began to edge the canoe toward the left bank. His muscles strained and he felt his heart jump as he aimed the canoe into the rapids.

Additional Suggestions and Strategy Lessons
Graphic/Sound Relationships

There is no evidence in Tim's reading to indicate a persistent problem with graphic/sound relationships. However, if a teacher feels that a student has such difficulties, he should consider a substitute for isolated word drill. The student might enjoy graphophonic exercises if he were to read (perhaps into a tape recorder or as a member of a choral reading group) some of the jingles and poems that have alliteration or middle and end rhyming elements. The following paperback books offer poems that have a simple sentence structure and reflect the interests of children:

All Day Long (McCord 1966)

Arrow Book of Poetry (McGovern 1964)

Faces and Places: Poems for You (Hopkins & Arenstein 1970)

Pop Corn and Ma Goodness (Preston 1969)

Take Sky (McCord 1962)

When We Were Very Young (Milne 1924)

Wind Song (Sandburg 1960)

Habitual Associations

There are certain word combinations that many readers habitually confuse, such as *brought/bought* and *for/from*. Sometimes these confusions do not affect meaning to any great degree and can be ignored. However, if the association hinders the reading process by misdirecting the reader either syntactically or semantically, the confusion should be dealt with.

Through/though is often a source of trouble for readers. One reader was presented with the word *through* in isolation. She said, "Th-, though, mmm thong?" The *r* was pointed out to her, and she said, "Oh, yes, thought!" The same reader was given the following passage. Her miscues are marked:

ⒸM—   Ⓡ
Mother said that even though I had not cleaned up my room

the
that I could watch ˄television. It was as though my dreams had been

Ⓒ   *th—*
answered because my favorite program was on.

listing
ⓊⒸ*list*
I looked through the television listings in the newspaper to

Ⓒ *sta-*
find out what channel the program was on. When I was through

with the paper, I folded it neatly and put it away because I didn't want Mother to have any reason to get angry with me.

Ⓒ *An*
Although I felt guilty for not cleaning my room I enjoyed the

Ⓒ *th-*
program. I thought that it might be a good idea to clean it up now.

Through the support of strong syntactic and semantic clues, the reader can overcome problems with habitually associated words.

Syntactic and Semantic Relationships

Some readers spend so much time attempting to pronounce a word that they lose the thread of thought. The following is an example of this:

> *$genly*
> *$gerly*
> *gently he cried*
> *g-g-gen cried*

. . . untied the dogcart that generally carried loads of wood to the house.

Although the reader was able to make a reasonable graphophonic match, the flow and the sense of the passage were soon lost. The reader would have maintained the meaning of the sentence if he had omitted the word *generally.* Only occasionally does an author build on a word so that the reader is tipped off to the meaning of a passage by his understanding that single word. If it is significant, an author will provide contextual clues and repeat the vital word.

A reader will reduce his omissions of unknown words as he gathers meaning from context. He must make sense of his reading, and he must allow the syntax of the sentence to help him make acceptable substitutions.

A student may feel that he is cheating if he substitutes his own word for the author's. However, he will begin to see the possibilities of such a strategy when he compares two ways of expressing the same idea. For example:

> Yesterday it rained. From time to time there were brilliant flashes of lightning and loud rumbling of thunder. Large balls of hail came down.

> Twenty-four hours ago we had some precipitation. Intermittently there were brilliant scintillations of static electricity and intense ruffled reverberations due to the expansion of the air. Massive globules of sedimentary ice came down.

With such exercises, the reader sees that an idea can be expressed in various ways. He also begins to realize that the *author* does not say everything, for reading is not passive. The reader has a responsibility for *thinking* as he is reading.

It is hoped that the examples given above can provide the teacher with some general guidelines in ways to base instruction in reading on miscue analysis and its linguistic base; however, the examples should not be seen as restrictive or as final models. I hope they will encourage teachers to develop materials that help children use all the cueing systems of their language more proficiently.

References

Goodman, Yetta M. & Burke, Carolyn L. 1972. *Reading Miscue Inventory manual: Procedures for diagnosis and evaluation.* New York: Macmillan.

Goodman, Yetta M., Watson, Dorothy J. & Burke, Carolyn L. 1987. *Reading Miscue Inventory: Alternative procedures.* New York: Richard C. Owen.

Hopkins, Lee B. & Arenstein, Misha (Eds.). 1970. *Faces and places: Poems for you.* New York: Scholastic.

McCord, David. 1962. *Take sky.* Boston: Little, Brown.

McCord, David. 1966. *All day long.* Boston: Little, Brown.

McGovern, Ann (Comp.). 1964. *Arrow book of poetry.* New York: Scholastic.

Milne, A. A. 1924. *When we were very young.* New York: Dutton.

Preston, Edna M. 1969. *Pop Corn and Ma Goodness.* New York: Viking.

Sandburg, Carl. 1960. *Wind song.* New York: Harcourt, Brace & World.

Reader-Selected Miscues: Getting More from Sustained Silent Reading

Self-evaluation is the major aim here. Whole language teachers value the reader-selected miscue procedure as an authentic assessment because it is:

1. *Learner-referenced; the focus is on the reader in relation to his or her own performance over time and over different texts and genres.*
2. *Student-driven; the reader directs the evaluation by deciding which miscues are shared or discussed with classmates and teachers.*
3. *Always within the process of reading and therefore never violates the integrity of language; the strength of this procedure lies in its immediacy and relevance.*
4. *A process that teaches; everyone benefits.*
5. *Noncompetitive.*
6. *Multileveled in that it assesses the reader's strategies, the text, and the effect of instructional procedures.*

The reader-selected miscue procedure is consistent with whole language beliefs about language, learning, and curriculum, but most important, it makes everyone involved a researcher and a learner.

Originally published in *English Education* 10 (1978), 75–85. Copyright 1978 by the National Council of Teachers of English. Reprinted with permission.

I have a friend who recently came into an unusual professional inheritance. She was asked to replace a teacher who was moving from the city, leaving behind a class of junior high students involved in a well-organized sustained silent reading program. My friend accepted the position and was surprised to learn that everything her predecessor told her about the class was, at first observation, entirely accurate—the students became quickly involved in their reading by selecting from the variety of materials available at their desks, read eagerly, and appeared to enjoy the daily experience of getting deeply involved in a variety of authors' messages ranging from simple to serious. Most teachers would delight in a classroom of students busily reading, but my friend was determined to find a fly in the pedagogical ointment. Her questions were endless, but the three most often repeated were: How can I be sure the children are mastering the skills of reading? Won't I have better control if I have daily reading groups? Am I really doing my job?

To support these questions, my friend pointed out that these were, after all, kids with a history of reading failure, and it wasn't reasonable to expect them to read without acquiring the basics. And to teach basic word-attack and comprehension skills, the daily reading circles seemed the most civilized, orderly, and accountable kind of organization. As far as the ego-involved question of doing a job was concerned—well, what would other teachers, parents, and administrators think of a teacher who spent precious class time modeling reading (McCracken and McCracken 1978) instead of instructing?

These were thorny questions from a dedicated teacher who was learning day by day that her students could never go back to an instructional mode that focused attention on splintered-off units of language through phonics and word-attack drills. Her students were now involved with whole language; that is, they read complete stories, newspaper and magazine articles, brochures, baseball cards, and books of all descriptions.

The students convinced their new teacher that they were, more than ever before, reading with zest and confidence. They did not, however, convince her that she could do no more for them than provide a rich environment of written material and act as their adult model of an avid reader. As good as it was, this teacher wanted more mileage from sustained silent reading.

Reader-Selected Miscues

Miscues, to review briefly, are deviations from the printed page made during oral reading (Goodman 1967). Miscues in this context will be defined as including those deviations that cause the reader problems while reading silently. The term *miscue,* substituted for *error* or *mistake,* is an especially good one for the activity presented here since the neutrality of the term encourages both the reader and the teacher to withhold judgment about a miscue's cause and its "interference" with the reading process until it is analyzed.

To her students' delight, my friend extended the daily sustained silent reading time from twenty to thirty minutes in order to accommodate the collecting of reader-selected miscues (RSMs). Before the reading period, students were given several two-inch-by-eight-inch bookmarks and asked to read as usual, but when they encountered difficulty to place a marker in their books at the troublesome point and continue their reading. Ten minutes before the close of the reading period, the students examined their miscues and selected three that in the long run caused major problems; that is, caused them to lose meaning or to be distracted from their reading. The students wrote each sentence containing a selected miscue on a bookmark, underlined the trouble spot, wrote their name, book title, and page number, and returned the three bookmarks to their teacher. Any remaining time after completion of this task was spent in reading; those who had not encountered problems continued reading the few extra minutes.

(Young children and students just starting the RSM activity can write the miscues directly onto the bookmark. This facilitates daily collection and quick categorizing on the teacher's part. Older readers can keep a log of miscues and turn the log in to the teacher each week.)

The first step in the RSM activity—inserting bookmarks at trouble spots and going on with the text—promoted in students several important attitudes about reading and about themselves as readers. First, the reader, not the teacher or other reading-circle mates, is in the driver's seat. No one is on hand to call attention to errors or to provide help. The reader and the author are allowed their own conversation without interruptions from outsiders. Second, the student realizes that everyone, even the most proficient reader, makes miscues; no one expects or strives for performance perfection in reading. Third, the reader has automony in selecting and rejecting material. No one can tell students that despite real needs and strong motivations they must discard a book when they have made five errors on one page ("The 'Greasy Hand' Readability Test" 1975). The *reader* decides if the miscues cause loss of meaning or interest, if they diminish determination or reduce staying power. Fourth, readers become their own monitors; that is, the students become actively involved in the meaning-seeking process. They must constantly match up text information with the information in their own heads, and they do this by insisting that whatever they read make sense and that the wording be acceptable to them. Finally, a "keep going" strategy becomes legitimate. The student is asked not to break the flow of reading by stopping to ask for help or to check the dictionary. Students sometimes feel that they have cheated if they continue reading not knowing every word on the page, but the little confession of inserting a bookmark allows them to continue, absolved.

In the next step of the reader-selected miscue activity, the students examined their previously marked miscues and selected three that caused the most trouble in terms of losing meaning and disrupting language flow. At this point in the activity the students qualified rather than quantified their miscues—they were not asked to count errors. Instead, with the teacher's guidance or on their own, the students decided that many of their miscues could be ignored because they no longer represented meaning loss. That is, they learned that through continued reading, the word or concept in question became clear. When readers pressed on, they gave the author an opportunity to provide more information through inference, reference, substitution, ellipsis, example, and definition. Through the efforts of both the author and the reader, communication was achieved—and they did it on their own.

The following were reported by my friend's junior high students as examples of gaining *immediate* text information and combining that with their own knowledge—resulting in comprehension of the word or concept. The unknown words are underlined; related explanatory text is italicized.

He's on this cafe au lait kick where he has to *heat the milk separately and then pour it simultaneously with the coffee into a mug.* (Source: *It's Not What You Expect*)

All that was visible of this alien Wisconsin were slivers of bright sky and fragments of green and gold fields, and just a twinkle, off to the left, of the loch—*lake,* she corrected herself wearily. (Source: *The Secret of Stonehouse*)

The jodhpurs were her dearest possessions, even though they had been handed down to her from a neighbor's cousin in Doddenkirk. They were a *soft black material, with black leather patches inside the knees,* and they had been handtailored in London. (Source: *The Secret of Stonehouse*)

"You *new* here, right? *Stranger* here?. . . A haole, dat's a *stranger. White like you. Not brown like me.*" (Source: *Make No Sound*)

Where did they get their food, anyway? "It is pauper's share," his grandmother answered shortly. He wished he had not asked. He hated the picture of his grandmother following after the reapers in the field, *scrabbling for the sheaves they dropped,* which had by law to be left for <u>paupers</u> to gather. (Source: *The Bronze Bow*)

Romey said he knew where there was a big spread of <u>lamb's-quarters</u> which is *a potherb, something like spinach.* (Source: *Where the Lilies Bloom*)

Readers discovered, too, that it was not necessary to understand every word in the discourse; some omissions did not change text meaning. Extensive vocabularies are desirable, but often readers have more to lose than to gain by interrupting their reading to look up or ask about word meanings. By continuing to read, the student can gain additional information from the text and decide at the close of the reading if a missed word needs attention. A junior high boy decided that the following omissions were unimportant to the total meaning of his story. He chose to read on.

"I'm glad all animals can't speak," said Lightfinger, "we'd have *meningitis* within the week. . . ."

. . . and a sheet of *corrugated* iron covered the main doorway.

The *facade* of the building was painted over in grey. . . .

It was a typical Borrible hideway, *derelict* and decaying. . . . (Source: *The Borribles*)

Looking into miscues instead of looking for errors gets readers off the hook. Through enlightened investigation, readers began to understand that they often change the author's message, not because they are lazy or careless readers (as they may have been told), but because something in their own personal background is momentarily influencing them. When students are relaxed about their reading, they enjoy sharing with each other those silent and oral miscues that directly reveal their origins in the reader's immediate context (such as signs just read, snatches of recent conversations, recurrence of hunger, or the subject of a movie just seen) or origins that are linked to pervasive or lingering forces in the reader's environment (such as concern with dating, current heroes, familiar expressions, brand names, lines from commercials, poetry and songs, getting a job, or making it through school). For example:

                         Scotch
A second later he was out again, carrying a roll of sticky tape.

        tail
You haven't got the law on your trail, have you?

By looking into miscues instead of counting errors, readers begin to recognize that the author may have unwittingly caused them to stumble. The following examples reveal that unexpected syntax, conceptual overloading, and lack of text cohesion can cause trouble (even when they don't provide miscues). For example,

> The driver folds the seat in half ∧ a second. (Source: *I'll Get There. It Better Be Worth the Trip*)

> Few *debutantes* have been the *recipients* of such *mass masculine* interest upon their presentation. . . . This somewhat unusually large attendance at a *rather usual miracle* was due to the fact that, like any *prima donna*, she *heralded* her arrival and then kept her public waiting almost two weeks. (Source: *Karen*)

> Or rushes in to *pal with an example*, when that's what the teacher *points me out to be*. Hardly anybody wants to hang out with *a guy* who keeps showing *him* up all the time. (Source: *Henry 3*)

By looking into their miscues instead of counting their errors, readers begin to appreciate their own contributions to the reading act. They become aware of their own correcting procedures, what causes the correction, as well as when it is necessary to correct and when it is inefficient to do so. Additionally, their own strengths become obvious when they are able to make appropriate substitutions based on text information combined with their own knowledge. The junior high students could easily express why they had corrected the following miscues or why they had accepted their own substitutions.

Ⓒ*Carter*
Old company letter says |Custer in debt before famous last stand|

(Source: newspaper headline during Carter presidency)

hang-up
. . . thought about names and gaining of them, a major preoccupation with him. (Source: *The Borribles*)

change
But Donald was in a good mood now, and she didn't want to jeopardize it. (Source: *The Secret of Stonehouse*)

Ⓒ
|They made ⟨for⟩ an empty house. (Source: *The Borribles*)

A girl in the back laughed just a little too long. Mr. Rawling merely
stopped
flicked his eyes at her and she subsided. (Source: *The Boy Who Could Make Himself Disappear*)

With practice, the students could easily determine that some miscues were so detrimental to the reading act that the reading flow was interrupted and meaning was distorted or slipped away, while other miscues did not cause any damage to their conversation with the author.

A Typical First Collection of Reader-Selected Miscues

When twenty readers turn in three RSMs each, the teacher has a wealth of data from which to glean information concerning students' reading behaviors. The task now is to categorize the miscues in an effort to find similar problems and a basis for forming group instruction. Usually the first collection of RSMs reveals that many problems are caused by unknown names, foreign words, and the dialect variations of the author or of one of the author's characters. Following are samples of reader-chosen "problem" words taken from the first collection of my friend's junior high class:

The moon was clear of clouds again and glinted on the nearby Thames. (Source: *The Borribles*)

She had an odd name—Malthace. (Source: *The Bronze Bow*)

In the distance Kiser Pease, high on his tractor, was creating clouds of furious, black dust. (Source: *Where the Lilies Bloom*)

. . . Frederick Douglass said that spring, in Rochester's Corinthian Hall. . . . (Source: *Her Name Was Sojourner Truth*)

. . . hid herself behind a flowering rhododendron . . . (Source: *Where the Lilies Bloom*)

. . . someone started to sing the Marseillaise . . . (Source: *When Hitler Stole Pink Rabbit*)

"The Mayor of Paris has decided to award prizes for the twenty best French compositions written by children taking the certificat d'etudes," she explained. (Source: *When Hitler Stole Pink Rabbit*)

Oliver was making smoked oyster sandwiches on kommisbrot with Boston lettuce. (Source: *It's Not What You Think*)

Thieves they are, just like us, only they call it finding. A copper would call it stealing by finding. (Source: *The Borribles*)

"Lord have mercy, look at him. He's sicker'n a dog. He don't even know we're here, he's that sick." (Source: *Where the Lilies Bloom*)

"Chillun, I talks to God, and God talks to me." (Source: *Her Name Was Sojourner Truth*)

"Aye, go it, lass," Heather sang. (Source: *The Secret of Stonehouse*)

And off in the distance were the volcanoes. Farthest off, with snow on top of it, was <u>Mauna Kea</u>. . . . Nearer were <u>Mauna Loa</u> and <u>Kilauea</u>. (Source: *Make No Sound*)

"I <u>spik</u> you later. Now I spik <u>dis lil malihini</u> . . . What your name? . . . <u>Bruddahs</u>? Two <u>mo' Baxters</u>, yeah? . . . We be back <u>bumbye</u>." (Source: *Make No Sound*)

On top of <u>Tepeyac</u> Hill in the one-time village is a small chapel. (Source: *Fiesta Time in Mexico*)

The last step of the RSM activity involves discussion with students who have similar reading problems. When the readers who made the miscues above discussed their RSMs, they were first of all surprised to discover that their problems were common ones shared by other readers. They talked about spending a great deal of time trying to determine the pronunciation of words. After the teacher helped them with naming strategy lessons (Goodman and Burke 1972), the students decided that it was better to substitute a nickname, a nonword, a letter, or a synonym for the unknown name or word and to continue their reading. If the word was foreign, they felt it important to know this, but it was not necessary to be able to pronounce it. The following examples helped the readers understand the naming strategy:

Val
It is called the Valkyrie. (Source: *B-70: Monarch of the Skies*)

But to continue my story, you see I've not finished yet, when we
Pren
arrived at the Prenungracht. (Source: *The Diary of Anne Frank*)

Man   *Rich*
Manfred von Richtoven was born in Silesia. (Source: *Flying Aces of World War I*)

L
Lavenia, get on with your spinning. (Source: *The American Book of Horse Stories*)

The students concluded that if they continued their reading, they could make their own decisions about whether or not they needed or wanted to learn to pronounce a particular name or word. For example, one reader whose hobby was marine life felt it important to be able to pronounce *Cyanea Capillata* in, "The largest of the jellyfish is Cyanea Capillata." The other students agreed that because of his interests he would enjoy researching the Cyanea Capillata, including learning how to pronounce the name, but for them it would be a waste of their reading time and effort.

Dialect mismatches caused readers problems until they saw that they could "translate" from the author's to their own preferred expressions, all without loss of meaning. Readers shared the following dialect preference substitutions:

there
"I forgot my sack. I left it back yonder." (Source: *Where the Lilies Bloom*)

among
There are good technicians amongst them. (Source: *The Deserters*)

right away
The water got deep straightaway. (Source: *The Deserters*)

Way   *long*
"Clear up in the foothills? That's a fair way, all right." (Source: *Tuck Everlasting*)

started
I took a basket and some knives and lit out for Trail Creek. (Source: *Where the Lilies Bloom*)

The members of the instructional group as well as the topics of discussion changed daily. The groups were built on need, and the students liked the idea of knowing that their selected miscues were going to be taken seriously and considered carefully.

My friend took her professional inheritance and increased the profits beyond her own expectations. By continuing a linguistically sound, student-centered procedure—sustained silent reading—and by adding an activity that provided personal and immediately applicable information—reader-selected miscues—she was able to promote her students' proficiency and interest in written material of all kinds.

References

Goodman, Kenneth S. 1967. Reading: A psycholinguistic guessing game. *Journal of the Reading Specialist, 6,* 126–35.

Goodman, Yetta M. & Burke, Carolyn L. 1972. *Reading Miscue Inventory manual: Procedures for diagnosis and evaluation.* New York: Macmillan.

The "greasy hand" readability test. 1975. *The Reading Letter, 1,* 2.

McCracken, Robert A. & McCracken, Marlene J. 1978. Modeling is the key to sustained silent reading. *The Reading Teacher, 31,* 406–8.

In College and in Trouble— with Reading

With unbelievable determination and with lots of encouragement on the part of caring friends, Jerry made it! He and his wife, Angela, now live in St. Louis where he works as a claims adjuster in an insurance office. Sometimes I run across something that Jerry wrote when we were working together and I think how lucky I was that he had the gift of persuasion and that he used it to talk me into learning with him. He may be one of the best teachers I've ever had. (Of the book I gave him for graduation, Leo the Late Bloomer, *Jerry said, "The story of my life!")*

How does it feel to be bright, twenty-one, good-looking, a star athlete, and lucky in love? In more cases than we care to admit, "Miserable" is the answer. Miserable, because of bad luck in learning to read.

Recently CBS television's news program *Sixty Minutes* presented a segment in which star athletes discussed their inability to read and the resulting problems they faced during and after their eligibility years. They described a miserable situation.

Jerry, a student at my school, saw that television show, and the shoe fit so well that the following morning he arrived at my door; a friend had told him I might have some new ideas about reading.

Originally published in *Journal of Reading* 25 (1982), 640–45. Reprinted with the permission of the International Reading Association.

Within minutes Jerry had dismissed all my protests: I don't tutor; I've got classes to prepare for; I have a pile of papers to read and letters to answer; you probably aren't serious anyway.

He persisted, so I picked up a story from the top of a pile on my desk and gave it to him, hoping he wouldn't be offended by the child-ish text that was undoubtedly far too easy for him. I wasn't prepared for what I heard. (Jerry's substitutions are written above the text, in-sertions are marked with a caret, omissions are circled, pauses longer than ten seconds are marked with a large P, and repetitions are under-lined and marked with a circled R.)

A Day at Home

Weston
Wes—
Bobby P *Wa—* P *wa-stick*   *start*
One day Bob Watson was sick. He had to stay home from school.

(R) *started*   *look+ed*   *win+dow*
He stayed in bed all day. And he looked out the window to see what

ha+pen+ning
was happening in the street.

said   *said*   P
He saw Mrs. Miller go to the store. He saw Mr. (Burke) bring the

said   *good + man*
mail. He saw Mr. Goodman bring the milk.

said   *draining*
s—   (R) *started drinking ing*
Then he saw something bad. He saw dark smoke ∧coming out of the

Bobby   *way*
window of Mrs. Miller(s) house. Bob knew that (no) one was in the house to see the smoke. (Time: 3 min. 5 sec.)

As Jerry struggled through the passage, beads of perspiration formed on his brow, his body appeared to tighten and shrink, and he hunched close to the page, alternately jabbing his finger at the words and clutching the sides of the book. After he had sounded his way to the end, he could tell me almost nothing about the story. The reluc-tant teacher succumbed.

In our first session, Jerry talked about his past humiliating expe-riences with reading and learning to read. He talked about how from the first grade, failure and deception had grown into a monster that was, in his mind, sure to breathe fire as soon as he was no longer eli-gible for sports. The Burke reading interview (Goodman, Watson &

Burke 1987) combined with questions about his school experiences prompted honest and helpful (for future instruction) answers. Jerry believed that in order to read he must sound out letters, syllables, and words; know the meaning of every word; put the words together; and, finally, read the sentence with good expression. Jerry knew teaching jargon. He told me about beginning and ending consonant blends, "dip-thongs," root words, vowels that go walking, eye exercises, skill builders, kits, and reading machines. He concluded his résumé of attempts to learn to read with, "I've got dyslexia." To keep from crying, I asked who he had caught it from.

At this point I knew I wanted to work with Jerry, but we had to lay down some ground rules. Our views of reading were so different that he might want to seek help elsewhere. For starters, no more mention of dyslexia, sounding out, flash cards (Jerry carried a pack of "basic words" in his pocket), or "I can't read." Additionally, home game or out-of-towner, he was to read an hour every day, write fifteen minutes a day, and meet with me once a week. He agreed, and I threw his dog-eared, pizza-stained Dolch Basic 220 in the wastebasket.

Jerry's determination, intelligence, and sense of humor made our weekly meetings a joy. We were engrossed, we were learning, time flew, and we always parted tired. We learned that reading is usually fun, learning to read sometimes isn't.

Every session was different, but we always began with talk about things that interested Jerry most—sports and learning to read. My comment on his classy display on the sports field was followed by his mini-lecture on some aspect of the last game (all in the attempt to diminish my cultural deprivation). Talk turned to things Jerry had read or been unable to read during the past week. We tried always to talk first about his successes.

In each session we attempted to include (1) time for Jerry to read, (2) time for us to read together, (3) time for us to write together, and (4) time for me to read to him.

Jerry Reads and Writes

Jerry read from his daily journal, from something he and I had written earlier, and from material that would help build fluency and confidence.

The first entry in Jerry's journal was a list of signs found in his print world:

Corrs
Pizza factory
No shoes no shirt no service
League

Tires
Batteries
Employee only
Ken's

In time Jerry produced near-sentences and sentences.

Home work bef-ur Tuesday
do you done all your time to school work
do you no how to talk a test?
I have a night class to morrow at 7:00 to 9:45

And later he wrote connected discourse with semantic intent.

I was so tir aftr practis today that my body aked. I bet someone mad
a fortune on wirlepool baths. I dont care if they did I give them my
lives savings.

Unless asked, I made no comment about spelling, punctuation, or
handwriting. We were, after all, learning to compose—to deal with
ideas and to write fluently without being distracted by attention to
surface-level features. I discouraged editing at first; later, at Jerry's in-
sistence, we spent time during each session discussing mechanics. Attention to form always occurred after the writing, not before or during
the process. When Jerry concerned himself with composing rather
than copying words, his journal entries reflected the real Jerry, complete with humor and intelligence. And with time and some editing
strategies Jerry moved toward standard spelling and grammar.

Jogging is something that a lot of people do nowadays. I do it but not
for the same reason most people do. I don't even like it but I do it
because I look good at it. Want proof? Tonight some really
goodlooking people wave their hands off at me in my Addeedas. I
going to keep on jogging. I owe it to the neighborhood.

Reading from his own journal, Jerry the reader and Jerry the
writer came together and the background gap was closed. When Jerry
had trouble reading his own writing, we reconstructed the situation:
What were you thinking? What did you intend to say? Build on what
you know and on the information available on the page.

Sometimes it was easier to read print that Jerry had collected for
one of his two books. Familiar advertisements, slogans, jingles, commercials, jokes, school cheers, and old sayings went into *Jerry's Sights
and Sounds*. Dozens of songs I had never heard of went into *Born to
Boogie*. These built his confidence (and shook mine).

Jerry did his daily reading with a pencil in hand. In order to keep
moving along in the story, he simply underlined the trouble spots and
continued reading. During our sessions he read from his marked book

and we discussed some of his problems. This procedure provided the opportunity to offer strategies that were immediately applicable. Following are some suggestions for Jerry's recurring problems.

1. Trouble with names of people and places: Assign a temporary abbreviation or nickname and keep going.

2. Trouble with a label for a concept: Try anything that makes sense, whether it "sounds out" right or not, or say *blank* and keep going. Don't worry about unlocking words—concern yourself with unlocking ideas.

3. Trouble with a wandering mind: Get ready to read by reviewing what has happened in the text earlier and by guessing what will happen next. Constantly monitor incoming information to make sure it is compatible with what you already know.

4. Falling into the "sounding out" syndrome: Remember that reading is constructing meaning, not constructing sounds. Don't tunnel in on letters—open up to ideas, and keep reading.

5. Reading too slowly and too much rereading: In most instances you have all the information possible to receive after the first glance, so let your mind, not your eyes, take over. Keep tying ideas together with ideas. Don't slow down—speed up and keep monitoring.

6. Poorly written material or text that is too structurally or conceptually difficult: Even great readers can look like poor readers if they are asked to handle poorly written text or something for which they have little or no prior experience. If you have given the author and yourself every chance to construct meaning, and for all your efforts you continue to be confused and bewildered—stop reading. Spend your time on material that is sensible and well written. In the event you must get the information contained in a difficult text, demand help. Help can come in the form of someone reading to you, selecting easier material on the same topic that will provide good background information, being cued in on the author's style and organizing structure, and discussing the concepts in the text.

Jerry and I Read Together

Selection of the material that Jerry and I read together depended largely on text predictability and Jerry's interests. The two of us were living proof that in order to read, both interest and good strategies are needed. For example, neither of us alone was a good reader of *Sports Illustrated*. I wasn't interested in the subject and Jerry used inefficient, uptight "attack skills." I needed to know something about Abdul-Jabbar, how Staubach should have been picked for the All-Pros, split-cane fly rods, and the difference between NBA, NFL, and RBI. And Jerry needed to learn about taking risks, building meaning with the author, and being cued not only by letters, but by on-the-page and off-the-page (context of discourse and context of situation) information.

Jerry and I assisted each other by discussing what we knew about the subject of the article and by predicting the author's message, all before we began reading. We then read aloud together, with Jerry often trailing slightly behind, sometimes reading exactly with me and sometimes, when concepts and language were supportive, moving to the lead. I needed, in order to comprehend the articles, Jerry's knowledge; he needed strategies with print.

Together we read useful language that Jerry found on posters, signs, ads, menus, directories, class schedules, how-to-do-it directions, and forms. This functional print caused him to consider the context of the print and led to important questions: Where did I find this? What do I expect it to say? How do I expect it to be worded and organized?

Jerry needed material that would build his fluency and independence. I wanted to use text that was structurally unambiguous, had repetitive and cumulative phrases, and lent itself to deletions for which Jerry could predict words, phrases, sentences, and ideas. I found all these in some poetry and stories for children. The question now was whether Jerry would be embarrassed and turned off by the childish format and content. As it turned out this intelligent twenty-one-year-old was not in the least offended by the children's literature. He loved the illustrations, picked up on themes, and thoroughly enjoyed becoming the author of wordless picture books. I felt vindicated when Jerry looked up from *The Biggest Bear* to comment, "Geeeez, I missed all this."

Jerry became a more determined and confident reader by joining me in reading the following books with predictable language: *Millions of Cats*, by Wanda Gag; *Drummer Hoff,* by Barbara Emberley; *Don't Forget the Bacon,* by Pat Hutchins; *Six Foolish Fishermen*, by Benjamin Elkin; *Hush, Little Baby*, by Margot Zemach; *May I Bring a Friend?*, by Beatrice S. de Regniers; and *Good Night Owl!*, by Pat Hutchins.

Jerry and I Write Together

Confident that with help Jerry could write about things that interested him, we began writing: Jerry used his brain and I used my pencil. First we discussed our story. I asked questions that a potential reader might

ask, questions that encouraged the author to present ideas in a clear and
cohesive manner. By discussing before writing, Jerry saw that writing
was not talk written down. It was necessary to shore up, reconsider, cut
out extraneous verbiage—that is, to edit in his head before dictating.
With the author hanging over my shoulder, I wrote Jerry's stories. He
read them back, sometimes editing and sometimes (to his dismay) having trouble reading parts of his own creation. When this happened, we
pieced together the author's intent and organizing pattern and prayed
for memory to help; with persistence he read his own work. Following
are Jerry's dictated directions for backgammon. Changes made in his
first rereading of the story are written above the text.

Backgammon

Every player has

~~You have~~ a certain amount of chips and a certain order to put them
number
in. You have dice and whatever ˄you roll on the dice you have to
Be
move the chips. ~~You have to~~ be sure you don't leave a man open. If
you leave a man open there is a chance of getting hit. When you get
hit you have to get on the hump. (That's the middle of the board.)
To get off the hump you have to roll a number that's open. When off
go
the hump, proceed on and try to get all your men on your side of the
board. That's when you start taking them off. The player who takes
all his men off first wins the game.

I Read to Jerry

Without fail, whether our session was forty-five minutes or two
hours, I read to Jerry. Our selections were intentionally varied: an
ongoing adult novel (we loved Ken Follett's spy mystery *Eye of the Needle*), a children's book (we cried through Wilson Rawls's *Where the Red
Fern Grows*), a folktale (Jerry selected stories from *Grains of Pepper:
Folktales from Liberia, The Jack Tales,* and *Grandfather Tales*), a passage
from one of his textbooks, the yellow pages, the newpaper, and popular magazines. Listening to reading allowed Jerry to relax and enjoy
language and to experience a variety of themes, styles, and organizing
structures. We discussed a passage only if he chose to. As I read, Jerry
alternated between attending so closely to the print that I had to move
his head out of my line of vision, and sitting hunched with his head
down staring at the table or floor.

He was relaxed but not passive; he monitored the new messages, constantly relating them to something already known, and he worked hard at predicting the author's next move.

Conclusion and Summary

After ten months, Jerry was still not out of the woods but was well on his way to becoming a language user who could read a variety of texts and who could express himself in his journal, letters, and stories. In our first year we experienced frustrations, setbacks, plateaus, spurts of rapid progress, and finally steady success. Jerry was motivated and bright, and had a sense of humor that got us over the tight spots. We also had *real* language on our side, language in the form of jokes, plays, poems, signs, stories, letters, notes, and books.

In summary, Jerry learned, first of all, that he was neither stupid nor sick and that indeed he could read some things. We began his stepped-up venture into print by using the language Jerry was most familiar with—his own. He also read professionally authored material that was structurally unambiguous, predictable, and dealt with known concepts. Never was Jerry offered text that was less than complete. That is, I never asked him to fight the abstractness of letters, sounds, syllables, and words out of the context of discourse and situation.

Writing experiences and reading experiences complemented and supported each other. Jerry was involved daily in writing about his own life, and weekly he wrote jokes, songs, stories, and letters with me. Revision and editing emerged gradually and naturally.

Jerry was given many reading strategies, but one of the most helpful had to do with handling "unreadable" material. When the author failed or when Jerry didn't have the background to cope with the concepts, style, labels, or format, I encouraged him to stop reading.

Jerry's major sports season is underway now and I won't see him for a month or two, but in an effort to assure me that he wouldn't break his reading and writing training, he parted (temporarily) with, "You know, reading is like riding a bike. You gotta keep going or you fall off. I got me a good start and I'm gonna keep on keepin' on!"

Note: Jerry gave his permission for me to tell our story.

Reference

Goodman, Yetta M., Watson, Dorothy J. & Burke, Carolyn L. 1987. *Reading Miscue Inventory: Alternative procedures.* New York: Richard C. Owen.

Strategy Lessons
(with Paul Crowley)

The unfortunate title of this chapter comes from, "How Can We Implement a Whole Language Approach?" is a constant reminder of the wisdom behind Ken Goodman's warning about becoming a "wholier than thou" whole language teacher. Just when we were sure we had the exact language for our ideas, Paul and I found that we had called whole language an approach *rather than what we believe it to be, a* philosophy *that embraces theories, beliefs, and practices about learners and learning, teachers and teaching.*

For more on strategy lessons that are consistent with a whole language philosophy, teachers may be interested in Reading Strategies: Focus on Comprehension, *(2nd. ed.) by Yetta Goodman, Dorothy Watson, and Carolyn Burke (Katonah, NY: Richard C. Owen, 1996).*

Ken Goodman has identified *reading strategies* as what the reader does when the eye hits the page: the reader samples print, predicts what is coming, confirms those predictions, corrects if necessary, and integrates new with old information. Now we want to use the word *strategy* in another, but related, way. Readers use certain strategies when they read, and some of these strategies are more effective than others.

Reprinted by permission of Dorothy Watson and Paul Crowley. From Chapter 8, "How Can We Implement a Whole Language Approach?" in *Reading Process and Practice: From Socio-psycholinguistics to Whole Language,* edited by Constance Weaver (Portsmouth, NH: Heinemann, A division of Reed Elsevier, Inc., 1988), pp. 258–67.

When a reader encounters an unfamiliar word, for example, there are choices to be made; these choices are strategies. When Mynett came to the word *gargoyle* while reading, she could have sounded out the word, broken it into syllables, related the word to a familiar word, looked it up in a dictionary, skipped it, stopped reading, or asked someone else. Mynett decided to use the strategy of asking someone else. Successful readers use various strategies at different times, depending on the context of text and context of situation.

We now want to discuss *strategy lessons.* These lessons are first of all whole language; that is, all the systems of language support the reader in the attempt to proficiently and efficiently sample, predict, correct if necessary, confirm, and integrate meaning—in sum, to read. Strategy lessons take advantage of the strengths of a reader, and they are often brief and always to the point. Equally important, they lead to a discussion of the reading process.

In order to introduce specific strategy lessons, we need to look at a specific learner. We will move from Gregg's reading below to a strategy lesson that will help him and other inefficient readers in their attempts to construct meaning.

Naming Strategy

Gregg read a story about an elephant named Sudana who was sick and needed to be given sulfa for her fever. The word *Sudana* appeared throughout the story and Gregg miscued on the word each time it appeared. These are some of his miscues:

Expected Response	*Observed Response*
Sudana	1. (omitted "Sudana")
	2. S-
	Shadu
	Shadan, Shadan
	3. Sh-
	Shutten
	4. Shana
	5. Shoud
	6. Shata
	7. Shur
	8. Shadon
	9. Shana
Sudana's	10. hers
Sudana's	11. Shadon's
Sudana	12. Shadon

In the same story, Gregg also made repeated attempts on the word
sulfa:

Expected Response	*Observed Response*
sulfa	1. s-
	shovel
	2. suchful
	3. shana
	4. shiffle (subvocalized: "or
	something")
	5. shum
	6. snafen
	serman (shook his book)
	7. surn
	8. surum
	9. surm
	10. surm

Gregg focused a great deal of attention on small, abstract units of
language, particularly symbol/sound relationships. Multiple attempts
on *Sudana* and *sulfa* exemplify a strategy that he used throughout this
and other stories—a sounding-out process. Gregg took a long time to
finish the story and his reading was hesitant and choppy. At one point,
when he had a great deal of difficulty with the word *sulfa,* he shook the
book in frustration. Nevertheless he was able to retell most of the story: Gregg knew that the main character was an elephant, female, and
that her name was "Shana, or something"; and he was able to tell that
the elephant was sick and that the doctor made numerous attempts to
give her medicine and finally succeeded. In addition to these major
propositions, Gregg remembered a number of details as well.

Gregg was an *effective* but *inefficient* reader: effective in that he
could successfully retell the major propositions of the story, but inefficient in that his reading was slow and laborious.

What does this suggest for Gregg's reading program? Whole language instruction always begins with what students are doing *right*
and builds on these strengths. Successful readers take ownership of
their own language and are empowered by an understanding of what
they can do and where they are headed. Gregg needs to view language as a process he can comfortably and confidently direct by using
strategies that will help him become more efficient.

Judged only on his oral performance, Gregg would probably be
considered by many to be a poor reader. Analysis of his miscues and
his retelling, though, indicate a number of strengths. Consider Gregg's
substitution of *hers* for *Sudana's.* These words have no graphic or
sound similarity; at this point, Gregg abandoned the sounding-out

strategy and put in something that fit grammatically and semantically. Gregg probably wasn't aware that he deviated from the text; he had adjusted his focus to meaning and let the sense of the story he was constructing offer him the support that was lacking in the smaller cues. Gregg's previous reading instructional model would describe such a departure from the text as an "error" that needed to be corrected. On the contrary, Gregg should be made aware that what he did was linguistically sophisticated and positive because it made sense.

Gregg needs to move more fluently through a text in order to make reading less frustrating; he needs to *keep going*. "Keep going" strategies hold readers' attention to meaning and to cues that move them fluently through text. The two questions that successful readers have in the back of their minds as they read are: Does this sound like language? and Does this make sense? Gregg's miscues on *Sudana* indicate that he needs a "naming strategy" so that when he encounters a proper name, he will substitute for it whatever name he wants and then stick with that substitution throughout the text. The important concept is that it is a name, not how the name is pronounced. *Mr. Przybilski* becomes *Mr. P.* Successful readers use this substitution strategy, allowing them to focus on meaning, not pronunciation. A lesson promoting this strategy involves the teacher's briefly conferring with the student or talking with a group having similar needs about choices to be made when something unfamiliar is encountered in a text. Reading is not an exact process, but Gregg's previous instruction indicated that it was, by focusing on exact oral reproduction of the text. Gregg must receive confirmation that it is acceptable to substitute a placeholder that makes sense.

Readers are flexible when they use a variety of strategies for handling a variety of texts; reading *instruction* involves engaging students in lessons that demonstrate the use of these strategies, and *reading itself* provides the opportunity to practice these strategies in the context of whole language.

For students who are bound to the text and will not move away from overreliance on symbol/sound cues, the following strategy lesson helps them use both semantic and syntactic information.

Selected Deletions

When readers not only overuse *graphophonemic* information but also are reluctant to skip words that give them trouble or unwilling to substitute something that makes sense, words and phrases can be omitted from the text to encourage linguistic risk taking. This "keep going" strategy lesson is a modified cloze procedure and referred to as *selected deletions*. It encourages readers to sample from *all* the available linguistic and pragmatic cues except the graphic cues of the deleted text item.

The passages used for selected deletions can be professionally authored or teacher-made; they must be cohesive and well organized. The teacher considers the reader as well as the text when selecting the items to be deleted. Deletions should be structurally and semantically unambiguous. The first sentence of the passage is kept intact to allow the reader to get information about the passage and to gain confidence. It is important to delete only highly predictable words, especially for reluctant readers, so they can move fluently through the text. Some deletions can be replaced by a number of different possibilities. When this is done, the student sees that meaning is not altered by putting in something that makes sense, even if it is not the original text item.

Words can be deleted by opaquing the items or by omitting them when typing the text. Teachers should always try the activity themselves after all the deletions have been made; too many omissions or the omission of certain words can make this a difficult procedure, thereby defeating its purpose. After the words have been filled in by the students, the original text can be distributed for comparison and discussion about the process.

Gloria on Jupiter

Gloria was the first explorer to land on Jupiter. When she returned to _____, she met with many important _____. One of these was the President _____ the United States. Gloria _____ the President talked a long _____.

"Congratulations, _____! Everyone is very, _____ proud of you."
"Thank _____, Mr. President."
"Are you happy to be back on _____?" asked the _____.
"Yes! I got very lonely on that _____ trip!"
"Do you _____ to go again?"
"I'd _____ any time you _____ me," said Gloria.
"What would _____ like to take with you on your next trip to Jupiter?" asked the President.
"Good _____ are always nice!" said Gloria.

Successful readers know that real authors will help them by building concepts from the unknown to the known. If, for example, the label (word) for a concept is unfamiliar to readers, the cues in well-written text will support readers in their attempts to make reasonable guesses at meaning; if there are no supportive cues, the word may not be important. When readers negotiate meaning with the author, they are learning from the text. In traditional classrooms, students are often advised to look up words in the dictionary before they have tried to make some guesses. But going to the dictionary not only interrupts the reading process, it often provides misleading definitions and keeps readers from gaining information; it is not what successful readers do. Proficient readers use the dictionary and other outside sources to *confirm* their predictions when there is sufficient ambiguity about an important concept and when interest is high; vocabulary usually develops naturally during reading.

The following selected-deletions text was developed for a boy who, upon seeing the title, decided he could not read the selection because he did not know the word *sampan*. (Interestingly, though, he could pronounce it.) He noticed that it occurred repeatedly through the text, but his teacher could not convince him that he could read it, so she created a selected-deletion version by removing *sampan* wherever it occurred. It was not long into the reading that he inserted *raft,* then *boat,* and finally *houseboat* in the blanks.

Rain on the Sampan

Rain raised the river. Rain beat down on the _____ where it lay in a long row of _____ tied to the riverbank. Rain drummed down on the mats that were shaped in the form of an arched roof over the middle of the _____. It clattered hard on the four long oars lying on top of the roof of mats.

The rain found the bullet hole in the roof of mats. Thick drops of water dripped through the bullet hole onto the neck of the family pig, sleeping on the floor of the _____. The little pig twitched his neck every time a big, cold drop of water hit it, but he went on sleeping. . . .

Rain raised the river. The _____ swayed and bobbed on the rising water. Voices drifted from the other _____ in the long row of _____ and muttered among the drumming rain. Tien Pao closed his eyes and almost slept, and yet he didn't sleep. He sat sagged against the mats, dreamily remembering the hard days just past, the hard journey.

It had been a long journey. Tien Pao had lost count of all the days and nights. But all those nights when the horns of the new moon had stood dimly in the sky, Tien Pao and his father and mother had pushed the _____ on and on against the currents of the endless rivers. (From *The House of Sixty Fathers*, by Meindert DeJong)

Proper names can also be deleted. In the earlier strategy lesson, Gregg was encouraged to use a naming strategy to help him deal with the proper name Sudana. If students are reluctant to use this strategy, the name can be deleted from the text.

This selected-deletions strategy lesson helps students use context clues from text to determine the unknown words. The grammar of the sentence is the basic structural cue to draw upon.

Schema Stories

Texts also have *story grammars* that give readers information about meaning; *schema stories* is a strategy lesson that focuses on story grammar. Just as selected deletions require readers to supply omitted words in text based on meaning and *sentence* grammar, schema stories require readers to reconstruct the order of a text based on meaning and *story* grammar.

The choice of material for a schema story is important. It must have highly predictable structures such as "Once upon a time . . . ," "The *second* giant . . . ," or "*At last* he reached Grandmother's house." Directions for science experiments and other content area selections having predictable structures also work well as schema stories.

A schema story is divided (physically cut apart) into sections, each of sufficient length to allow students to consider meaning in the text. After the text is divided at clearly predictable cutoff points, each section is distributed to individuals within a group. As students read, they direct their attention to the cohesive features of the text, consider prior information, and predict subsequent text. The teacher invites the person who believes he or she has the first part of the story to read the section and to explain why it is the beginning. If everyone agrees, the procedure continues. If two people both believe they have the subsequent section, both sections are read and a group decision is made.

There are at least two modifications of this strategy lesson. The first involves each student's receiving all sections of a story and reconstructing that story. The students then compare their reconstructions with those of the other students and discuss the process. Another alternative involves several groups. Each group receives a section or sections of the text and proceeds as a group through the procedure mentioned above.

Schema stories provide the opportunity for talk about language and texts. Readers see not only that texts teach them but that the meaning of text is supported by a structure that they can understand and use.

Determining Lessons

Whole language involves learning on the part of teachers as well as students. Teachers learn by reflecting on what they know about language and learning in light of what children do from day to day.

Figure 1.
Jan's worksheet.

VOWEL DIGRAPH ea

The vowel digraph ea has three sounds: long e, short e, and long a. If a word is unfamiliar, try each

of the three sounds. You should then recognize the word. Show the sound of ea on the line after each

word. Show the sound of a short e with an unmarked e.

−14 (−41)   KEY: EACH e   HEAD e   GREAT a

1. TREATMENT ē	25. CREAKING ē	49. TREACHEROUS
2. STEADIER a ✓	26. JEALOUSY ✓	50. HEADQUARTERS
3. STEALTHY ✓	27. APPEAL e ✓	51. CLEANLINESS
4. TEAK ā ✓	28. DECREASE ē	52. MEANT
5. GREATEST ā	29. BEEFSTEAK e	53. UNDERNEATH
6. WREATH ē	30. PEASANT e	54. BREAKTHROUGH
7. DEALT e	31. PEACEABLE e ✓	55. REPEAL
8. CONGEAL ē	32. REVEAL	56. STREAKED
9. SHEATH ✓	33. WEAPON	57. WEATHERED
10. CREASED ā ✓	34. CLEANSING	58. MEANTIME
11. MEASLES ē	35. BEAGLE	59. EAGERNESS
12. BEACON ā ✓	36. SNEAKERS	60. EAVES
13. BREAKNECK ā	37. FEATHERY	61. THREATENED
14. HEATHEN e ✓	38. FEAT	62. LEASED
15. HEAVENLY e	39. FLEA	63. LEASH
16. EASEL ē	40. MEANWHILE	64. BREAKWATER
17. SWEAT ē ✓	41. CEASE	65. DEAFEN
18. UNHEALTHY e	42. HEAVILY	66. EASTERN
19. SEASONING ē	43. PEALED	67. RETREATING
20. CHESAPEAKE ✓	44. WEASEL	68. BLEACHERS
21. STREAMLINED ē	45. DREAD	69. DEATHLESS
22. TREACHERY ē ✓	46. EATABLE	70. HEADACHE
23. DEFEATED ē	47. INCREASING	71. LEAKY
24. PHEASANTS ē ✓	48. DEALER	72. SNEAKY

Finish your work! (−41)

The purpose of *determining lessons* is to help the teacher reflect and search for patterns that make sense. For example, it may appear that a student needs to focus on an isolated skill. Before breaking language apart for instruction and drill on that skill, it is important for teachers to *determine,* in the context of continuous discourse (whole language), whether or not the skill needs to be studied in isolation. By giving the student whole language, teachers support the reader with all the cues that readers draw upon as they read. Consider Jan.

Jan, a fourth grader, was successful in school and considered herself a good reader. These views were shared by her teacher and parents. Jan and her mother were understandably concerned when she brought home the worksheet shown in Figure 1.

At first glance, it could be assumed that Jan is at fault: she doesn't have sufficient "readiness skills"; she isn't trying her best; she wasn't paying attention; she needs more work on the vowel digraph *ea*. Rather than operating on limited information, it is crucial to analyze Jan's performance; otherwise the "victim" may be blamed and punished.

The first requirement is to consider the task Jan is asked to do. It becomes immediately apparent that this worksheet has many problems. Even if a teacher believes strongly that isolated drill on the vowel digraph *ea* is important, the seventy-two items on this worksheet constitute excessive practice. Directions for any activity should be presented carefully and clearly. Consider the directions on this worksheet:

> If a word is unfamiliar, try each of the three sounds. You should then recognize the word. Show the sound of *ea* on each line after each word.
> KEY: Each $\bar{e}$ Head e   Great $\bar{a}$.

Because of her poor marks on the worksheet, Jan cried herself to sleep; her mother consulted a reading teacher. Rather than depending on the check marks and scanty numerical information on the worksheet, the reading teacher went to the informant—Jan. Jan followed the directions; she tried "each of the three sounds" (which she called "each e," "head e," and "great a") and when she recognized a familiar word, she wrote the symbol representing the sound of the familiar word: *teak* became *take, beacon* became *bacon, sweat* became *sweet, heathen* (appearing before *heavenly*) became *heaven,* and *appeal* became *apple.* Many of the words were unfamiliar to Jan regardless of the particular sound of the *ea.* She was confused by *peaceable* because she didn't know which *ea* to mark. This student was not sloppy in her work; she struggled a great deal with each item, using her own linguistic knowledge and logic. It is ironic that after encountering unknown words such as *stealthy, congeal,* and *sheath,* Jan did not expect this worksheet to make sense to her and consequently did not even recognize words with which she was familiar. For example, Jan's father and uncle went pheasant hunting regularly but she missed *pheasants* on the worksheet.

In order to determine whether Jan really had a problem with the vowel digraph *ea,* the reading teacher asked Jan to read the passage shown in Figure 2.

Does Jan have a problem with the vowel digraph *ea?* Obviously not. She omits *steady* when the word doesn't affect the meaning and occurs in an unfamiliar construction, *steady leash.* Later in the text, however, Jan reads *steady* in a more semantically predictable context, "Babe and Bingo's steady stream of barking. . . ." *Deafening* is the only

Figure 2.
Determining lessons for Jan.

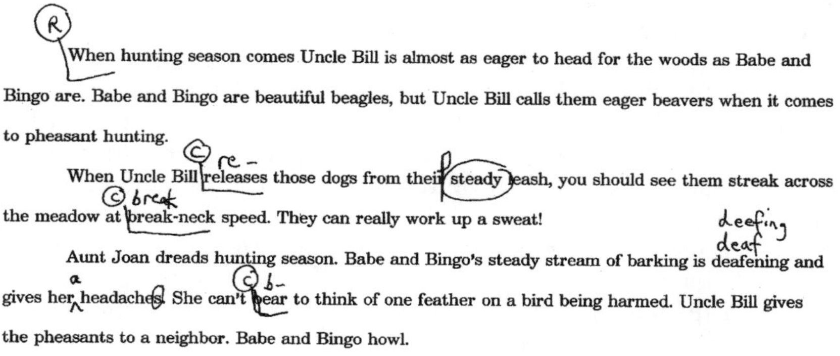

(R) When hunting season comes Uncle Bill is almost as eager to head for the woods as Babe and

Bingo are. Babe and Bingo are beautiful beagles, but Uncle Bill calls them eager beavers when it comes

to pheasant hunting.

When Uncle Bill releases those dogs from their steady leash, you should see them streak across

the meadow at break-neck speed. They can really work up a sweat!

deefing
deaf

Aunt Joan dreads hunting season. Babe and Bingo's steady stream of barking is deafening and

gives her headaches. She can't bear to think of one feather on a bird being harmed. Uncle Bill gives

the pheasants to a neighbor. Babe and Bingo howl.

---

other word with the *ea* digraph that Jan miscues on; she substitutes *deaf* and abandons it for the nonword *deefing*. Her explanation: "When two vowels go walking, the first one does the talking." With a sensible, predictable whole text, Jan becomes a much better reader. Rather than making reading hard by giving her a worksheet that raises her anxiety, wastes her time, and makes her feel stupid, her teacher should make reading easy by giving her good literature.

When language is stripped of its context and left with the bare bones of symbol/sound relationships, readers are in potential linguistic trouble. By relying on quality literature and maximizing the linguistic strengths of readers, teachers will find that the need to determine whether skills should be drilled in isolation will disappear.

ERRQ

(*E*stimate, *R*ead, *R*espond, *Q*uestion) is a strategy lesson that helps reluctant readers make a commitment to a text and personalize their reading. When students think of themselves as poor readers, they tend to avoid reading. The focus of instruction at this point must be on helping them feel successful. By assisting readers in monitoring their pace and comprehension, this activity offers these readers an opportunity to prove to themselves that they do indeed have linguistic strengths and control of the reading process.

Readers begin by *estimating* how far they can read in the text with understanding in a given period of time; they make a check mark at this point. This requires them to "stake their claim" and to make a decision about the text and themselves; the teacher doesn't make an assignment, the students do. Next, they *read*. The personal decision concerning the amount of reading to be done moves readers along and challenges them to go beyond their own expectations.

When students reach the place they've checked, they *respond*. The response should be brief and related to the reader's life and literary experiences, such as giving her opinion of a character, how he would feel in the same situation, or whether it reminds her of another piece of literature.

Finally, readers ask a *question* that can lead into a discussion or a written dialogue about the selection. This can be a question about something readers don't understand in the text, or a question that pulls the text beyond the page, as in raising issues concerning a character's motivation, for example. The teacher can ask readers a question, but this is optional.

Reading is neither "getting the author's meaning" nor an independent response of the reader; rather it is a transaction between the reader and the author's text. This strategy lesson capitalizes on the reading transaction and moves students to active, personal reading. In ERRQ, as in all whole language strategy lessons, the reader is supported by the text, by the task, and by the teacher. Reading is made easy.

The Classroom Environment

We have mentioned earlier that the whole language classroom is littered with literacy. Perhaps we should talk about the classroom environment as a strategy. Access to literacy and student ownership of the environment is crucial. The classroom is for everyone; teachers don't talk about "*my* room," "*my* pencils," "*my* rules"; rather they talk about "our room," "our pencils," "our rules." The bulletin boards are conceived, designed, and produced by students and teacher. Such boards often become idea boards as well as sounding boards; one student's product becomes another student's motivation to read and write. Tools, materials, references, and books are organized, but all over the classroom—wherever children might need them. The distribution and maintenance of materials is everyone's responsibility, and, at the end of a busy day, everyone restores and readies the environment for the next day. Whole language teachers "read the environment" by looking at it from the children's point of view: Can students get materials? Are there places for quiet work? Are there places for groups to work

that won't bother others? Are there places that invite trouble? Loughlin (1983) says that the outcome of a functional literacy environment
assures self-growth, but that the environment must be established.

Reference

Loughlin, C. E. 1983. *Reflecting literacy in the environment* (Publication 16:3).
Grand Forks, ND: Center for Teaching and Learning, University of North
Dakota.

Part Three

Curriculum Models (1980–1990)

Process Paradigm:
Grades Six Through Nine

I've just visited a sparkling new middle school that opened in our district a few months ago. As I watched the students in a variety of settings, and as I listened to them in their discussion of Roll of Thunder, Hear My Cry *and* May the Circle Be Unbroken, *I sensed the energy and potential of these contemporary youngsters.*

As I talked with the students, I became nostalgic, thinking of the students I taught years ago in Kansas City. Suzanne Davis and her students reminded me of why I loved teaching these emerging adolescents: after all these years, I still get a kick out of discovering how smart they can be and how much they can grow when they're in a warm and accepting community of learners. And yes, I even appreciate their humor.

I think—I hope—this piece has useful suggestions for the modern middle school kids. If not, I'm sure they will quickly let us know.

This article describes a process curriculum for middle school and junior high school students. To do this it is necessary to focus on the students and on the teacher, for from them stems the curriculum. We

Previously published in *Three Language Arts Curriculum Models: Pre-K Through College,* edited by Barrett Mandel (Urbana, IL: National Council of Teachers of English, 1980), pp. 91–100. Copyright 1980 by the National Council of Teachers of English. Reprinted with permission.

will first look at the typical, if hypothetical, process-oriented (sometimes called naturalistic, humanistic, or creative) teacher, then at the
students, and finally at some activities that might go on in their teach-
ing/learning world.

The Teacher

At some point in their careers, potential process-oriented teachers become consumed with curiosity about why their students are succeed-
ing, slipping away, or standing still. When our hypothetical teacher, Joe
Green, was himself in junior high school, he received instruction in
what was referred to as the language arts and later as English. As it
turns out, the instruction he received had a great deal to do with learning to identify parts of sentences, spelling words on a graded spelling
list, punctuating innumerable sentences, reading a prescribed list of
books, and memorizing the same elegant poems his older brother had
memorized ten years earlier. There were variations, within limits, but
for the most part Joe received a ready-made curriculum, and by prevailing standards he was a successful student. In his undergraduate
methods courses in college, he "gained insights" into how his own junior high teachers had helped him produce. His student teaching was
déjà vu—junior high revisited—and his first years of teaching were attempts to teach as he was taught and as he was taught to teach.

   Reflecting on his own schooling, our hypothetical teacher vacillated
from feeling slightly cheated to feeling irreparably misled: cheated because he did not reflect with joy on his own schooling and misled because at the close of each day he sensed that his own students were
in a continuous retreat from language and literature. The language
arts he had hoped to bring to life in the minds and hearts of his students were languishing for want of proper staging. Then, one day,
right before the concrete of the preexisting curriculum had hardened,
our hypothetical teacher began to look around. That is when he
stopped teaching as he had been taught and began searching for
a solid foundation on which to build a lively language arts curriculum.

   The process-oriented teacher has special viewpoints about language, literature, learners, and learning. When our hypothetical
teacher began to look for alternatives to preformulated guides, he
found it necessary to rediscover literature for children and youth, to
investigate pedagogical research, and to investigate current information related to language. As his study progressed, he developed a guiding belief: language is alive and well and resides in the heads and on
the tongues of students as well as in the plays, prose, and poetry writ-

ten for young people. It dawned on him that by the time children enter the sixth grade, they have used their language to inform, proclaim, persuade, gossip, tattle, double-talk, sweet-talk, and outtalk—when they were motivated to do so. Our hypothetical teacher learned two important things: first, students use language when they need to and, second, the meaning attributed to their discourse does not reside in sounds or in print, not in glossaries or dictionaries, but rather in what they and those in their worlds say it means. A third truth followed: as surely as young adolescents and their worlds are changing, so is their language changing. From a realization of these truths came a teaching/learning fact: it is not profitable for children to deal with letters, syllables, words, or any other units of language abstracted from the whole of language in its fullest context. Indeed, to understand what language symbolizes we must first be concerned with the concept, the reality, rather than with the symbol. If students understand what is being talked about, they can then use their language to help categorize, classify, and label. To introduce labels, rules, and nonsituational facts prior to reality is to pander to nonsense and to invite blank stares, yawns, and frustration.

Another important notion held by our teacher has to do with individuality. When students are encouraged to share their world and to tell about their lives in their own preferred language, the entire class can only become richer and wiser. In addition to adding another resource to the classroom, such contributions give teachers creditable information about their students' motivations and needs and allow them to find out if students are communicating with one another and the teacher with them. They know that the greater the overlap in their worlds, the greater the chance for communication and the interchange of ideas. However, even when experiences are the same, they are aware that individuals perceive those experiences differently and describe them differently. Who is to say which perceiver is right or wrong or, indeed, if anyone is right or wrong?

But what of errors and mistakes? Perhaps when dealing with language learning we should accept Kenneth Goodman's (1972) more positive term, *miscue*, usually applied to reading. When a student reads something that deviates from what is printed, a miscue has been made, and until that miscue is investigated, it can't be labeled good or bad. Isn't it possible to talk about miscues in listening, speaking, and writing as well? A process-oriented teacher encourages students to forge ahead into situations in which they must take risks, hypothesize, and—quite likely—miscue.

At all times our hypothetical teacher attempts to find out what students are trying to do; he understands that if care and attention are given to the process (the risk taking, the hypothesizing, the miscue-ing) by which learners make sense of their world, the results of such endeavors will be meaningful, important, and satisfying for both teacher and learner. Denial of a learner's tentative attempts, along with concern for achieving someone else's preconceived objectives and emphasis on production, misdirects the learner and distorts the learning process. Such attention causes students to doubt their own motivations and choices and inhibits even the most tentative explora-tion. This is not to say that learning stops when the product rather than the process is treasured; rather, the lessons students learn are unexpected and unwholesome: (1) that they have little or no voice in their schooling, (2) that there is a prescribed body of knowledge they are expected to master, and (3) that there are certain acceptable ways of acquiring that knowledge.

Our process teacher is an incurable kidwatcher. He can't help himself; it is an addiction that not only delights and informs him, but is the bone and marrow of his curriculum planning. Yetta Goodman (1978) reminds us that the basic assumption in "kidwatching" is that development of language is a natural process and that the teacher should keep two questions in mind: (1) What evidence is there that language development is taking place? and (2) When a student pro-duces something unexpected, what does it tell the teacher about the child's knowledge of language? Goodman also advises that good kid-watchers have up-to-date knowledge about language and that they understand the role of errors in language learning; errors are not ran-dom, and if we know enough about language and the language user, we can explain those errors.

Finally, our hypothetical teacher is instinctively a nongrader, and finds it difficult and unnatural to reduce a child's efforts to a black squiggle on a report card. Where is the motivation when we label a group of students with a C? Where is the process and growth when a student gets an A? Where is the context when we indicate that a child is a B student? On the other hand, our teacher has bulging folders of students' work, dated notes, and memories—all of which are used as data for discussions of the pupils' strengths and needs.

The Student

Children between the ages of eleven and fifteen have been described in interesting, diverse, and sometimes unprintable terms. To make our task of learning about the learner easier, we will again produce a hy-pothetical character—this time a student who finds herself in an eighth-grade classroom with a teacher who is interested in why, how, and what she is thinking and doing. This can be unsettling for a youngster who for seven years has come to expect a cycle of test, prescription, readiness, drill, retest, and remediation.

Our hypothetical student spends the first few weeks being very ill at ease. She is uncomfortable working with a partner and in small groups, and when she does work alone, it isn't on the ever familiar purple worksheets or exercise books, nor is it even answering questions at the end of the chapter. Uprooting, redirecting, and beginning anew are tough, and our young student inches through her prevailing malaise by demanding the past, testing the innovator (something must shatter his calm determination), acting up, refusing, resisting, pouting, keeping a distance, eavesdropping, waiting, watching, listening, offering a comment, writing a thought, opening a book, and finally giving it a tentative try.

Our young student discovers that she has something to say and write and that she can talk and write without fear of interruption or put-down. Her ideas are valued, her suggestions are considered, her humor is appreciated, her doubts are explored, and, strangest of all, her mistakes are investigated—not counted. Slowly, our student becomes accustomed to having her strengths as well as her weaknesses pointed out. The weaknesses—learned through the curious investigation of miscues—point the way for the next attempt. For the first time in her schooling, our young student hears that you learn not only by getting it right but also by getting it wrong.

Another source of discomfort for our student has to do with major changes in the reward system. In the past the student relied on immediate approval or disapproval; there was no waiting to find out about correctness. She knew, too, that there was the final reckoning; stars or spaces, smiles or frowns, and letter grades awaited. One year she received poker chips for jobs well done, and these were traded in for free time, extended play, or Friday movies. Once in remedial reading class she received candy for doing workbook exercises. By contrast, in this new class she gets encouragement that is realistic. Now strange things begin to happen as she starts the processes of reading and writing. First, the student is encouraged to use her own strategies; no one gives her the word or constructs the sentence. She gives the whole thing a try without interruption for corrections or changes. She is never asked to read or write snippets of language about things she knows or cares little about, but now works with whole, meaningful discourse. After a while, our student begins to pay attention to receiving and producing something sensible. That leads to another curious thing: making sense is its own reward.

If the full potential of language is to be realized, it must be used in as many situations, private and public, as possible. The "sociability of language" calls for our hypothetical student not only to enjoy the privacy of reading and writing but to share, communicate, and grow with others. Giving and receiving does not mean parading a polished production that can be compared with other polished productions. Sharing can take place in a natural, comfortable way when students work cooperatively, giving and receiving ideas, venturing speculations, and making discoveries as they work on mutually rewarding projects. But the notion of cooperative activity is easier said than done for our young student. She is familiar with competition in which her book reports, other writings, and scores are compared with those of her classmates. She knows how to hide disappointment; hurt feelings are nothing new. Now she is asked to abandon the familiar for the untried—leave competition on the playing field and accept cooperation as a way of academic life. Fortunately, the cooperative spirit takes hold quickly when students find joy in some creative venture such as dramatic improvisation, sharing readings and writings with other readers and writers, or participating in a research project with others who are participating just as fully.

In summary, a process-oriented curriculum calls for teachers who invite students to explore and expand their own private and public linguistic powers in an atmosphere that is natural and fulfilling; the students in this setting come to think of themselves as joyful receivers and producers of stories, plays, songs, poems—all forms of worthy and useful language. Both learner and teacher pay respect to the ideas and language of the other; they never cease asking questions of each other; and in a cooperative environment, they use language and experience to generate new questions, new ideas, new experiences, and new ways of expression—to achieve personal growth.

Invitations

In preparing for their students, teachers will find it helpful to consider any plan of action as a series of invitations that learners may accept or refuse. Teacher beckons and, if the plan is considered important and worth their while, students will respond, become involved, and extend invitations of their own. To make the invitations appealing, teachers must constantly look to their students for ideas and inspiration.

The activities that follow have been accepted by many who are taking their first intrepid steps toward a process-oriented classroom. Reasons for success vary and have to do with the student, the teacher, and language. First—and this is a good rule of thumb for selecting any activity—the endeavor must involve whole language for the whole child. *Whole language* means that there is no artificial separation of language arts into instructional categories of listening, speaking, reading, and writing and that the systems of language (graphic, phonemic, morphemic, syntactic, and semantic) function as the unified process students enjoy and use. The term *whole child* acknowledges that the learner has a life outside the classroom and that the emotional as well as the cognitive life of the learner will be given consideration. A second factor contributing to the potential success of these activities is that they are *present*- rather than *future*-related. Unless long-range goals can be made relevant for a student's life as it is right now, the goals are unrealistic and deflect the learner from important and attainable ends. The last reason for the success of these activities concerns the teacher's perceptions with regard to discipline. Cautious and beginning innovators have reason to fear, stultifying as that fear is, that their classes will be scenes of uncontrolled confusion. These four activities are relatively tidy—appropriate and productive, noise notwithstanding.

Reading to Students

Reading is a manageable and natural starting point. It evokes a feeling of family in which special stories, sayings, even jokes, are shared and a tradition is built. Reading to students takes the pressure off those who have trouble with print, and it allows listeners to bring their experiences to the author's experiences. Students can comfortably speculate on what will happen next based on their own background; they can discuss the messages they received from the author, noting differences in what each one gained; and they can use the experience to lead them to talk, improvise, and read and write further. A student who is comfortable only with basal-reader prose quite likely will have trouble when first confronted with the language and organization of other texts. Hearing a variety of discourse exposes students to the diverse cognitive frames of reference used by authors in all modes of prose and poetry. Reading to students—every day without fail—sets a tone of sharing and a comfortable rhythm for students and teachers alike; it puts imaginations in motion and helps nurture a love of literature. That's a good place to start.

Students Reading

Sustained silent reading has many advocates, and it is no longer necessary to point out that students learn to read by reading, that to become hooked on books it is essential that they regularly devote large amounts of time to reading. It does appear necessary, however, that we investigate how students become hooked on reading. Left alone in a library bursting with informative and delightful books, most children will find their way to suitable reading material. However, some students not only need to learn how to select their own books but also would benefit from suggestions for selections from adults and other students. In *Growth Through English* (1966) Dixon points out that "a predetermined list of reading assignments leaves no room for individual growth and initiative, but throwing the library at the student is no real opportunity for free choice. Stage by stage, teachers can set up a framework of choice within which they help pupils find their own purposes" (p. 85).

A selection procedure called *Mine, Yours, Ours* provides such a framework for the reader. Students are encouraged to have three selections available at all times: *mine,* selected by the reader for whatever purpose deemed important; *yours,* judged by the teacher, librarian, aide, or parent to be of interest to the student; and *ours,* a selection mutually agreed on by the student and a teacher, parent, or another student. Such a selection procedure allows children to consider, suggest, reject, and select reading material for themselves and others.

Improvisation

Britton (1970) indicates that dramatic play is a special form of talking-and-doing—a way of dealing with other times and other places. Britton is not talking about a scripted and staged drama but rather improvisation in which students make do with the tools (materials, ideas, situations) at hand. Britton warns that improvisation as some teachers organize it is no more than a story retold in action and that success is measured in terms of getting the story right, all deteriorating into trivial detail. Britton encourages "exploration in the face of a situation in which much is known; the exploration is a realization, a bringing to life" (p. 141).

Moffett (1968, pp. 288–91) suggests three situations for improvisation. In the first, students can elaborate on an action that took place in their reading. The children select and recapitulate some of the action as they remember it, but at the same time they invent changes. Their improvisation can serve as an alternative to comprehension testing and critical literary analysis. Moffett's second suggestion for improvisation, a way to interest and prepare students for reading a particular book, is to abstract some key situation from the book, sketch a similar situation, provide some detail, and lead the students into an improvisation of the episode. This activity helps develop experience into which students can fit information and ideas as they meet similar situations in print. Finally, Moffett suggests a type of improvisation that might be described as a spontaneous discussion from which moral, social, or psychological issues can evolve. The discussions might involve a jury deliberating over a verdict, a family settling a matter of television watching or dating, or a group considering membership rules. In any case, Moffett suggests that in such improvisations students become aware of how their ideas are rooted in the roles and characters they are portraying. Such improvisation leads naturally to talk with a partner, small group discussions, private writing, and possibly further group action.

Writing

At least three conditions are essential before children will write: they must feel they have something to write about that is worth the effort, they must feel they can get their thoughts on paper, and they must have the opportunity to write. The first condition requires experience both in and out of the classroom. Students should be encouraged to think of themselves as resources, experts perhaps, in areas such as making pottery, camping, football, popular dances, the solar system, the life of a historical person, gardening, or fixing flats. Through beginning-of-the-year questionnaires, attention to material read, and discussions, teachers can find out what their students are interested in and perhaps good at. The point in having children write about something they know well and are interested in is that it puts the emphasis of writing on the message rather than on the form of writing. Graves (1978) suggests that a way to emphasize the student's reason for writing rather than the form in which it appears is the process-conference approach. In this procedure, several brief individual conferences of one to five minutes each are informally conducted. Graves recommends that in the first two or three conferences, the teacher ask leading questions (How did you get interested in this subject? What else do people say about sharks? Have there ever been shark attacks in this area?) and give encouragement (You have a good start with what you have just told me. Many people talk about sharks, but few have actually seen them. You certainly have good information about sharks. I suspect very few people know what the Coast Guard is up against). About the fourth conference, the teacher reviews a written draft and makes suggestions about arranging ideas, deleting irrelevant and less pertinent information, and eliminating fuzziness. In the final conference, the student mentions any "weird spellings" and punctuation problems. Form *will* be attended to if the student feels that the writing is worth "checking out."

Final Thoughts

The goals of a process curriculum stress the students' use and enjoyment of language in all sorts of situations; it means never being at a loss for language. If this sounds too general, then it must be pointed out again that it is the process, the means, that we focus on in such a curriculum. The selection of means (activities, materials, methods) is not difficult if the notion of whole language for the whole child is kept in mind. It isn't difficult to see that keeping a journal, having a conversation, comparing feelings and reactions to a movie, writing letters and petitions, writing and singing songs, telling stories, and reading to a friend involve students and their language, totally.

There are problems with this approach. Many find it threatening to step into a new and undefined world. Even adventurous young adolescents want to cling to the past; it may be deadening, but it is familiar. In the beginning, teachers may find themselves issuing invitations that few want to accept. It falls to the teacher, then, to spark the imaginations of parents who don't realize that the basics they are so eager for their children to acquire must involve useful language, not dry-run activities; to educate administrators about the promise of language expansion and the strictures of reductionism; to ask their colleagues to suspend judgment about their program long enough to get a good perspective; and to beckon students to come, take a chance, explore, and discover the power and joy of language.

References

Britton, James. 1970. *Language and learning.* New York: Penguin.

Dixon, John. 1966. *Growth through English.* Reading, England: National Association for the Teaching of English.

Goodman, Kenneth S. 1972. The reading process: Theory and practice. In Richard E. Hodges & E. Hugh Rudorf (Eds.), *Language and learning to read: What teachers should know about language* (pp. 143–59). Boston: Houghton Mifflin.

Goodman, Yetta. 1978. Kidwatching: An alternative to testing. *National Elementary Principal, 57,* 41–45.

Graves, Donald. 1978, April. Balance the basics: Let them write. *Learning,* 30–33.

Moffett, James. 1968. *A student-centered language arts curriculum, grades K–13: A handbook for teachers.* Boston: Houghton Mifflin.

Language Arts Basics: Advocacy versus Research
(with Peter Hasselriis)

Although we don't hear "back to basics" as much today as we did a decade ago, the issue still exists. Today, the back-to-basics advocates demand a prescriptive curriculum "with a strong dose of skills." Once I asked a woman what skill it was she was so concerned about. After a very long pause she announced, "Syllabication."

The back-to-basics advocates are afraid that

> *if Johnny doesn't get a daily dose of directly taught phonics, he will never be able to read.*

> *if basals are not used in reading and if a textbook is not used for all subject areas, some critical fact will be missed. (E.D. Hirsch has conveniently identified the really important ones.)*

> *if Mary invents her spelling, she will forever let her mother know that she loves her with a note that says, I LV U MM.*

> *if students spend time selecting and discussing an idea of their interest, it is lowering standards and academic expectations.*

> *if learners engage in talk it is probably "time off task." The teacher talks and students listen.*

Teachers have responded to these and many more concerns expressed by parents, colleagues, and even students. I suppose the important thing to remember is that these advocates, like ourselves, love children and want the best for them. It falls on us to persist with a sane and respectful conversation with them.

Previously published in *Contemporary Educational Psychology* 6(1981), 278–86. Copyright 1981 by Academic Press. Reprinted with permission.

The back-to-basics thrust in teaching the language arts has been marked by a great deal of emotion and misinformation. On an emotional level, it appears to be a reaction against what is viewed as a move toward permissive, open, child-centered schools and classrooms. Intellectually, it appears to be characterized by a view that there are serious problems with what young people are being taught and that those problems can be solved by implementing teaching materials and methods that were held to have been taught in past years and that are no longer being taught. These "basics," moreover, are held to be necessary for gaining control over broader goals. (The ability to spell words correctly is held to be basic to writing, knowledge of phonics generalizations is seen as basic to reading, and miscue-free oral reading is viewed as basic to other reading proficiencies.)

Language Arts Basics: Advocacy

Back-to-basics advocates appear to view reading as a product consisting of discrete skills that must be mastered in sequence. They call for elementary school teachers to stress instruction in phonics and in other aspects of reading that tend to be fragments of the total act rather than integrated activities having comprehension as their principal focus. In a "basic" reading program there is a great deal of teacher direction and materials that incorporate repetitive drill. Much time is spent on teaching "skills," which, when mastered, will enable students to read at a designated "grade level."

Basic programs in the other language arts appear to have a similar focus. Students diagram sentences, choose correct words to be placed in blanks, underline parts of speech, and work on other such skills that when mastered will enable them to write.

Oral language is handled similarly. Back-to-basics advocates view regional dialect as "incorrect" language that needs to be corrected. Students are therefore asked to complete exercises in which they must choose the correct word for a sentence. Most of us have worked through a lifetime's supply of such sit/set, lie/lay kinds of exercises.

Back-to-basics programs, reflecting what many strident voices in society are demanding, place a great deal of emphasis on penmanship and spelling, again emphasizing skills that must be mastered in order to assure proficiency at higher levels.

Language arts teachers are under pressure to teach grammar and the classics. Grammar instruction is considered to be traditional grammar in which the emphasis is on identifying parts of speech. Such study is expected to help students become proficient readers and writers. Students' required reading is strictly prescribed and generally consists of works that are neither contemporary nor controversial. *Ivanhoe, Silas Marner, Julius Caesar,* and *Macbeth* are examples that come to mind.

Language Arts Basics: Research

From our perspective, the back-to-basics movement is more of a nonmovement than a movement—a nonmovement in which we find instructional fragmentation of a static bloat of unnecessary information. In order to change a nonfunctional nonmovement into a vigorous course of action, we need, first of all, to identify the real basics as the students themselves and their language. With this clarification we can immediately reject skills, drills, mastery programs, and the technology of the uninformed curriculum makers, for they have nothing to do with students and their language. Fortunately, when we abandon the "back-to-basics" curriculum we are not cut adrift, floundering about for wise information on which to build our program and invite our students. Rather, when we discard the technocrats' baggage, we find energy and spirit to investigate the information provided by language theorists and researchers.

We have chosen the following researchers/theorists/educators to help us describe an active, real basics program for at least three reasons. First, they are known and respected for their professionalism and clear studies; second, their views are consistent and compatible; and third, they probably would not take offense at being dubbed kidwatchers (Goodman 1978) and listeners rather than subject experimenters.

From Vygotsky (1962, 1978), Halliday (1978), Smith (1975), Britton (1970), and Yetta and Kenneth Goodman (Goodman & Goodman 1977; Goodman 1978) we hear again and again that our attention must indeed be directed to students and to their language. These theorists tell us that we must look at students in their entirety: their motivations, interests, stories, songs, games, jokes, and jargon. We must explore the potential meaning symbolized in the string after string of words that are heard, spoken, written, and read in diverse settings, societies, and cultures. That is, we must investigate how language users make meaning and under what circumstances they make it.

Following are seven if-then statements that direct us toward some basic instructional procedures. These procedures are followed by further arguments and suggestions for activities that are consistent with the theoretical principle presented.

If-Then Statement 1

If we know from theorists that linguistic order is created internally, cannot be imposed upon the learner, and is constructed by the learner through social interactions in which the user's *intent* is clear—then it is basic that we

1. Reject unnatural activites, assignments, and materials that impose unnecessary information on the learner and that have no hint of meaning off the page, out of the kit, or outside the classroom in which they are found.

2. Replace contrived, isolated, and impersonal drill with expanded personal and social activities in which students can hear and read the situation as well as hear and read the speaker and author—in order to construe meaning.

Advocates of skills-oriented basal readers, phonics workbooks, spelling lists, programmed instruction, and the like seem to share a view that teaching involves showing students examples of the "right" way to use language. Unfortunately, such views not only place meaning and the unique differences among students as users of language in the background, but they also pay no regard to the pragmatics; that is, the context of the situation in which language is used.

Because language functions in situational contexts that dictate form, activities such as language experience stories, spontaneous conversations (including written conversations), role-playing, and scripted and extemporaneous drama allow learners to get a feel for the intent. That is, they understand why language is being used in the particular way it is being used.

If-Then Statement 2

If we know from theorists (Britton 1970; Goodman & Goodman, 1977; Smith, 1975) that we often underestimate and underrepresent students' knowledge and their ability to use language and that what learners experience and know *before* they listen, speak, read, and write powerfully affects their ability to construct meaning—then it is basic that we

1. Reject a deficit view of the students' language in which our attention is on the half-empty rather than the half-full container.

2. Come to know and respect the learners' store of knowledge and use this information as a guide in planning curriculum.

3. Use our energies and knowledge in planning a learning-by-doing

curriculum in which students become comfortable with new ideas and concepts and unfamiliar labels before they are asked to read and write about them.

Often a deficit view of students comes about from educators' looking at standardized test scores rather than looking at students. In a study conducted by Allen (1978) we learn that only 42 of the 255 items on a popular reading test are designed specifically to find out how well the pupil can comprehend text. Scores on the subtests were, for the most part, not indicative of the actual reading proficiency of students. Such tests are widely used and often direct the curriculum. For example, students who score below 80 percent on the sound discrimination subtest are to have remediation in sound recognition, even though we know that children and adults constantly demonstrate an ability to read despite low scores on the sound discrimination subtest. Assessments of this sort rarely give information upon which teachers can build curriculum. Activities that allow children to show, tell, and demonstrate their abilities are far more informative.

A student who thinks Loretta Lynn exemplifies the state of the art in vocal tone production will run from Luciano Pavarotti as if Pavarotti were rabid. There is an elitism in many schools that would place Loretta Lynn and Harlequin Romances, and many other forms of art that are highly regarded and sincerely respected by many persons, at the negative end of the "cultural" continuum. Luciano Pavarotti and Shakespeare would probably be placed quite readily on the positive side. Constructing curricula and lessons exclusively around Pavarotti and Shakespeare would typify what many critics seem to expect schools to do, thereby leaving students with a heightened conviction that school is so far removed from their world—the real world, as they see it—that putting a great deal of physical or psychic energy into it is a waste of time. If the critics, schools, researchers, and students start communicating with one another, we will begin to observe schools in which students are using language in ways that they perceive to be both valuable and enjoyable. We will, moreover, begin to observe astonishing amounts of improved writing, speaking, listening, and creative thinking.

If-Then Statement 3

If we know from theorists that risk taking is a necessary part of all language learning—then it is basic that we

1. Reject any program that is devoted to simplistic exactness, prescription, and mastery.

2. Encourage informed risk taking by urging students to explore and ultimately control language by using it in large amounts at all appropriate times.

3. Teach students that they can learn as much from getting it wrong as from getting it right.

Kenneth Goodman (1967) calls reading a psycholinguistic guessing game in which the reader interacts with the text, and (based on what the author has written and on the reader's prior knowledge) takes a guess—a risk—and reads. Figure 1 is a miscue analysis of a second grader who kept getting it (the word *camera*) wrong, kept on taking risks, kept on gathering information from her own information network and the author's, and finally got the concept and the label straightened out. (A circled R indicates repetition and a circled C indicates correction, while the numbers indicate the lines in the story on which the word *camera* appeared.) The point to be made here is that Edie's risk taking was encouraged; the teacher did not stop her after each miscue to give her a basic skill strategy. Rather, Edie was allowed to construct meaning by interacting with the full text.

If-Then Statement 4

If we know from theorists that students learn to speak, listen, read, and write by engaging in a great deal of speaking, listening, reading, and writing—then it is basic that we

1. Carefully scrutinize our curriculum and exclude all dry and dispirited activites that take time away from practicing oral language and literacy.

2. Provide as part of the curriculum (not as a reward, as "enrichment," or an elective) significant amounts of time to discuss, read, and write.

3. Become kidwatchers and listeners and, as a result of watching and listening, guide our students toward successful reception and production of language.

Schools need to implement whole-school emphasis on language development and to explain to all teachers why this should be done. Every class should be organized in such a way that students spend the majority of their time engaged in conversations, panels, and discussions and in reading and writing whole stories, poems, books, and plays. Teachers should serve as models in such programs as sustained silent reading (McCracken 1971) and in all other "languaging" activities.

Figure 1.
Edie's miscues.

---

caramel

220 ▪I▪ll get the camera now.▪

301 For a week Penny, Sue, and Jack took the

caramel ©anywhere

302 little camera everywhere.

caramel

404 She left the camera on the grass.

caramel

406 Now she walked to the camera.

ƒ tumped
ƒ~ tripped

408 She thumped the

caramel

409 camera with her white fur paw.

Ⓡ

410 Sue came out just in time to see Kitten

caramel

411 playing with the camera.

604 Kitten took that picture! I found her with

Ⓡcamera!

606 the camera.

715 It was

716 more fun to play with than a camera.

If-Then Statement 5

If we know from language theorists that when students read and listen they are constructing (not reconstructing) meaning just as surely as they are constructing when they are speaking and writing—then it is basic that we

1. Reject evaluative procedures that demand a template answer or cloned response that is an instant replay of the speaker's or author's message.

2. Place students in situations in which they can construct meaning from meaningful discourse; construction from nonsense is nonsense.

3. Enjoy diversity of interests, texts, and language, and encourage students to acknowledge and use their background of experience to translate and understand everything they hear and read.

Educators are encouraged to ask students to explore language within the discipline of general semantics. General semantics stems from the work of Alfred Korzybski (1933) in the 1930s and has been popularized by such persons as S. I. Hayakawa (1972), Stuart Chase (1951), Wendell Johnson (1946), and, in more recent years, Neil Postman and Charles Weingartner (1969). Closely aligned with the thrusts of general semantics are the National Council of Teachers of English's concerns with "uses and misuses of language" as these are examined by its Committee on Public Doublespeak. *Language and Public Policy* (Rank 1974) and *Teaching About Doublespeak* (Dieterich 1976) are NCTE publications on this topic.

General semantics examines language within a context of social interaction and thus helps students become acquainted with the multitude of ways in which business, government, educators, and others use language to persuade, manipulate, and otherwise influence people. General semanticists would argue that an evening spent studying how langue is used in traffic court might be of much more value than spending the same amount of time doing workbook exercises on subject/verb agreement.

In any event, students need to use language in truly functional ways. If they are asked to write, it must be evident to them that what they are writing is valuable, either to themselves or for an important outside purpose. (A message needs to be sent, for example, a record kept, a thought captured before it's forgotten, or an order written and sent.)

If-Then Statement 6

If we know from language theorists that having control of language (being able to use it, play with it, learn through it) is amply rewarding and motivating in itself—then it is basic that we

1. Exclude external rewards such as stars, coupons, M&Ms, and extravagant praise from our language arts program.
2. Help students enter into language using situations in which they can succeed and consequently be rewarded and motivated to use more and more language.
3. Value and help students value their own work as well as that of other learners.

Children begin to value language when they see that adults value language. Students need to experience a teacher who is experiencing language—that is, a teacher who is reading and writing right along with his or her students. When a principal comes into a classroom and reads during the silent reading period, the students know that reading is special—even the principal does it.

When students see their poems and stories in print (anything from a class paper to a polished school district publication), they know that their language has been taken seriously and is valued.

If-Then Statement 7

If we know from language theorists that home is where language starts—then it is basic that we

1. Know something of the language, experiences, and values of the family and community.
2. Share with parents information gained from research on language development.
3. Suggest to parents whole language activities such as silent reading time, singing, playing, talking, and writing together that will complement and support the school curriculum.

Teachers who explain to parents the basis of invented spelling (Read 1975; Chomsky 1979), the theory of miscues in reading (Allen & Watson 1976), the difference between real composing and superficial grammar drills, and the harm in attempting to eradicate dialect find the experience rewarding and in return for their efforts are supported by informed parents. The teacher who refused to identify her students by a "reading level" was told by her colleagues that the parents would demand to know their children's ranking. When the teacher outlined the problems, restrictions, and uselessness of such categorizing the parents expressed their relief; they were tired of big sisters reminding little brothers that they were "dismally below level."

Conclusion

Back-to-basics advocates lobby for schools that are product centered, with the products being mastery of skills, correct and neatly done drills and exercises, standard dialect, perfect penmanship, and other forms of conformity.

As we have shown, language researchers and theorists have given us a basis on which to lobby for schools that are student centered. Language activities in such schools will be characterized by respect for learners, their language, their motivations, and their strengths. Such language will be functional and valued at all times by students, parents, and teachers. Ironically, it will turn out to be language that is also more "correct," and thus more satisfying to those among us who appear to be certain that form is more "basic" than content.

References

Allen, P. David & Watson, Dorothy (Eds.). 1976. *Findings of research in miscue analysis.* Urbana, IL: National Council of Teachers of English.

Allen, V. 1978, November. Riddle: What does a reading test test? *Learning,* 86–89.

Britton, James. 1970. *Language and learning.* New York: Penguin.

Chase, Stuart. 1951. *Roads to agreement: Successful methods in the science of human relations.* New York: Harper.

Chomsky, Carol. 1979. Approaching reading through invented spelling. In Lauren B. Resnick & Phyllis A. Weaver (Eds.), *Theory and practice of early reading* (Vol. 2) (pp. 43–66). Hillsdale, NJ: Erlbaum.

Dieterich, Daniel (Ed.). 1976. *Teaching about doublespeak.* Urbana, IL: National Council of Teachers of English.

Goodman, Kenneth S. 1967. Reading: A psycholinguistic guessing game. *Journal of the Reading Specialist, 6,* 126–35.

Goodman, Yetta M. & Goodman, Kenneth S. 1977. Learning to read is natural. In Lauren Resnick & Phyllis A. Weaver (Eds.), *Theory and practice of early reading* (Vol. 1) (pp. 137–54). Hillsdale, NJ: Erlbaum.

Goodman, Yetta. 1978. Kidwatching: An alternative to testing. *National Elementary Principal, 57,* 41–45.

Halliday, M. A. K. 1975. *Learning how to mean: Explorations in the development of language.* New York: Elsevier.

Halliday, M. A. K. 1978. *Language as social semiotic: The social interpretation of language and meaning.* Baltimore: University Park Press.

Hayakawa, S. I. 1972. *Language in thought and action* (3rd ed.). New York: Harcourt Brace Jovanovich. (Originally published 1939)

Johnson, Wendell. 1946. *People in quandaries.* New York: Harper & Row.

Korzybski, Alfred. 1933. *Science and sanity.* Lakeville, CT: International Non-Aristotelian Library.

McCracken, Robert A. 1971. Initiating sustained silent reading. *Journal of Reading,* 14, 521–24, 582–83.

Postman, Neal & Weingartner, Charles. 1969. *Teaching as a subversive activity.* New York: Delacorte.

Rank, Hugh (Ed.). 1974. *Language and public policy.* Urbana, IL: National Council of Teachers of English.

Read, Charles. 1975. *Children's categorization of speech sounds in English* (Research Report #17). Urbana, IL: National Council of Teachers of English.

Smith, Frank. 1975. *Comprehension and learning: A conceptual framework for teachers.* New York: Holt, Rinehart & Winston.

Vygotsky, Lev. 1962. *Thought and language.* Cambridge: MIT Press.

Vygotsky, Lev S. 1978. *Mind in society: The development of higher psychological processes.* Cambridge, MA: Harvard University Press.

Bringing Together
Reading and Writing

Outside the classroom, integration of the language acts is a given. No one would ever think of intentionally separating reading, writing, listening, and speaking: we reread the grocery list we've written, if we don't listen during a conversation we're sure to get into hot water, we take notes as we talk things over with a study partner or listen to a tape on a given subject. If it seems natural to combine all the language arts, we don't hesitate. When kids walk into a classroom they may experience the fractionation of language: stop talking and finish your work (written, of course), listen to my lecture and take notes that I'll check for accuracy, present (talk) your report, read the assignment and then write answers to the questions at the end of the chapter. This piece presents a rationale for making language learning meaningful by building classroom experiences on Halliday's functions of language. The strategies are ones that teachers have deemed helpful and on which they have developed many integrated experiences suitable for their students.

Reading and writing have to do with meaning and with people—their languages, their intentions, their expectations, and the situations in which they find themselves. Eight-year-old Angela tacitly understands

Originally published in *Teaching Reading with the Other Language Arts*, edited by Ulrich H. Hardt (Newark, DL: International Reading Association, 1983), pp. 63–82. Reprinted with permission of the International Reading Association.

Figure 1.
Angela's bathroom rules.

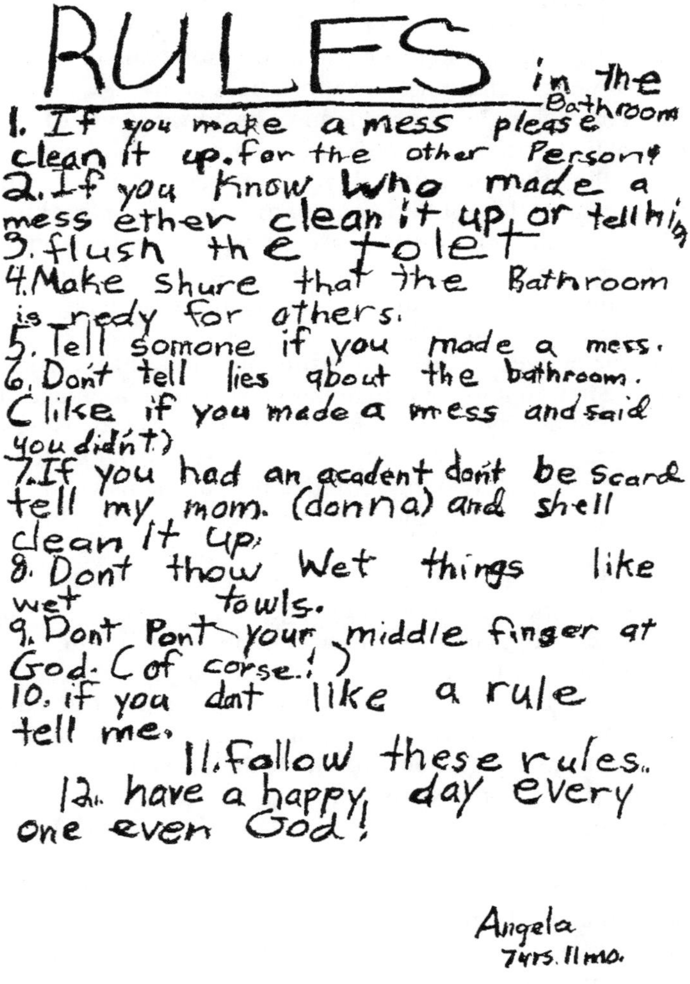
RULES in the Bathroom
1. If you make a mess please clean it up. for the other Person
2. If you know who made a mess ether clean it up, or tell him
3. flush the tolet
4. Make shure that the Bathroom is redy for others.
5. Tell somone if you made a mess.
6. Don't tell lies about the bathroom. (like if you made a mess and said you didn't)
7. If you had an acadent don't be scard tell my mom. (donna) and she'll clean it up.
8. Dont thow Wet things like wet towls.
9. Dont Pont your middle finger at God. (of corse.!)
10. if you dont like a rule tell me.
11. Fallow these rules.
12. have a happy day every one even God!

Angela
7yrs. 11mo.

this and is therefore an easy receiver and producer of meaningful messages. For example, when the need arose within a social context to convey a personal message to her brother (who needed to be reminded of the virtues of tidiness), Angela chose language that represented her meaning (reality), and wrote Rules in the Bathroom (Figure 1). When the receiver of this message, four-year-old Matthew, saw his sister's note taped to the bathroom door, he had no doubt that the message was for him. And he was able to accurately predict its content. The lesson Matthew learned from this experience was not the one Angela hoped for (the bathroom wasn't much tidier after his visits). Rather, Matthew learned about language and its use: someone intended to tell me something; under similar circumstances someone had sent this message to me before, orally; someone was now sending the message by way of paper and magic marker; the content of the written message will be like the content of the oral message; the conventions of the oral message (loud talk accompanied by finger shaking, foot stomping, and calling in Mother) are different from the conventions of the written message (print, numbers, lines, spaces, words, sentences, punctuation marks, and quiet); reading and writing, like speaking and listening, are useful tools.

Using the above as preface, it is the intention of this article to do two things. First, to apply a functional view of oral language acquisition to reading and writing, which will be done by focusing on the two processes as mutually supportive linguistic social systems. And second, to suggest classroom activities that are consistent with the theoretical base presented and that will advance reading and writing processes.

The model in Figure 2 may help us with both tasks. It is a compilation of several notions about language and language users that includes the following: language is social and learned in the context of meaningful situations (Halliday 1975); language users receive and produce information and perceive both language processes to be active (Goodman 1982; Graves 1983); and active writers *intend* certain meanings and use certain conventions while active readers *expect* certain meanings and certain conventions (Smith 1982).

In this model we see that the language processes of listening, reading, speaking, and writing are developed and practiced in the sociolinguistic settings of home, school, and community, all of which are embedded in and influenced by the culture of the language user. Undergirding this is the assertion that reading, like listening, involves anticipating meanings and conventions. Such expectations guide the reader in the selection of on-the-page and off-the-page cues that lead to constructing a message. Writing is similar to speaking in that it involves wishing to say something and then producing cues for someone else to use in resolving that intention. Reading is basically receptive, writing basically expressive, but both are transactive. That is, in both there is a lively negotiation between the writer and the unseen reader or between the reader and the unseen writer in which the potential of both writer and reader is affected. Writers broaden the

Figure 2.
Model of a functional view of language.

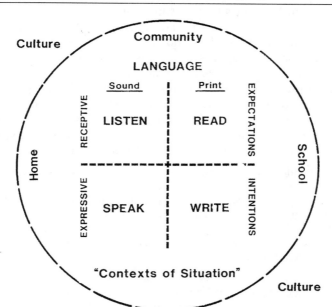

potential of their readers if they are aware of their audience's lives and linguistic backgrounds and then use language and conventions that take advantage of the readers' knowledge. Readers affect the text potential when they bring appropriate life and linguistic experiences to the passage. Certain texts can shrink the potential of readers, making them appear to be poor readers. Certain readers can diminish the potential of a text, making the text appear to be poorly written. On the other hand, when readers with background knowledge and reading strategies that push toward the construction of meaning come to well-written text, the potential seems limitless. Reading and writing are transactive processes that involve action, as well as change of both text and reader (Rosenblatt 1978).

Our next consideration is the contexts of situations in which these transactions occur. Like listening and speaking, reading and writing are acquired because they are functional and because they occur in meaningful social settings. As children play and work with others in their societies of home, school, and community, they find it necessary to express their meanings for a variety of reasons and in a variety of ways. Halliday (1975) has described seven functions through which a child acquires oral language or, in his terms, "learns how to mean." These seven functions have inspired others (Goodman & Goodman 1976) to draw parallel functional motivations for learning to read. A third parallel follows easily—motivations for learning to write. Halliday's categories are appealing because they give teachers an idea of the underlying forces (I want, do as I tell you, tell me why) that motivate children into the sociolinguistic acts of reading and writing. That is, we can easily see how natural it is, how it follows directly from a functional motivation, for children to write and read notes, signs, letters, rules, autobiographies, language experience stories, and newspaper articles. Halliday's point (1978) is important:

> We do not experience language in isolation—if we did we would not recognize it as language—but always in relation to a scenario, some background of persons and actions and events from which the things which are said derive their meaning. This is referred to as the "situation" so language is said to function in "contexts of situations" and any account of language which fails to build in the situation as an essential ingredient is likely to be artificial and unrewarding.

Returning to the model, two points need to be considered, as they directly affect reading and writing instruction. The first has to do with the use of visual cues in reading and writing. These visual cues include letters and combinations of letters, punctuation marks, italics, lowercase and uppercase print, and even the white spaces between words. Strangely, this utilitarian, surface-level, information-relating system of the language can present major problems for the reader and writer—if it becomes the focus of instruction. Warning against such a visual emphasis, Smith (1972) suggests that if writing is seen as a matter of reproducing letters and reading as a matter of identifying them, then mastery of phonics can become the goal of reading instruction, and precision in spelling, letter formation, or filling the page with print can become the prevailing concern of writing lessons. This kind of "alphabetic puritanism" neglects the meaningful intent of writers and the meaningful expectations of readers and is a prime bone of contention for educators who are disturbed by the misplaced emphasis of "back to basics" proponents.

The second issue raised by the "integrated language arts" section of the model has to do with the order in which children acquire language modes. The model challenges the notion that children learn to write only after they have listened, spoken, and read. Current research (Clay 1975; Goodman & Cox 1978; Harste, Burke & Woodward 1981; M. King 1979; Wiseman 1979) indicates that children can experiment with writing as soon as they can hold a pencil or make marks in sand. At a

1976 conference on reading, Carol Chomsky gave accounts of children who were writing—using invented spellings—before they knew how to read. Chomsky argued that expecting children to read before they write is an imposition that hinders their willing involvement in language and takes the fun out of learning. Ferreiro and Teberosky (1982) add that if children are to understand the writing system of their culture, they must be able to do more than name letters and utter sounds. Ferreiro and Teberosky say children must actively construct the writing system—by writing. If children become authors as they become readers, they discover through experience that writing and reading are related, with meaning and use as the link between them. To children who learn the processes simultaneously, print is no mystery and requires no manipulation (sounding out, dividing words into syllables, finding *the* main idea) to be understood. Authors are the first readers of their own work. Children who write messages they perceive to be sensible are not likely to accept nonsense when they encounter the work of other authors. They expect their own print to have a semantic intent and they will demand it of others.

Read's landmark research (1975) provides insights into the phenomenon of preschool and kindergarten children's learning to spell. The invented spellings of these young children reveal their intuitive strategies: they discover that a letter (often from their own names) can spell a sound, and they begin to spell words based on the sounds contained within the letter names (for instance, if the name of the letter *h* contains the /ch/ sound, then the invented spelling for *chair* for some children would logically begin with the letter *h*). If, as Read indicates, the spelling creations of children are not whimsical and haphazard but, instead, are indicative of their sophisticated understanding of phonology, and if these spellings can in fact be categorized, then it seems reasonable for teachers to encourage their students to use spelling variations. This does not mean we are not interested in standard spelling. It means that our first interest is to encourage children to express meaning—reality. Standard spelling will develop as children are more and more actively involved in using language through reading and writing.

Just as children are encouraged to use what they know about life and language when they read, they are encouraged to do the same thing when they write. Six-year-old Tracy does exactly that when, while waiting to see the nurse, she writes in her journal, "My stomach feels like it is going twenty miles an hour in circles" (Figure 3). Tracy has a message and she uses her knowledge of speech sounds and print to invent spellings so that her message can be written.

Proficient readers and writers consider all the pragmatic and linguistic information available to them. If for any reason one of the cue-

Figure 3.
Tracy's journal entry.

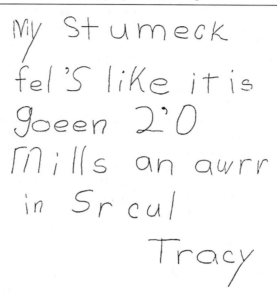

My Stumeck
fel'S liKe it is
goeen 2°0
Mills an awrr
in Srcul

Tracy

ing systems available to children (graphophonemic, grammatical, or semantic) is not used, the process may falter, stop, or end in nonsense. The following example indicates that Jane (age ten) was attending to the graphophonemic system (making letter-sound matches) while ignoring other important linguistic cues. Her miscues are written above the typescript.

            pizzas   *chin*
There will be prizes for children who take the best pictures. You
      show   *pizzas*   *f-framly*
should see those prizes. All the family stood around him when the
           Now   *l-l-led*
prints were done. How they laughed at some of the pictures!

Sammy (age eight), who was asked to write about a class trip, neglected to use the grammar of language as a frame for his meaning. He elected simply to list correctly spelled words. Because he avoided grammatical structures, we can only guess at his meaning.

Zoo Trip

Yesterday	Animals	Feed	Tigers
Zoo	Zebra	Jump	Fun

If we compare Sammy's "story" with Angela's Rules in the Bathroom and with Tracy's journal notation, we can infer that intention and instruction may be the keys to what and how children write. If Sammy had a purpose in his writing, he was unable to make it known to his readers, because his writing instruction seems to have focused mainly on correct spelling and neat handwriting. Angela and Tracy intended to get their meanings across and they were encouraged to use language to do it.

Activities That Bring Together Reading and Writing

The second purpose of this article is to present activities that are compatible and consistent with what we know about language and language users and that will support both the reading and writing processes. The activities mentioned are but a few in which the student can be author and reader, producer and receiver of messages.

Books Without Words

When asked, children will explain that books without words, unlike their other picture books, "don't have any writing in them." Such an oversight encourages children to become authors and to share their stories with others. After children give voice to their story, they write their own text or dictate it to the teacher. The story is then clipped to the appropriate page. Some particularly good wordless books for this activity are *Bobo's Dream*, by Martha Alexander; *Look What I Can Do*, by Jose Aruego; *What Whiskers Did*, by Ruth Carroll; *The Chicken's Child*, by Margaret Hartelius; and all of Mercer Mayer's excellent books without words. Richard Abrahamson in his "Update on Wordless Picture Books with an Annotated Bibliography" (1981) gives us information on high-quality books without words. Books with good illustrations but with meager texts ("Mat sat on the cat") can also be used if a teacher will snip off or cover up the "nontext" and then ask children to write real stories.

Bringing Familiar Language into the Classroom

Children's familiar language appears in many forms: jump rope rhymes, cheerleading yells, songs, sayings, poems, jokes, riddles, commercials, and family stories. Children enjoy writing and illustrating their own familiar language, a process that can begin by dictating it to the teacher, who writes it on the board. Everyone reads it and adds it

Figure 4.
Greg's venture into the familiar.

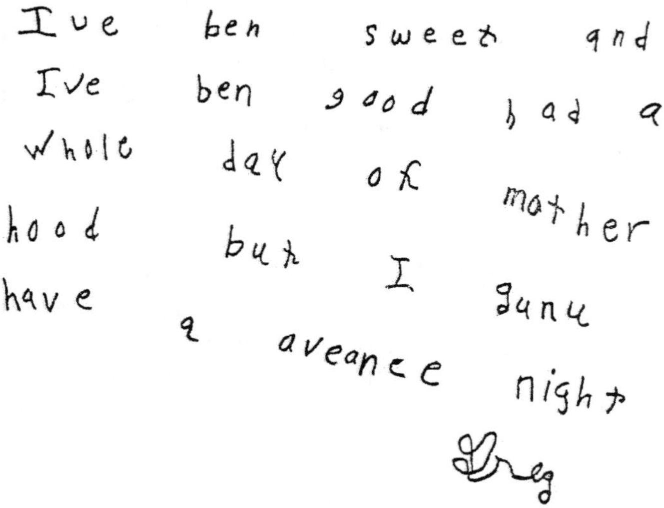

to their own and to the class book. Figure 4 shows one of Greg's first writing ventures, language so familiar that it had to be shared, said, written, read, and even acted out. (For those whose memories don't stretch back to the late 1970's, this comes from a popular perfume commercial of the time.)

Written Conversations

Written conversations are pen-and-paper talk between a teacher and a student in which the teacher initiates the conversation by writing a message to the student. The student reads the message and writes a reply. Sometimes it is necessary to read the dialogue to the student, but as the conversation becomes more predictable, the student usually will not need this help. Figure 5 shows a conversation between a teacher and a first grader.

These pen-and-paper conversations tacitly point up the similarities and differences between oral and written language. The written conversation necessitates some editing of the oral message—you simply don't/can't write down everything you might include in an oral conversation. Carolyn Burke and her students at Indiana University have developed this activity for use with very young children as well as adults (D. King 1983).

Figure 5.
A written conservation between Kyle and his teacher.

Your baby rabbits are so cute! Thank you
for bringing them. How are they today?

They are fin How are

your KIDS   One girl is not feeling

very well but the other one is fine. She

is singing in a play tomorrow night

That is hrs

What are you doing today?   Weeken
What are you working on? week
What work?

(worKing oN deT TadeTs

Where did you get dot to dots?

FROM YOU

Me! No! I don't remember that. What else
are you doing?   a POTea
What is the poster about?   me
What does it tell about you? I'm a semr
What else? a diver
How did you learn to dive?
all You GaT To do is Jeeaq

It would scare me to jump. Do you
jump off a high board? Yes

You're brave! What do you like
to do most of all? Peiy

What do you play?

Fello The leTr

Who do you play follow the leader

with?

my Fecs

Extended Literature

The world of children's stories and books is a natural source for the integration of the language arts. One example will sufficiently illustrate the point. Stephen Kellogg's *Can I Keep Him?* (1971), a favorite of Jane Decker's Title 1 reading students, tells the story of a small boy's attempts to talk his mother into letting him keep (among other animals) a dog, a fawn, a bear, and a python. His mother persistently refuses him, each time providing a reasonable argument, such as, "No, dear. Tigers grow up to have terrible appetites. They eat enormous amounts of food, and sometimes they eat people. We could never afford to feed a tiger." In addition to delightful illustrations and a captivating story, Stephen Kellogg provides the repetitive refrain, "Can I keep him?" for beginning readers to chant. This unambiguous, predictable sentence allows insecure readers to participate in reading the story.

Decker's first and second graders loved *Can I Keep Him?* and used it as a model to write their own letters asking if they could bring animals to reading class. Decker's replies to each student were read, shared, and reread. (See Figure 6.) The treasured letters were collected and compiled, and now a new book, *Can I Bring Him to Reading?*, is a class favorite.

Language Experience

Children experience, talk about their experiences, and then write about them with the help of a "talking secretary." Teachers serve as talking secretaries as they urge authors to clarify their thoughts by asking questions that a potential reader might ask and by simply listening and responding to the telling of the author's experiences. Talking secretaries never control the composing process. This tried and proven language experience activity is a basic in promoting the writer as reader and the reader as writer. And, because there are no sociopsycholinguistic gaps between the writer and the reader, there are no roadblocks in the construction of meaning. This is not to say that students can always reread what they have written. They may need to consider again their motivation for writing, what they intended to say and what they wrote first; in other words, they may need to reconstruct the original writing experience in order to read their own composition.

Team Stories

Writing a text with a partner or as a member of a team provides a situation in which the strengths of individual members can support the

Figure 6.
An exchange of letters.

Dear Mrs. Pecker
I have a dog and I want
to bring him to reading. He will
not runaround and he will not
bark and he will not clime on nobody
can I bring him to reading.
                          Renee

Dear Renee,
   No, you cannot bring your
dog to reading. I'm sure
he would not bark, climb
on anyone, or run around,
but dogs have tails. Tails
knock books and papers
on the floor.
                    Mrs. Decker

entire team. As children discuss their story, they impose structure on
it; that is, they use a grammatical frame. Brown (1977) suggests that
this sense of story influences comprehension. Roulette stories are one
form of team stories in which team writers don't discuss their text but
contribute to a growing discourse when it is their turn to do so. The
readers/writers of the roulette story quickly see the need for links between their portion and the existing text, then the need for a plot and
a central character emerge. These beginnings for group members can
grow into individual creations with all the basic structuring principles
of true narratives.

Interviewing Friends

Students first discuss what they would like to know about other students and what they would like others to know about themselves. The teacher acts as a scribe, writing their interview questions on the board: What sports do you like best? What do you do on Saturday? What is your favorite book? How would you describe yourself? What are you afraid of? These and suitable follow-up questions help prepare for a productive interview. Spontaneous and informal conversation precedes the interview as the partners take snapshots, draw pictures, or cut out silhouettes of each other. These pictures, often accompanied by fingerprints (another way of showing one's uniqueness), are placed on posterboard or on the cover of an individual's book (e.g., *The Biography of Tony Jones*). If a poster is made, some identifying characteristics and bits of information (has brown eyes, loves basketball, never misses *Mork and Mindy,* read *Where the Red Fern Grows* five times) can be added and used by the partner when introducing the Student of the Day. If the interviewer decides to produce a book, chapters can be written by different class members (including the teacher), and one chapter might be an autobiographical frame in which the subject fills in the missing parts with details of his/her life. These pupil-produced books become an important part of the classroom library and are read and referred to again and again.

Conclusion

The activities listed above are supportive of both reading and writing and are consistent with the following notions about learners and their language:

1. Language is learned in meaning-filled contexts by individuals who want and need to use it. In other words the language an individual learns and uses must function in real social situations and must be important to the learner.

2. Reading and writing are transactions in which both the reader and writer are active and are capable of modifying each other's potential.

3. "Alphabetic puritanism," overattention to form, and isolated lessons in one of the language modes or in one of the language systems decompose language and are nonfunctional and time-consuming practices that can be referred to only as meaningless and defeating.

4. The processes of reading and writing can be learned simultaneously, each strengthening and supporting the other.

5. Readers and writers must concern themselves with meaning—both in receiving and in producing it. If there is no meaning there is no impetus for using language.

References

Abrahamson, Richard. 1981. An update on wordless picture books with an annotated bibliography. *The Reading Teacher, 34*, 417–21.

Brown, Ann. 1977. *Knowing when, where, and how to remember: A problem of metacognition* (Technical Report No. 47). Urbana, IL: Center for the Study of Reading. (ERIC Document Reproduction Service Document ED 146 562.)

Chomsky, Carol. 1976, April. *Approaching reading through invented spelling.* Paper presented at the Conference of Theory and Practice of Beginning Reading Instruction. Pittsburgh: Learning Research and Development Center, University of Pittsburgh. (ERIC Document Reproduction Service Document ED 155 630.)

Chomsky, Carol. 1971. Write first, read later. *Childhood Education, 47*, 296–99.

Clay, Marie. 1975. *What did I write?* Portsmouth, NH: Heinemann.

Decker, Jane & her students. 1979. *Can I bring him to reading?* Columbia, MO: Grant Elementary School.

Ferreiro, Emilia & Teberosky, Ana. 1982. *Literacy before schooling.* Portsmouth, NH: Heinemann. (Original work published 1979.)

Goodman, Kenneth S. 1982. *Language and literacy: The selected writings of Kenneth S. Goodman* (2 vols.). Boston: Routledge & Kegan Paul.

Goodman, Kenneth S. & Goodman, Yetta M. 1976, April. *Learning to read is natural.* Paper presented at the Conference of Theory and Practice of Beginning Reading Instruction. Pittsburgh: Learning Research and Development Center, University of Pittsburgh. (ERIC Document Reproduction Service Document ED 155 621.)

Goodman, Yetta M. & Cox, Vivian. 1978. *The development of literacy in young children.* Washington, DC: Basic Skills Group, National Institute of Education.

Graves, Donald H. 1983. *Writing: Teachers and children at work.* Portsmouth, NH: Heinemann.

Halliday, M. A. K. 1975. *Learning how to mean: Explorations in the development of language.* New York: Elsevier.

Halliday, M. A. K. 1978. *Language as social semiotic: The social interpretation of language and meaning.* Baltimore: University Park Press.

Harste, Jerome C., Burke, Carolyn & Woodward, Virginia. 1981. *Children, their language and world: Initial encounters with print* (Final Report).

Bloomington, IN: Department of Language Education, Indiana University. (ERIC Document Reproduction Service Document ED 213 041.)

Kellogg, Stephen. 1971. *Can I keep him?* New York: Dial.

King, Dorothy. 1983. Written conversation. In J. Collins (Ed.), *Teaching all children to read* (pp. 65–68). Liverpool, NY: New York State English Council.

King, Martha. 1979. Toward a theory of early writing development. *Research in the Teaching of English, 13,* 243–53.

Read, Charles. 1975. *Children's categorization of speech sounds in English* (Research Report #17). Urbana, IL: National Council of Teachers of English.

Rosenblatt, Louise. 1978. *The reader, the text, the poem: The transactional theory of the literary work.* Carbondale, IL: Southern Illinois University Press.

Smith, Frank. 1972. Phonology and orthography: Reading and writing. *Elementary English, 49,* 1075–88.

Smith, Frank. 1982. *Writing and the writer.* New York: Holt, Rinehart & Winston.

Wiseman, Donna. 1979. A psycholinguistic description of the reading and writing behavior of a selected group of five-year-old children (Doctoral dissertation, University of Missouri at Columbia, 1979). *Dissertation Abstracts International, 40,* 4982A.

Readers and Texts
in a Fifth-Grade Classroom
(with Suzanne C. Davis)

It has been a decade since Ralph Peterson and Karen Smith and her students introduced me to the exciting and dynamic learning experience referred to by many teachers as literature study. *Ron Schlimme, the principal of Lee Elementary School in Columbia, Missouri, encouraged Suzanne Davis, who taught fifth grade, and Marilyn Andre, who taught first grade, to give it a try. Because of the courage and influence of these two teachers, major curricular changes have taken place in the teaching of literacy in the district and beyond.*

The first morning of the new school year was typically hot and humid. Little wonder that Suzanne Davis's fifth graders were incapable of much enthusiasm when their teacher began talking about a new reading program. Showing no signs of hearing the word *new*, the children politely settled down, fully expecting to hear the familiar. Most of them, after all, had been in Suzanne's classroom the year before and

Originally published in *Literature in the Classroom: Readers, Texts, and Contexts* (Urbana, IL: National Council of Teachers of English, 1988), pp. 59–67. Copyright 1988 by the National Council of Teachers of English. Reprinted with permission. The authors are indebted to Ralph Peterson, Arizona State University, whose conceptualization of the use of literature in classrooms has been the basis of this project; and to Debra Crouse, University of Missouri, whose research field notes are incorporated here.

knew that reading meant basals, workbooks, and endless skill sheets. There was also no doubt about what was expected of them as readers: they were already categorized as poor, average, or good and assigned to ability groups according to the end-of-level basal reader test given the previous year. Their reading performance had always seemed to reflect and confirm their poor, average, or good labels. Why should it be any different this year?

Suzanne's students were in for a surprise: the familiar was not forthcoming. Their teacher held up four paperback books, *Where the Red Fern Grows, Island of the Blue Dolphins, Ralph S. Mouse,* and *Nothing's Fair in Fifth Grade.* She proceeded to tell a bit about each book and then asked each student to select one book to read. She explained that there would be no low or high groups, no worksheets to fill out, no vocabulary words to find in the dictionary before reading, and no questions to answer at the end of two or three pages. The children would, however, be expected to read silently a great deal, to think about their books and their reading, to talk with others who were reading the same book, and to write about their books and their reading.

Suzanne and her students embarked on a year of extensive and intensive reading. They read a lot of quality literature, and they reflected and responded to the literature by making connections between it and their own lives and between the books they currently were reading and the literature they had read in the past. In Suzanne's words, it was a year neither she nor the students would forget.

Reasons for the Literature Project

Suzanne felt that something was missing in her traditional basal reading program. The children were learning to read, but in the case of some it seemed as if they were learning despite the program. Furthermore, her program had inspired little if any enthusiasm or love of reading. Writing, other than fill-in-the-blank or an occasional story starter, did not exist in the program.

Aware of her students' lack of interest, and at the same time intrigued by the new research in reading and writing, she was eager to test a model of literacy instruction that insists that language presented to children must be as alive and whole as the children using and learning that language. Suzanne made a decision: she would no longer expect children to become proficient and eager readers by presenting them with small units of language in regulated and controlled pieces (preselected paragraphs and stories with stilted syntax and controlled vocabulary). That approach would be replaced by increased reading of trade books, talking in small groups with others reading the same books, and bringing the reading process to conscious awareness by talking about what readers do to become more proficient. Another major change in the reading instruction involved having the children and the teacher write about what they read, about their reading (the process), and about things important to them.

Literature Study Groups

The term *literature study groups* (LSG) states exactly what the activity involves: real literature for children, high-level thinking about the literature, and readers meeting together in small groups to talk and think about what they are reading. In most upper elementary LSG programs, there are three or four groups in the classroom. Members of a group, those seven or eight students who choose the same book to read, meet with their teacher for thirty or forty minutes twice a week.

Literature study groups provide a curricular framework in which students can read extensively. In Suzanne's class, each student read approximately sixteen books throughout the year for his or her study group. On average, the LSG program also promoted the reading of approximately twenty-two non-LSG books, which were borrowed from the library, brought from home, or ordered through book clubs.

Books chosen for the study groups are selected on the basis of children's interest, quality of the text, and availability. (Although availability is a factor, no book is selected just because it is accessible.) The teacher introduces five or six books to the students by briefly discussing the title, author, plot, and so forth. During this introduction, the teacher challenges students to explore new genres and subjects— to extend their ability to make meaning in unexplored territories. Students bring their background of life and literature to this discussion and select a title for personal or social reasons. On the basis of their first or second choice, the children are assigned to groups. The most proficient and the least proficient readers sometimes select the same title and are therefore in the same group. Groups are never formed on the basis of reading ability or test scores.

Response to Literature

Students are expected to read, read, read—a great many books. But just as important as *extensive* reading is *intensive* reading. The LSG program does more than add another title to a list of books read or another segment to the bookworm elongating itself around the room. Children are asked to slow down, move back and forth between their lives and the text life, to consider meaning embedded in characterization, mood, pattern, ordering of time, circumstance of setting, even conventions of print. In other words, they are encouraged to participate in higher-order thinking—anything that helps them live through the literature experience, learn from it, and value it.

When students and teacher come together in a small group, the emphasis is on sharing impressions, ideas, and problems encountered in constructing meaning from the text. At this point it becomes evident that readers are as important as authors. When a topic surfaces that holds a common interest and has the potential for deepening perceptions, the teacher's help shifts from sharing to dialogue. Through dialogue (a shared experience that encompasses critical thought), the group discloses and constructs meaning. Through group power, meanings of the text held by individuals are expanded. In a cooperative undertaking, readers reflect on the importance of events, both within and outside the text, that move the story and themselves forward.

Before the group discussion, students are invited to respond personally in their literature logs, which they receive the day they select their first LSG book. It is made clear to the children from the outset that they are free to write as personally, specifically, or generally as they care to in their logs. They are encouraged but not required to write and to share their writing with the study group. In Suzanne's class, some children were comfortable with the writing and sharing, while others cared only to write and not share their thoughts. Occasionally, when there was little or no time for learning log entries, a few minutes either before or after the discussion group were devoted to writing. Toward the middle of the year, many students wanted to read the entire book before they responded in their log.

Suzanne never asked students to do anything she was not willing to do herself. As an authentic member of the group, she read all of the books and responded in her own log. The necessity of the teacher's participating in this way became apparent early in the year. The dialogue could never have been as intense and as important if any members, including the teacher, had failed to read the literature. Suzanne's sharing was always an invitational demonstration. It was never presented as *the* model toward which the students must strive. Rather, sharing was simply her honest response to the literature. She wrote in her log and shared it as a way of making her own connections with the literature, contributing to the group, modeling writing, and inviting the students to write. Following are two entries from Suzanne's learning log:

September 25
I began reading *Island of the Blue Dolphins* today. When I first began reading this book, I didn't think I was going to like it very well. Some of the names were unfamiliar, and I wasn't sure how I was supposed to pronounce them. I decided to settle on one way to pronounce each name and continue reading. Once I quit worrying about how to pronounce each name, I began to become more interested in the story.

I thought it was interesting that the people on the island had a real name, a secret name that is seldom used, and a common name that is used most. It might be fun to have a secret name that had a certain magic to it when used!

I stopped reading today at the point where the leader of the island left the island in search of a country he knew as a boy. He's going there to make a place for his island people. I have a feeling he may not return.

April 1
When I began reading *The Book of Three* I wrote in my log that it was difficult to pronounce the names and to keep the characters straight. It seems odd to me now that I could have gotten the characters confused. The characters were easier to keep straight along about the fourth or fifth chapter. Once I figured out my own strategy for pronouncing unusual names, then I could get on with the business of reading and getting to know the characters. I think only Lloyd Alexander himself knows how to pronounce them all correctly anyway!

I said earlier in my log that when I started this book I didn't know if I liked C. S. Lewis's or Lloyd Alexander's books better. I've now decided that's like trying to choose between rocky road and burgundy cherry ice cream—impossible! I like them both!

I must confess. I've always been afraid of reading high fantasy or science fiction. I was always afraid I would never really understand it and people would think I was dense. I enjoy this high fantasy of Lloyd Alexander's and I can't wait to read the next one. He is a creative author and uses such good description and imagery that I was drawn into the book and felt I was right there with the characters.

Alexander has a subtle way of getting you to think about something that could be a rule to live by. For example, when Gwydian discusses what brought the fall of the Horned King (on page 216), he says, "Once you have courage to look upon evil, seeing it for what it is and naming it by its true name, it is powerless against you, and you can destroy it." Somehow, that really struck me and I think there's a powerful message there.

Not only does Suzanne write about the content of the story and how it makes meaning for her, but she writes about the reading process and the strategies she uses to help her make sense of the story and derive a message from it. The impact of a teacher's sharing such information is powerful. Imagine the surprise and relief of an unsuccessful reader on learning that teachers also have problems when reading. As Brice's entries indicate, he learned from his teacher's example and accepted the invitation to write in his log:

> *December 19*
> I just finished *The Witch of Blackbird Pond*. It was a terrific book. I would recommend this exciting book. The author did a terrific job of portraying characters. The author always kept secrets from the reader. This book is for all ages, well thats what I think. Now I know why it got the Newbery Medal. My two favorite characters are Nat and Matthew Wood. I liked how Nat became the captain of a ship that he called "The Witch." That was a neat name to me. Now I'll tell you why I said Matthew Wood. I like how Matthew changed. For instance, he stood up for Kit 3 times at the end. I think that he just got more used to Kit.

> *April 1*
> I finished *The Book of Three* last Friday. It was the best book I've ever read! Except for *Where the Red Fern Grows*! I think Lloyd Alexander is one of the best authors that I know of. He is a very adventurous writer. I think Eilonwy is selfish. I wouldn't be surprised if she wanted to be *queen of Prydain*! Flewdur Flam is a pretty nice sort of character. He sounds like a nice sort of guy. Gúrgi is kind of a wierd sort of thing. He runs up trees like we run on the ground. Taran was sort of a coward at the beginning but in the end he was very courageous. I think that Lloyd Alexander made a terrific ending when Gwidion came to Taran's room and Lloyd kept Gwydion alive. I'm thinking of writing a story similar to this one.

What Was Learned

In the past year we have seen children become proficient and avid readers by having the opportunity to read real literature and to respond to it through discussion and writing. The children and the literature have taught us a great deal.

1. We have a sharper definition of *extensive reading*. Students are placed in a context where they are surrounded by literature. They see other students and their teacher spending a great deal of time with their noses in books, not only books from the literature study groups, but from the library and other sources as well. Children are encouraged to live through different kinds of literature and to make connections among plots, themes, characters, illustrations, and authors.

2. We have a sharper definition of *intensive reading.* It is not enough to read many books; the reading must be personalized in a way that taps children's worldviews in order to construct meaning and ownership through reading. In intensive reading, children return to the text to explore relationships, find links with their past experiences, build on previous readings, and explore what it is that makes the story.

3. The literature that students are asked to read must be of value. It can be professionally authored or written by classmates or the teacher, but it must have integrity. Trivialized text does not lead to future readings or to reading in depth. When children are invited to reflect on what they have read, something must be there to reflect on, to mull over, to savor. The issue of basal readers cannot be ignored. On the basis of an extensive study in Suzanne's class that included a miscue analysis of her fifth graders' reading, we have learned that the basals did not meet the interests and cognitive-linguistic needs of these readers.

4. Reading is both a personal and a social activity. Children must have time to read silently, personally. They must also have the opportunity to talk with others about books. From social interaction, children find that others have similar and different interpretations and opinions. Through confrontations with ideas, forms, and perspectives other than their own, members of the group are challenged and grow.

5. Reading groups to which children are assigned on the basis of traditional reading test scores are harmful to their linguistic and social health. Literature study groups provide a safe harbor for all readers to take risks, contribute, and become more proficient and more avid readers. Esteem for self and others is kept intact.

6. Many times it is useful for the student to bring the processes of reading and writing to a conscious level of awareness. One group discussed the use of parentheses, while two other students saw the need to bring in resource books to find out more about tarantulas, the topic of their LSG book. The students often talked about what they did when they came to something unfamiliar in a story, how they handled unknown concepts and unpronounceable words. They discussed the roles of writers and readers. All of these discussions occurred in the context of the "teachable moment."

7. The role of teacher is crucial. Literature study groups do not have much of a chance if the teacher fails to accept his or her primary role as a contributing member of the group, understanding that no member has the right to dominate. However, the teacher is the

teacher, and there is no better, more natural place to gather information about students and their learning than in the literature study groups. It goes without saying that teachers teach. It may, for example, be critical that the teacher spend time with a small group or the entire class, talking about how readers can look at the relationship of characters in a story or discussing the framework of a good detective story or illustrating by using excerpts how understanding the setting of stories may help readers understand the motivation and behavior of characters.

8. Reading and writing are mutually supportive. Writing helped the students focus and extend their understanding of the text. Reading gave them background, motivation, pattern, and convention for their own writing.

9. Teachers must be actively involved in the literature study groups: they must read the books and respond to the literature in both discussion and writing. Suzanne usually read the books before she introduced them to the students, but the children enjoyed it when she read along as they were reading. Authentic participation can happen only when teachers do what they ask their students to do—read and write.

10. Involvement of group members in real dialogue takes time, patience, knowledge, and experience. Most students and teachers expect any "discussion" to be teacher directed, teacher controlled, and even teacher centered. In literature study groups this cannot be the case if intensive reading is a real goal. For Suzanne, initial sessions were sometimes discouraging when the discussion seemed to be going nowhere or had nothing to do with the book. Discussions must be more than question-and-answer periods, bull sessions, or chitchat. Ways of involving children in dialogue, promoting real questions, and making appropriate comments continue to be basic concerns.

11. Making writing a part of the literature study program requires time, patience, knowledge, and experience. For some children, inviting them to write about their reading and then giving them time and facilities for the activity is enough incentive to set them immediately to the task. For most it is not enough, however. Through writing, teachers and students can help each other read intensively. The literature log provided Suzanne's students with the means for writing; she made sure they had time to write daily, and she gave an invitational demonstration by sharing her own writing with group members. Ways of involving children in response to their books through writing continue to be a basic concern.

This year with real kids and real literature has been a rejuvenating experience for everyone involved, including children, researchers, parents, and other teachers. It has been a time of learning for all. But for the teacher who had the most to gain or lose from the experience, it was also a time for taking risks. Suzanne Davis did just that. In the process she gained a confirmation of her practical theory of literacy and lost her hesitancy in speaking out for a curriculum that intrigues, enlightens, and empowers students.

We strongly recommend that teachers (because they know their students) choose the books to invite their children to read. Although Suzanne will change her list each year, the following were her first-year LSG books:

Louisa May Alcott: *Little Women*

Lloyd Alexander: *The Black Cauldron; The High King; Taran Wanderer*

Clyde Robert Bulla: *Shoeshine Girl*

Betsy C. Byers: *The Summer of the Swans; The Cybil War*

Beverly Cleary: *Ralph S. Mouse*

Vera and Bill Cleaver: *Where the Lilies Bloom*

James Lincoln Collier: *My Brother Sam Is Dead*

Margaret Davidson: *Helen Keller's Teacher*

Marguerite de Angel: *The Door in the Wall*

Barthe DeClements: *Nothing's Fair in Fifth Grade*

Jeannette Eyerley: *The Seeing Summer*

Paula Fox: *The One-Eyed Cat*

Kenneth Grahame: *The Wind in the Willows*

Madeleine L'Engle: *A Wrinkle in Time*

C. S. Lewis: *The Lion, the Witch, and the Wardrobe; Prince Caspian*

Jack London: *The Call of the Wild*

Jane O'Connor: *Yours Till Niagara Falls, Abby*

Scott O'Dell: *Island of the Blue Dolphins*

Katherine Paterson: *Bridge to Terabithia; The Great Gilly Hopkins; Jacob Have I Loved*

Wilson Rawls: *Where the Red Fern Grows*

Willo Davis Roberts: *The Girl with the Silver Eyes*

Marilyn Singer: *Tarantulas on the Brain*

Doris Buchanan Smith: *The Taste of Blackberries*

Elizabeth G. Speare: *The Witch of Blackbird Pond*
J. R. R. Tolkien: *The Hobbit*
Jules Verne: *Around the World in Eighty Days*

Reference

Kinder, Sandra J. 1989. Literature study groups: Effects on readers' proficiency, concepts of the reading process, and attitudes (Doctoral dissertation, University of Missouri-Columbia, 1989). *Dissertation Abstracts International, 51,* 1562A.

Alternative to Basals: Story and Inquiry

I teach an undergraduate course that investigates methods and
materials of teaching reading, including a skills-based and a
whole language curriculum. Among other activities, we devote
time to the basal reader and to literature study. I remember showing a basal reader series with all its ancillary materials and seeing
the eyes of my students light up. Here was the answer to their
prayers—everything anyone wanted to know about reading could
be found in that teacher's manual. Never again would they say, "I
don't know how to teach reading." It was all laid out for them,
step by step. So complete. So scientific. Then we would turn to
whole language experiences, including literature study. There was
no kit of activities, no hierarchy of skills that could be learned from
any given book. Here was too much fuzziness, too much work.

It took a while, but I finally learned that I couldn't just tell
undergrads about these two resources, they had to experience them.
It was not until we did an entire basal reader story, complete with
exercises, that the students realized how draining and depressing
the work was. Even when I told them that most teachers omit the
exercises, they found too many faults with the way the stories were
selected and presented. They were appalled to find stories that had
been tampered with. They began to share their own experiences
with basal readers. These teacher/learners were ready for an alternative to the conventional program. I remember the first time I
had a class try literature study. They had choice; their ideas about
every aspect of the book that they found interesting were explored.
They talked not only about the literature and about the reading
process, but also about how the discussion groups contributed to

the community feeling in the class. Literature study within a whole language curriculum became worth the effort. Now, these young educators talked about the excitement and the challenge of literature and learners. As one student put it, "We will have so much literature in my class that the basals will never be missed!"

I was asked once by a somewhat-exasperated-with-me school administrator what could possibly replace a basal reader program. A related but far less skeptical question is sometimes asked by experienced teachers: *How* do we replace the basal program with real literature and authentic inquiry? The same concern is expressed in an almost desperate way by future teachers who, after considering existing models of reading and writing instruction, have decided in favor of student-centered, meaning-focused, and literature-filled programs but don't know what to do on Monday morning.

This paper is addressed to teachers who have thought deeply about language and learning, have inquired about them within their own classrooms, have explored literacy research, and who have decided that the use of a basal reading program is neither consistent with all that *they* know, nor is it compatible with all that *their students* know. The following suggestions are for teachers who have rejected workbooks and worksheets, and have sent the basal readers back to the storage room or have ripped any acceptable material out of them and made "skinny books" for the classroom library.

If there are no more basals and therefore no more worksheets, workbooks, and three-level reading groups, what then will take their place? I propose that story in the broadest and deepest sense of the term and *inquiry into story,* when utilized in a whole language classroom community, will promote maximum rather than minimal literacy learning. Uncompromised (nonbasalized, real, important to the learner) stories written by professional authors, students, family, or teachers can easily replace and outdistance prescribed, precollected, and often compromised materials contained between two covers of a single hardback book.

Story in the form of poetry, narrative, essays, fairy tales, magazine and newspaper articles, reference materials, pen pal letters, plays, jokes, rhymes, and riddles should be as pervasive and important within the classroom community as in the larger community. Story as it represents the culture of students is a defining artifact in the cultural circles (Paulo Freire's term) of the classroom.

If students are expected to think on a "higher order," to read with understanding, and to write with clarity, they must be at home with uncompromised story. The invitation to such story is a continuation of home language use: reading and telling stories (including students sharing family and community stories), singing, joking, and playing with language. Such sharing of stories among students, teachers and family is the solid ground on which learners stand in order to become proficient and eager readers and writers.

But what of more organized strategies in which it is clear that students are learning to read? Literature study as one strategy, in place within a whole language curriculum, promotes the growth of proficient and enthusiastic readers and writers. It also appears to observers as if "reading is being taught."

Let's first investigate a possible organizing structure for young readers, perhaps kindergarteners and first graders. Shared reading using oversized "big books" (or large-print charts of poetry, songs, or students' stories) provides the social setting for kids helping kids learn to read. Within this snug small-group setting, learning to read is as natural as learning to speak (Holdaway, 1979). Children are invited to enter the story with a great deal of support from other learners, from their teachers, and from the predictable language of the text. Don Holdaway calls the first shared reading of a big book "discovery reading." Children are invited to join in the reading of repetitious, cumulative, or other highly predictable portions of the story as the teacher guides the reading by moving his or her hand under the enlarged text.

The teacher invites the children to predict words or events, but leaves the questioning and commenting to the students. This listening/reading experience involves no criticism or competition. If small books are available, these are distributed after the first shared reading. The children read these books on their own, with a partner, with the aid of a recording, with special teachers or visitors, or at home with family members. When the group meets for a second reading of the big book, more children will confidently take part in the reading of the story. The discussion is an invitation for a learner to comment on illustrations, patterns within the text, interesting or unknown words and concepts, as well as to talk about the author and illustrator and the relationship of the story to the students' own writings. If it is appropriate, there are discussions of story conventions such as theme, setting, plot, and characterization. All talk emerges naturally and must contribute to the understanding and love of the story.

Is phonics a part of this program? Dorothy Menosky once commented that whole language teachers utilize phonics with a small p; they don't teach Phonics with a capital P. If it is appropriate and useful, within the supportive context of the entire story, teachers act accordingly and suggest to readers that they focus on letter-sound relationships. Likewise, if attention to punctuation, capitalization, spacing, or line and story directionality is needed to aid comprehension, the teacher discusses them at the appropriate time. Brief and spontaneous sessions calling attention to conventions emerge naturally from students' needs and should never detract from the enjoyment of the shared book experience.

Hundreds of wonderful books are now available for young readers and are increasingly accessible through library exchange programs and book clubs. Money previously spent on basals can be used to build a fine collection of paperback books and big books. Teachers involved in literature study must become familiar with valued children's literature. Familiarity with stories, along with knowledge about predictability, literary quality, and literary elements, are indispensable. Teachers must feel comfortable when reviewing literature for their children and must be able to decide, for example, that *Chicken Little* (Kellogg 1965), *It Didn't Frighten Me* (Goss & Harste 1981), and *Brown Bear, Brown Bear* (Martin 1983) are very suitable for most children's early shared reading, while *The Shoemaker and the Elves* (Grimm 1960), *Drummer Hoff* (Emberley 1967), or *Why Mosquitoes Buzz in People's Ears* (Aardema 1975) are appropriate at a slightly later time. Obviously, picture books and big books vary in quality. Some books help learners feel the rhythm of language and are suitable for the joyful practice of reading. Other stories not only provide practice but invite students to bring their lives to the text for thinking and discussion with other readers.

When children move into chapter books, literature study takes on slightly different aspects; usually, for instance, there are very few, if any, big books available, and more meetings may be needed in order to fully discuss the book. After children read on their own, they then come together in a small group to talk with others who have read the same book. The purpose of the group discussion is to enter the story again, perhaps at a different level; to learn from others; and to intensify and clarify what the reader knows or wants to know. I once asked fifth-grader Courtney what she thought of literature study. She, after all, was a proficient reader who read widely and well; I suggested that she probably didn't need to talk to others about the story. Her reply was that although she read a lot of books, it was those books she talked about with others that she remembered and loved. She said that when she talked about the book with other kids and her teacher, "There is more to remember."

Teachers in a literature-filled program using shared reading and literature study have their work cut out for them. Not only must they know literature, collect multiple (seven to eight) copies of each title, read the literature, plan their overall literacy program, including evaluation, but they must also understand the dynamics of a learning community, especially as it relates to literature. Literature study groups are not basal reader groups—not even close. Children select their own groups by choosing the book they want to read; they are never identified as one of the three "bird" groups. It is often the case, in fact, that the most proficient and the least proficient readers are in the same group; they can learn a great deal from each other. Round-robin reading and interrogation of students are out; the teacher is another contributing member of the group. Literature study includes all the language acts of listening, speaking, reading, and writing; group members often respond to the literature they are reading by writing and drawing in their literature logs. In order to extend concepts addressed in the literature and to enter the story yet another time, projects that involve writing, drama, music, and art are often undertaken.

The following outline is one that many teachers may find helpful to guide their literature study. It should be modified to fit the learners.

Literature Study—Shared Reading

Clear the way: Collect multiple copies of many titles. Choose quality literature. Share information about literature study with parents, administrators, and others who are interested. Talk with students about the strategy.

Book selection: Introduce books to the children. (If three groups are planned, present four books; if four groups are planned, present five books; this allows for a wider range in choice.) Students make first and second choices and are assigned to groups based on their choices. Negotiate group membership with the students. Don't be tempted to make one group large and another small; more than eight members results in voices not being heard.

Shared reading: Use a procedure like that described above for the first reading of big books with young readers.

Personal reading: If students are reading chapter books, determine reading assignments with the group's members; a sizable portion of text should be undertaken. Make sure the children have time to complete the assignments.

Less able readers: Conference briefly with students about "close read-ing" and text that can be skimmed. Facilitate partner reading or listen-ing to portions of the story on tape. Perhaps the Title 1, special education, or speech teachers will include the story in their curricula. Talk with families about reading with the students. It is crucial that the less able readers come to the discussion prepared.

Highly proficient readers: Rather than reading beyond assigned pages, the advanced reader might collect information concerning some topic of interest within the story to share with the group, prepare a tape of the story, read other concept-related texts, or read other books by the same author.

Literature logs: The response log is a chronicle of the students' reflections on the literature as it relates to their lives and to other literature. The group members must feel comfortable with the logs and understand that their purpose is to deepen the learners' understanding of the story. Students might write in their logs as they read, or time can be devoted to writing before their group discussion. Teachers keep logs, too.

Dialogue: Dialogue is genuine sharing of information and responses with others who have read the same book. Dialogue allows learners to reenter the text for a more intensive exploration of it. Teachers sometimes feel that discussion groups fail to meet their potential. The following may help the teacher/group member in keeping the dia-logue powerful.

Starting the dialogue (invitations):

1. Wait and listen to the other members of the group.
2. Ask: What do you make of this story?
3. Who wants to start? Who will start?
4. Who will share from your log?
5. Comment on something in the story that is important to you. Wait and listen.
6. Before the meeting designate someone to begin the discussion.
7. Respond to an earlier agreed-on topic:

    What makes this book fantasy?

    Word play and interesting language.

    Writer's special techniques.

    Follow the development of one character.

Continuing the dialogue (more invitations):

1. Wait and listen to the other members of the group.
2. Comment on something important to you. Wait and listen.
3. What do you make of that?
4. What is this story really about?
5. Invite readers to ask one real question of the group. Demonstrate.
6. When did your heart beat faster?
7. Does this book matter to you? How?
8. Are you changed in any way? How?
9. Who should read this book? Why?
10. What one thing will you remember? What one character?

Closing the discussion:

1. How did we do?
2. How did I do?
3. What about next time? (Suggestions for improvement, assignments, etc.)

Projects: In order to return again to the literature and intensify and extend the story, students are often invited to engage in projects such as making tapes, posters, bookmarks, time lines, or maps. They also reflect on the story through song, dance, art, mime, or drama. These optional projects might be individual endeavors or be undertaken with partners or the entire group.

A whole language literacy program involves much more than story-telling and literature study. One major whole language literacy strategy, for example, involves using all of the language acts in order to research within the areas of science, social studies, or any topic of individual and group interest. Within a selected theme, students and their teachers consider all the areas in which there is research potential. Inquiry into student-selected topics involves the learner's reading a variety of materials, taking notes, conferencing with others, writing drafts, revising, editing, and presenting. Collections of texts that have unifying themes are an important feature of such inquiry.

In addition to constructing meaning through the use of logs, records, and reports, children become proficient readers by writing in all genres. The stories written by learners in the classroom are as important as those written by Beverly Cleary, Walter Dean Meyer, and

Katherine Paterson. The children's works are read not only by the authors themselves but also by partners, by those in their authoring circles, by other children in the school, and by students' families.

The alternative to a basal reading program is so appealing that one might wonder how anyone could resist. Such a program does, however, require giving up some conventional aspects of the curriculum: selected and controlled materials; children being tested and then labeled as good, average, or poor readers; drill on prescribed skills; workbooks and worksheets; teacher as controller; and the fragmentation of story and curriculum. Such a program, on the other hand, requires acceptance of a world of valued literature; children who view themselves as successful readers and writers; reading a great deal of literature and then thinking, talking, and writing about it; a seamless curriculum in which reading and the other language acts are a cohesive factor; and a classroom community of learners.

Is there an alternative to the basal? Ask your students. Ask yourself.

References

Aardema, Verna. 1975. *Why mosquitoes buzz in people's ears*. New York: Dial.

Emberley, Barbara. 1967. *Drummer Hoff*. Englewood Cliffs, NJ: Prentice-Hall.

Goss, Janet L. & Harste, Jerome. 1981. *It didn't frighten me*. New York: Willowisp Press.

Grimm, Brothers. 1960. *The shoemaker and the elves*. New York: Scribner's.

Holdaway, Don. 1979. *The foundations of literacy*. New York: Scholastic.

Kellogg, Steven. 1985. *Chicken Little*. New York: Morrow.

Martin, Bill, Jr. 1983. *Brown bear, brown bear, what do you see?* New York: Holt, Rinehart & Winston.

Part Four

Whole
Language
(1988–1994)

Whole Language Teachers
and Reality
(with Paul Crowley)

Whole language is a learning experience. We warm to the principles and practices of whole language because we are advocates for students and we find that what we've done in the past doesn't invite learning. Sometimes we get so caught up in our adventure that we forget to look over our shoulder to see whether anyone else is on the path with us. The students are there, but where are parents, administrators, colleagues, journalists, school board members, and legislators? As we reflect on our whole language presence, let's listen to those teachers who have invited all stakeholders into the whole language learning experience.

In complex technological societies, literacy is an empowering force. Those who read can find out what others know and those who write can share what they know; written language is an effective vehicle for the exchange of information, beliefs, and values across time and space. Whether one is reading a recipe or a petition, writing a letter

Reprinted by permission of Dorothy Watson and Paul Crowley. From Chapter 8, "How Can We Implement a Whole Language Approach?" in *Reading Process and Practice: From Socio-psycholinguistics to Whole Language,* edited by Constance Weaver (Portsmouth, NH: Heinemann, a division of Reed Elsevier, Inc., 1988), pp. 273–76.

to a cousin or to the editor of the newspaper, written language helps get things done. In George Orwell's *1984,* Big Brother wanted people literate only to the extent that they could comprehend government slogans and propaganda on a literal level; writing was a heinous crime. Suppressive regimes carefully control access to information and the dissemination of ideas through print. On the other hand, democratic societies take pride in freedom of information and freedom of the press.

There is an implicit contract between the community and the school that children will learn to read and write so that they will be independent adults. People who leave school illiterate can receive negative national attention. It is no wonder that reading—and more recently writing—instruction is closely monitored within the school curriculum. There are pervasive influences affecting what happens in a public school classroom; one such influence has to do with accountability. Teachers are accountable to their principals, principals are accountable to their superintendents, superintendents are accountable to the school board and legislators, and the school board and legislators are accountable to parents and other citizens. Other forces impacting on curriculum and teaching involve state mandates, district policies, departmental regulations, and expectations of principals and supervisors. The effects of these policies and expectations can be found in all classrooms.

Whole language teachers do not sacrifice the needs of children for the sake of political issues; they do, however, use their knowledge and expertise to understand these influences and to use them for the benefit of students. Breakdowns in communication can lead to power struggles that teachers too often lose. Consider the following scenarios.

Scenario 1

A father is curious about what his first grader is doing in school and asks about her reading class. "We don't have reading class" is her answer. That evening he visits his neighbor, a school board member, inquiring as to the whereabouts of the "First R" in first grade. The next day when the teacher is called into the principal's office to explain why she is neglecting to teach the basic skill of reading, she is in a less than advantageous position.

Her explanation is good: every day the children are read to or told a story. The bookshelves are filled with a variety of children's literature, content texts, resource books, blank paper, and writing utensils.

The children have been invited from the first day of school to read and write independently, and success is guaranteed. The children read for real purposes: for enjoyment, to find out about spiders, to find out what's for lunch, to read their friends' writing. There is no designated "reading class" because reading is a learning tool that is used all day, and when there is a need to talk about the process of reading, it is done individually or in small groups. The teacher explains that she doesn't view reading as an entity unto itself but as a language process that is used to explore and express the content being studied. Reading, in concert with writing, listening, and speaking, is not taught in isolation, but is learned and refined through use.

Reflection

People are uncomfortable with the unfamiliar. Parents in particular can become understandably concerned if they feel that their children's needs are not being met in school. The features of a whole language program are sometimes unfamiliar to people who are accustomed to traditional reading instruction, but parents and administrators can understand the theory and the practice of whole language. If the parents had been invited to learn about the curriculum at the beginning of the year and if information had been sent home concerning reading and writing in this classroom, the miscommunication could have been avoided.

Scenario 2

A first-year third-grade teacher is dismayed by the spelling books ordered the previous year. The guidebook instructs the teacher to introduce a list of ten words on Monday, have the students write the words ten times each, use each in a sentence, look up their definitions in the dictionary, and copy these in the space provided. On Wednesday the children are tested on the words, and failed words are drilled on Thursday and retested on Friday.

The teacher knows that this is not the way spelling is learned. The prescribed words are often unfamiliar and unimportant to the student, and are chosen by the author of the spelling textbook. The activities can be completed with little or no thought; the teacher knows that the children are easily bored with such activities and can become uninvolved in their learning, often leading to passivity or behavior problems. But the teacher believes the spelling books must be used.

Reflection

Did the teacher ask if the books really had to be used? (If so, how?) Or how much time had to be spent on the books? Do the directions in the teacher's manual have to be the curriculum? Did the teacher propose alternatives, such as using the spelling books as reference books? Can pages be skipped? Can students substitute words they want to learn for those chosen by the publisher? Did the teacher explain to her supervisors how she handles spelling in the curriculum? Informed teachers find out what is required by law or mandate and where they have freedom and autonomy. Administrators and supervisors respect professionals who can articulate their beliefs and knowledge, who have confidence in what they know, and who show a genuine concern for the needs and welfare of their students.

Scenario 3

The second-grade teacher walks into the teachers lounge during lunch complaining to the faculty about how terrible her students' writing is. She has drilled them on the correct formation of the lowercase *k* for a week now and there are still children who can't do it. They just need more drill. The language arts consultant is annoyed because by "writing," this teacher means "handwriting." The consultant tells her not to worry about such a trivial matter: writing is generating ideas, learning through language use, and expressing inner thoughts and feelings. She has the undivided attention of the teacher and all of her colleagues. Later she's the only member of the faculty not invited to that teacher's yearly Christmas party.

Reflection

Teachers must afford their colleagues the same consideration that they expect and that they give their students. When teachers are empowered by their beliefs, they want everyone to share their excitement. But others have their own beliefs and they too are seeking acknowledgment. People are less likely to change when their practices are attacked or when they are told that they should do things differently; individuals change because they see value in something else.

The well-meaning consultant embarrassed her colleague and questioned her expertise. Rather than taking an adversarial role with the other teacher, she might have simply shared student writings. This would have provided an opportunity to offer what she knew and to present children in a positive light, both in an unassuming matter.

Reflecting on Reflections

The problem common to these three scenarios is poor communication. Teachers must be open about what they know, and they need to find out what others are doing—really doing—if there is to be hope for positive communication. Teachers need to talk to parents, administrators, and other teachers in order to support each other's endeavors, always maintaining the child at the center.

Teachers need support. How frequently does someone come into the classroom to talk with teachers or to discuss curricular matters? Teachers often close their doors, hoping to be left alone. Whole language teachers have found it necessary to metaphorically "open their doors" to other teachers who can, in turn, share their own successes and problems.

Reflections on Whole Language: Past, Present, and Potential

Whole language teachers value their professional pasts and the personal journeys they have each taken. They learn and grow from all that is happening right now in their classrooms. The past and the present of whole language fill their heads with new ideas and fill their hearts with courage. The successes and problems of the past and present move whole language teachers into a future filled with hope.

Recently I sat in the lounge of an elementary school listening to a friend talk about her fifth-grade class and about herself. With genuine enthusiasm she told all about the reading and writing her students were doing. She told anecdote after anecdote, pointing up marvelous child logic and instances in which children helped each other rather than competed with each other in order to learn. And then she began to reflect on her own first shaky steps into a whole language literacy program. Just a year ago she felt that she didn't have a firm grasp on the theoretical base that supports a whole language program and therefore felt very unsure of herself as a whole language teacher. To add to her uneasiness, she knew that for some in her school district whole language either was unknown or was unpopular—just hearing

Originally published in *Oregon Council of Teachers of English*, 11 (Fall 1988), 4–8. Copyright 1988 by Portland State University. Reprinted with permission.

172

the words was like waving a red flag. On the other hand, she realized some advocates of whole language occasionally uttered the words in the self-righteous way a chip is placed on a shoulder: I dare you to knock it off! I dare you to disagree with all I know about language and language learning.

Nevertheless, the literature supporting whole language was compelling for this teacher; it rang true, and even more important, her students confirmed that it made sense to them. Within a year, with the help not only of her students but also of colleagues in her teacher support group, this teacher came to understand that a whole language (or meaning-centered, student-focused, literature-based) program meant that she and her students could become a community of learners in control of their own ways of knowing.

It became important for this teacher to define whole language. She said it was an important part of her professional development. She began to define the concept in *ways* (not *a* way, but *ways*) that were deeply imbedded in her own professional growth. For this teacher, at a linguistic level, whole language means that *all* systems of language (meaning, grammar, symbol-sound relationship) are involved in any literacy encounter.

Curricularly, whole language means that students—not textbooks or preformed guides or tests—are at the heart of teaching and learning; it means that students are invited day in and day out to read whole stories, poems, and books; to write their own stories, poems, and books; and to have conversations and conferences with teachers, senior citizens, parents, and other students. It means that language is learned as students *use it* in reading, writing, listening, and speaking about science, math, social studies, literature, sports, and anything else that interests them.

Culturally, whole language means that the students' beliefs, life styles, interests, values, and needs are valued and are a source of information and joy. Students of all cultures and all subcultures have a place in the society of the classroom, and their contributions are celebrated.

Socially and psychologically, whole language means that the individual thought and language of the child is nourished and enhanced in schooling situations that encourage peer support and interchange. Children learn language not in isolation but personally and in transaction with their world and all the people in it.

Instructionally, whole language means that the artifacts of real language—including ideas, stories, conversations, and writing materials—and the circumstances of real thought——hypothesizing, risk taking, organizing, getting it wrong, getting it right, categorizing, summarizing, pondering, changing, and a thousand other -*ings*—take the place of fragmented skill, drill, fill-in-the-blanks in an uptight, get-it-right classroom.

And *politically,* whole language means that teachers, through knowledge, become empowered, and they pass on that power to students, parents, and other teachers.

In other words, whole language is defined as a powerful point of view about students, language, learning, and teaching. And it is much more.

The Past

As the teacher told me what had happened to her and her students during the year, I began to think about other teachers and of my own path toward whole language. It occurred to me that, in keeping with whole language tradition and theory, whole language teachers have similar but never identical stories to tell. Our pasts, our presents, and our potentials are unique. I'd like to share mine with you, to tell my story of growth as a whole language teacher.

When whole language teachers talk about their past, it seems that they talk first about all the theorists, researchers, teachers, colleagues, and of course, students who have influenced them. I must do the same, and without hesitation the philosopher/educator who has contributed most significantly to my perspective on learners and learning is John Dewey (1940), who in all his work urged us to place students at the center of the curriculum and to make that center an appropriate and active (not passive) one for learners.

Like so many others, I have been touched by the revolutionary work of Louise Rosenblatt (1938/1976, 1978) who, in keeping with John Dewey, told us that when it came to reading, the powerful *action* that Dewey was talking about was actually a *transaction*—a transaction that involved a unique dedication on the part of the reader that evolved into a unique and moving experience that Rosenblatt described brilliantly as "living through the literature." Rosenblatt's insight helped me realize that no two people reading the same text could ever leave that piece with identical meanings, and that when readers truly transact with a text they are not the same at the end of the piece as they were at the beginning of the reading.

Leland Jacobs (1965) understood the power of this lived-through experience, and he added to it that we must invite children to live through literature that has the strength to touch them, the power to change them, and the energy-force to move them. Jacobs placed literature at the center of the curriculum right along with the student and the teacher.

Michael Halliday (1975) helped strengthen my whole language understanding by showing that we learn language by "learning how to mean"; that is, by creating meaning in functional, useful, and natural situations. And Halliday told us too that we needed others to help us make meaning. Halliday, in effect, directed us to pull down the dividers, to do away with the so-called individualized and programmed learning kits that separate student from student, even student from teacher. His research was reminiscent of the Russian psychologist Lev Vygotsky (1962, 1978), who advocated much earlier (his work was originally published early in the century) that learners are in the most appropriate position to help other learners. Vygotsky said that what children couldn't do yesterday, they could do today with someone else's help, and could do by themselves tomorrow. Students can make each other look a head taller simply by helping each other. Vygotsky broadened and enriched the curriculum by placing other humans in the center along with the learner, the teacher, and the literature. Halliday and Vygotsky told us of the importance of the *community of learners*.

Each individual's personal history and his or her growth into whole language will include others who in some way clarified a problem, answered a question, or caused the individual to reflect and rethink. For many of us those special teachers include Sylvia Ashton-Warner, James Britton, Frank Smith, Don Holdaway, Donald Graves, Donald Murray, Marie Clay, Charles Read, Emilia Ferriero, Yetta Goodman, Jerry Harste, Harold Rosen—just to name a few. And I suspect that there is one particular name that heads our individual list. For me that educator is Kenneth Goodman. Goodman built his studies on the work of predecessors who saw the child not as a subject but as a learner—valued and whole.

I remember in 1965 reading Goodman's "A Linguistic Study of Cues and Miscues in Reading," in *Elementary English* (now *Language Arts*). He did some unusual things in that research: he didn't ask the students to read short passages and then take paper and pencil to prefabricated questions that allowed only one right answer. Goodman refused to deal with what Don Graves calls faceless data; Goodman gave not only a face but a mind and a life to the data. He painted a picture of a learner. And in 1965 he did it by sitting down next to children (first and third graders) one at a time, chatting with them until both the child and he were comfortable; then he asked the child to read a complete story and tell about what had been read. Revolutionary. Goodman found out that these young readers could read in context over half the words that they missed on a list of words out of context, and that when kids backed up or regressed (in the eyes of most, regressions constituted making a mistake, and mistakes needed to be eradicated), they backed up for one overriding reason: to correct themselves.

I remember the effect that that research had on me. My first reaction was, "I knew that all along!" Then I began to make some theoretical memos (assumptions) based on Goodman's research, memos that could be changed, but for the time being would guide my emerging theoretically based teaching. These memos may sound commonplace today, but twenty-four years ago they were new and exciting.

1. This early research showed us that it is not necessary to introduce words out of context. Direct instruction of vocabulary that usually consists of flash-card drill or asking students to look up ten words in the dictionary, divide them into syllables, use them in "a good sentence," and (if the teacher needs more time to get the worksheets graded) place diacritical markings on the words is unnecessary and possibly harmful. This research articulated what we already knew—drilling on vocabulary is not the way we learn the concepts in our world or the labels (words) for those concepts.

2. The research helped us realize that direct phonics instruction is unnecessary. In fact, using rules or sounding out as the first reading strategy may keep learners from using integrative strategies that focus on meaning. We began to understand that rules don't help the reader. In truth, rules often confuse the learner—is it "Starve a cold and feed a fever" or "Feed a cold and starve a fever"? When it comes time to apply the rule we usually end up doing what we want to do.

3. This early research also helped us realize that we shouldn't do anything for learners that they can do for themselves; that learners need to grapple not with the impossible but with the delightfully difficult; that with the help of meaningful text, readers can use all the systems of language and their past experiences—to consider, reconsider, back up, take another shot at constructing meaning, and possibly get it right. Now, if readers are encouraged to use these risk-taking strategies, the teacher must refrain from correcting readers at the point of utterance; doing so can stop kids in their linguistic tracks. The teacher invites students to read good texts and then gives them time and a setting in which they can take linguistic risks.

4. Goodman's early research helped us to get over our fixation on eye fixation. We began to realize that it was the mind, not necessarily the eye, that doubled back, reconsidered, renegotiated, and constructed meaning.

5. Goodman's research of the sixties and seventies helped us understand that there is no hierarchy of skills in reading development. This finding had clear whole language implications: reading is not a matter of identifying the skill, mastering that skill, and then moving to a so-called higher step and mastering *that* skill. Nor is reading instruction a matter of getting kids to stop miscueing; rather, reading instruction is for the purpose of helping kids to get a handle on the reading process.

Getting a handle on the reading process involves some interesting phenomena. First, it's hard to get a good grasp if you're scared to death of making a mistake. Language users (whether with oral or written language) need to feel that they can take risks. When children take risks in order to construct meaning, their miscues begin to be higher-level (that is, the reader may not produce an exact replication of the text, but the miscue approximates the meaning and intent of the text and therefore the miscue makes sense). Second, the materials that are most appropriate for helping kids get a handle on the process are not prescribed reading programs that include workbooks, worksheets, and dittos (now called reproducibles), but real stories, poems, and plays written by real authors, including students themselves.

Each of us has our unique professional past. If we had only kept a journal of our early teaching experiences so that we could reflect on our past and share those moments that moved us into questioning the status quo, those times when we felt uncomfortable being in a powerless position of not knowing how to move away from a defeating curriculum, those times when we said that we and our students deserved more. If we had such journals to read we might find the names of theorists and researchers who have helped us, but we also might find the name of the third-grade teacher down the hall who gave us an article to read and then invited us to her teacher support group or the principal who made the road easier—not tougher—for teachers who knew what they were doing or the parents who said that their child had never read or written so much and had never had a happier year or the college teacher who said that there really was an alternative to programs driven by basal readers, language arts textbooks, and standardized texts.

The Present

We use both our public and our personal pasts to read the present. Both can strengthen us and give us focus. I teach an undergraduate course in which the students are asked to keep two journals—an individual one and one that is called a roving journal (Heine 1989), which is passed around among five or six students. I'd like to share an entry written by one of the students who at the end of the semester reflected on her past experiences and how those reflections helped her get a perspective on the present and the future. Laura writes:

> I was in the high reading group from 1st grade right through 6th. It was no big deal because for the most part the good readers were left alone. We got to read a lot of books—the bad news is that I had to write a book report after each book, so I never read as many as I could have or wanted to. But the real problem with the reading groups was that my first great love, Denny, was in the slow group. Although Denny never said a word about it, I think he knew he was thought of as a lousy reader, therefore a lousy student, therefore a lousy person—and too often he did his best to live up to his label.
>
> What I remember most vividly is that I was embarrassed for Denny. I hated that he had to do "puh and buh drill" and to meet in a reading group every day with the "dummies." The absolute worst day of my life was when Mrs. Clairmore paired Denny and me to do his flash cards. He struggled and I died. I think that may have been the only time in my entire life I ever doubted that I wanted to grow up and be a teacher. It never crossed my mind that there was a real alternative to labeling kids, assigning them to reading groups, and then drilling and skilling the poor readers.
>
> Now I know that there is a more humane and joyful way of teaching kids to read and write—a way that comes out of good research with real kids. I'm sorry and just a bit angry that it's come too late for Denny. Thank God, it's not too late for me, and, Mrs. Clairmore, wherever you are, I pray that it's not too late for you!

We know that the past can lead us, but we know too that it can mislead if we don't take control of the knowledge by constantly testing it—and by generating new information while confirming or disconfirming what we think we know. Someone else's habits must not rule us, and our habits must only be those rituals that help, not hinder, our students' learning.

But the real status of whole language has to do with our collective and personal *present:* Where are we right here and now in our own growth? As a group we're doing well if national organizations such as the National Council of Teachers of English and the International Reading Association are any indication. NCTE, an organization that has traditionally been student- and literature-centered, continues in that tradition by supporting whole language teachers. NCTE's *Language Arts* and *English Journal* are professional journals to which whole language teachers can turn. At the IRA convention in Toronto this year, all the whole language presentations were filled to overflowing, and we are beginning to see whole language–based articles in *The Reading Teacher* and *The Journal of Reading.*

Another indication that whole language is growing is the increasing number of teacher support groups emerging across the United States and Canada. There are at latest count [as of 1988]160 groups, ranging in size from two members to five hundred members, called by a variety of names, including TAWL (Teachers Applying Whole Language). These groups are, for many whole language teachers, the touchstone of sanity. When overwhelmed with prescribed curricula that include assessment procedures that mask what students can really do, support groups help teachers see beyond the blind spots to the bright spots in education. In 1988, in Winnipeg, a confederation of whole language teachers was established. Over Labor Day weekend an advisory board met in Tucson and put the finishing touches on a constitution. The first meeting of this international TAWL group was held on February 18, 1989, in Winnipeg. New York State had its First Annual Whole Language Conference the same year. Three thousand teachers attended the conference, and there were two thousand names on the waiting list.

Our personal present, as we work with students, confirms what the researchers, theorists, and those earlier practitioners told us. The present is with our students: only they can tell us if whole language is our hope or if it is only hyperbole.

What goes on in the home and in the classroom every day tells us that when valued children and valued literature are brought together in a safe harbor, learners will become successful and eager readers and writers. Sometimes they make us gasp, as in Dolores Welshmeyer's fourth-grade class:

> The children are reading Katheryn Paterson's *Bridge to Teribithia*. They come to their literature discussion group after just finishing one of the most moving scenes in the book. The children and the teacher are quiet . . . there is a heartfelt acknowledgment of the pain they are feeling. Finally Martha asks quietly—"How can we ever bear this?"
>
> Later the children talk about their personal experiences with death and move on to passages in the book that they love. Tony, after reading a few lines, says, "I know this may sound weird, and call me crazy, but do you ever hear music in your head when you're reading this book?" Jenny replied, "Oh, no, but I think I could now."
>
> The students were moved by Tony's question; most of them made a reference to it in their literature logs. Almost a month later John wrote: "I remember what Tony said about the music in his head when he was reading *Bridge to Teribithia*. He said we could call him crazy? Well, I didn't because I kinda knew what he was talking about, but I

never really heard it but I do now cause I have. I mean I did. I did. I mean I heard music. I wasn't reading *Teribithia*. It was *Come Sing, Jimmy Joe*. I heard it and it was good and it was country. And I knew it would be Katheryn Paterson who would let me hear it."

The Potential

Reflections on what is happening day in and day out in our class-rooms confirm and strengthen our beliefs, but they also help us think through what it was that brought us to that assumption. And those reflections not only give clarity to what we know, they help us put the future in focus and give life to it.

Because we have a whole language past (a personal and collective history), because we have a present (a confirming and modifying pro-cess that allows us to create and renegotiate our theoretical memos)—because of our whole language past and present—we can predict that our whole language future is indeed a powerful potential.

It's been observed that once a teacher begins to understand the power of whole language, she or he will be changed. For some the change seems to be 180 degrees overnight. For others the change is considerably slower. There is room for both the tortoise and the hare in whole language. Consider Kathy. Kathy writes in her journal:

> I watched Nancy all last year. She exuded confidence and when she began Literature Groups with her kids I knew it was going to be a success. That isn't to say that I was ready to do away with my basals. I was just ready to watch her and her kids. Sure enough, it was un-believable. I visited Nancy's class one day in November and heard those kids (4th graders) talking about the book they were reading by talking about themselves and about books they had read earlier in the year. What thoughtful comments coming out of the heads and hearts of those 4th grade farm kids!
>
> What is it with me? I see Nancy's success, but I'm still afraid to do away with the basals completely. Everyone says to be patient with myself and do what I can do. Well, I'm going to take them at their word. I know I can read to the kids every day, invite them to write (real writing) every day, and we will do literature groups twice a week. Until I make myself realize that all kids don't have to "See Spot run"—that's it!

I find this journal entry honest and encouraging. Kathy has the stir-rings of a commitment. She has entered the comfort zone of whole lan-guage teaching, unable at this point to risk the discomfort zone in which so many teachers find that suddenly they and their students are no longer bored and boring but excited and exciting learners and teachers.

Just as our personal pasts and presents differ, our dreams may differ as well, but they might be similar to these:

1. I dream that schools of education will recognize the new knowledge about language learning and offer that perspective in an integrated curriculum, as an alternative to a skills model of literacy.

2. I dream that school systems will stop pandering to the uninformed teachers and will, rather, recognize teachers who know what they are doing and allow those teachers to take back the curriculum and the classroom for the sake of students. I'm not asking that whole language be mandated. I'm asking that it be a real alternative.

3. I dream that assessment will become consistent with the curriculum and the theory on which the curriculum is based. It is tokenism, a nod at whole language, to say that teachers can develop whole language curriculum, but the children must pass the skills tests. Whole language teachers know how to gather and maintain that chain of evidence that assuredly describes learners. I look forward to the day when assessment begins with teachers' asking themselves at the end of the day, Did everything that went on in this classroom today make sense to the students and did it make sense to me?

4a. I dream that we will afford all those educators who are attempting whole language the same patience, support, and information that we have received—or should have received. In Ken Goodman's words, we don't take a "wholier than thou" stance with teachers who are moving slowly into a whole language program.

4b. On the other hand, I hope we will take a wholier-than-thou attitude with those publishing companies and curriculum engineers who advocate the whole language basal and with other profiteers who tell us that all of whole language can be boxed and labeled. We must take a wholier-than-thou stand against those who would use themselves rather than the students as our curriculum informants.

The whole language future? Our potential lies in the individual, the personal, the "this is me." Our potential lies in the partnership, the collaboration, the team support and effort, the "this is us." Our potential lies in the stories, those stories lovingly and carefully crafted by authors of literature for children and youth. Our potential lies in the parent, in the administrator, in the researcher, in the theorists . . . but our potential *will be realized* through the efforts of the teacher with the student. For it is the teacher who can open the book, unfold the story, and invite the reader. It is the teacher who can create the safe harbor where students can share their lives and their literacy. And it is the teacher, above all, who can join hands with the learners.

References

Dewey, John. 1940. *Education Today*. New York: G. P. Putnam's Sons.

Goodman, Kenneth S. 1965. A linguistic study of cues and miscues in reading. *Elementary English, 42,* 639–643.

Halliday, M. A. K. 1975. *Learning how to mean: Explorations in the development of language*. New York: Elsevier.

Heine, David. 1989. Teaching as inquiry: A sociosemiotic perspective of learning. (Doctoral dissertation, Indiana University, 1989). *Dissertation Abstracts International, 50,* 1278A.

Jacobs, Leland B. (Ed.). 1965. *Using literature with young children*. New York: Teachers College Press.

Rosenblatt, Louise. 1976. *Literature as exploration* (3rd ed.). New York: Noble & Noble. (Original work published 1938.)

Rosenblatt, Louise. 1978. *The reader, the text, the poem: The transactional theory of the literary work*. Carbondale, IL: Southern Illinois University Press.

Vygotsky, Lev S. 1962. *Thought and language*. Cambridge: MIT Press.

Vygotsky, Lev S. 1978. *Mind in society: The development of higher psychological processes*. Cambridge, MA: Harvard University Press.

Defining and Describing Whole Language

In 1989 I was surprised to discover that I could find no one who had specifically set out to define the term whole language. *Today it may be one of the most defined and described terms in education. We can thank our detractors. They were the ones who demanded that we detail again and again what we meant by that strange label.*

As I look at the thoughtful definitions and descriptions given by whole language advocates today, I realize again how much whole language teachers have learned from their professional experiences and how willing they are to share their very best practices and theory making with others. Teachers whose tentative first writings were for their TAWL newsletter now find their articles and books on the shelves of educators around the world. Teachers who would only quickly share with their TAWL group a single example of a student's work now speak to hundreds of educators at national conferences. These teachers are helping us all describe and define whole language as it evolves within our classrooms.

Whole language. Two words that have become a label for an exciting grass-roots teacher movement that is changing curricula around the world. Two words that have to do with teachers being heard and students becoming visible. Two words that conjure up diverse definitions and strong reactions. Two words that need clarification by way of definition and description. Two words that are much more than two words.

Why Define Whole Language?

Whole language, whatever it is—a spirit, a philosophy, a movement, a new professionalism—is leaving its imprint on students, educators, and parents from Wollongong, Australia, to Winnipeg, Canada, to Nashville, U.S.A.

Whole language teachers talk enthusiastically about students who have become eager and joyful readers and writers; teachers back up their claims by showing countless examples of pupils' creations. In more and more college courses, *preservice teachers* study the research and theory of whole language and expect to find practical application of the research and theory when they walk into student-teaching classrooms. *Parents* read or hear about literacy programs involving process writing, authors' circles, literature replacing basals, even invented spelling, and they ask for such a curriculum for their children. *Administrators* in increasing numbers are listening to and supporting teachers who advocate and can articulate the principles and practices of whole language. And *researchers and teachers* working together describe the new curriculum and the classrooms in which it is in place; they encourage other teams of educators to become involved in such collaborative inquiry.

Despite growing enthusiasm, some educators, parents, and researchers have serious doubts about the merits of whole language. Those on the periphery of the movement may be impressed with a second grader's interviewing techniques, be pleased with a school's increased circulation of library books, and even show amazement at junior high special education students' insightful discussion of a book they have read, but they have questions about the "basics" of this innovative literacy program. Many are willing to attribute students' increased interest in and love of reading and writing to the influence of whole language curriculum, but those same educators and parents become cautious, even fearful, when they cannot get a clear definition of a term that identifies a perspective on literacy that is felt so deeply and is moving so rapidly and with such great force into classrooms around the world. After all, advocates are asked, if whole language is not defined precisely, how can we know when it is happening, test the results of it, and report its influence?

No matter how much intellectual energy and practical experience go into the formation of a whole language curriculum—no matter how hard it is studied and worked at—if educators cannot talk clearly about whole language in terms of its theory and its practice, some critics will be quick to disparage it or discredit it entirely. An administrator once reported that she was pleased with the school's first-grade whole language curriculum but was surprised and dismayed that neither first-grade teacher could clearly define whole language. She readily admitted that she needed and was counting on their expertise and their words to help her talk with parents and with the superintendent about the program. It is not enough to say that whole language is something that all good teachers do and were doing long before the term emerged. Nor is it sufficient to call whole language an essence, a way of thinking, or something that has changed the lives of teachers and students. Such definitions may be accurate, even needed, but they leave the inquirer with the same question, What is whole language?

Whole language must be defined not only for those outside the movement but for whole language educators as well. Doing so helps teachers become mindful of three important dimensions of this powerful point of view: first, of the *research* in literacy and learning that is accepted as credible by whole language advocates; second, of the pedagogical *theory* that emerges from that research; and finally, of the *practice* that is consistent with the theory. For example, teachers cannot, from a basis in research in miscue analysis and writing as a process define whole language as an integrative use of the systems of language, and then in practice rely heavily on phonics for reading instruction and on parsing of sentences for writing instruction. If a teacher says that whole language involves integrating the language arts across the content areas, that teacher must then turn a critical eye toward the way listening, speaking, reading, and writing are used to teach math and science. If a teacher says whole language involves putting students at the center of the curriculum, that teacher must be able to show how children influence what happens academically and socially in the classroom. It is not enough to *define* whole language; educators must make sure that what occurs in classrooms is supported by and consistent with their definition.

By the same token, when publishing companies and curriculum planners say that their materials and methods are whole language, their definitions must be grounded in whole language research and theory. I have seen "whole language reproducibles" (ditto sheets), "whole language basals," "whole language reading kits," "whole language–directed reading activities," and "whole language worksheets to be used with literature," all advertised and promoted by "whole language" publishers and curriculum planners. I have also seen harmful imitations of materials that are regularly found in whole language classrooms; it can no longer be said that all big books and computer writing programs are suitable for whole language classrooms. It does not take a genius to detect the inconsistencies between what is stated about these materials and what in truth exists. The practice of such companies is in conflict with the research and theories of whole language and therefore should not be labeled as such.

A final need for a definition and description of whole language can guide us into the future—into an exploration of the potential of language and of learners. For example, when whole language is defined or described as student centered, meaning focused, and involving real literature, teachers are motivated to inquire into the curricular possibilities that can materialize when these three dimensions do indeed exist. Many whole language teachers have grown to realize that their definition of whole language is in process, that tomorrow it will be sharpened and refined.

Why Whole Language Is Difficult to Define

Whole language is difficult to define for at least three reasons. First, most whole language advocates reject a dictionary-type definition that can be looked up and memorized. Teachers have arrived at whole language by way of their own unique paths. Because of this, their definitions reflect their personal and professional growth, and their definitions vary. Additionally, to arrive at one's own definition, a teacher must enter what has been called a discomfort zone of whole language, uncomfortable because it requires great honesty in evaluating one's own past, as well as patience and time for reflection. Some educators are hesitant to take on such an introspective inquiry. If they do, the inquiry will reflect their own personal histories; the results will have similarities, but there will be significant and important differences.

Second, whole language is often difficult to define because many of its advocates are intensely passionate about it, while those who demand a definition may disapprove of it just as intensely. For whatever reason, the emotion against or for whole language could be so strong that it keeps opponents from asking reasonable and inoffensive questions or keeps advocates from providing nondefensive answers and an unambiguous definition. One of the most miserable evenings of my life was one in which I was questioned in minute detail about whole language. I perceived the questioning as an offensive and senseless interrogation, when in truth, it is possible that my passion clouded my judgment to the extent of misunderstanding the intentions of the questioners. At any rate, there was no possibility of clarification or meeting of minds—the emotion on both sides was too strong.

Third, the experts in whole language who can provide the richest answers to questions about it—the teachers—have not often been asked. Knowledgeable teachers remained silent. This has changed. Increasingly, whole language teachers are being consulted; they are receiving recognition for their experience and professional information. Acknowledgment of a teacher's abilities and encouragement to speak up often come first from the teacher's own support group (sometimes called TAWL—Teachers Applying Whole Language). Whole language teachers are now appearing on national and international conference programs and are writing for recognized professional journals about their experiences with whole language practice, theory, and research.

"Definitions"

All this is not to say that whole language or some major dimension of it cannot be defined. It can be. It has been. The following "definitions" were taken from works in which the authors discussed whole language, although I believe it was not their intention to present an all-inclusive definition of it.

> Whole language is clearly a lot of things to a lot of people; it's not a dogma to be narrowly practiced. It's a way of bringing together a view of language, a view of learning, and a view of people, in particular two special groups of people: kids and teachers. (K. Goodman 1985, p. 5)

> Those who advocate a whole language approach emphasize the importance of approaching reading and writing by building upon the language and experiences of the child. (Weaver 1988, p. 44)

> *Whole Language:* Written and oral language in connected discourse in a meaningful contextual setting. (Anderson 1984, p. 616)

> It is built on practical experience and the research of educators, linguists and psychologists. Whole language utilizes all the child's previous knowledge and his/her growing awareness of the aspects of language. (Southside Teacher Support Group, Edmonton [Canada] Public Schools 1985, p. 1)

> "Whole language" is a shorthand way of referring to a set of beliefs about curriculum, not just language arts curriculum, but about everything that goes on in classrooms. . . . "Whole language" is a philo-

sophical stance; it's a description of how some teachers and researchers have been exploring the practical applications of recent theoretical arguments which have arisen from research in linguistics,
psycholinguistics, sociology, anthropology, philosophy, child development, curriculum, composition, literary theory, semiotics, and
other fields of study. (Newman 1985, p. 1)

Whole language is a way of thinking, a way of living and learning
with children in classrooms. (Bird 1987, p. 4)

These definitions may lack sameness, but they never go outside
the boundaries of an acceptable definition of some dimension of
whole language. The definitions are diverse because the personal and
professional histories of the authors are different. This variety frees
those who have studied and practiced whole language to generate
their own definitions, then to revise their definitions again and again.

A few years ago I defined whole language primarily in linguistic
terms (Watson 1982). Language remains an important focus for me,
but involvement with whole language teachers, students, and researchers has made me realize that whole language is more than beliefs about
language. Through the years my definition has become more inclusive
and more helpful to me as a teacher. In truth, it became so inclusive (of
language, learner, teacher, curriculum, politics, and so on) that friends
suggested a short definition might be useful. For me that short definition became: whole language is a label for mutually supportive beliefs
and teaching strategies and experiences that have to do with kids learning to read, write, speak, and listen in natural situations. And it is much
more. Over the years, that definition has become: *whole language is a
perspective on education that is supported by beliefs about learners and learning, teachers and teaching, language, and curriculum.* This definition calls
for the following elaboration.

Because of the term itself, *whole language,* I begin with a linguistic definition that emphasizes the wholeness of language. On first
consideration, the words may appear to be redundant: Is language
not always whole? Who ever heard of half or three-quarters language? In natural situations language *is* whole and intact. In many
non-whole language instructional settings, however, language is broken into small segments in the belief that students can thus master it
more easily and that teachers can more closely monitor readers' and
writers' acquisition of it. Whole language is a point of view that language is inherently integrative, not disintegrative. It follows that language is learned and should be taught with all its systems intact. That
is, all the systems of language—semantics, syntax, and graphophone-
mics (call it phonics if you must)—are maintained and supported by

pragmatics (language in natural use) and must not be torn apart if language is to be learned naturally. Pragmatics includes the situational context in which language is used as well as the learner's prior knowledge activated in that situational context. Because language develops within a culture, the students' culture must be a consideration in the understanding of the language itself and in how language is learned.

Many educators define whole language first in terms of learners and learning. This is understandable, for if it were not for teachers' deep concern for learners, there would be no whole language movement. Whole language involves whole learners (with all their strengths and needs) who, when given real and continuous opportunities in safe and natural environments, can initiate learning, generate curriculum, direct their own behavior, and evaluate their own efforts.

Frank Smith (1973) said that to help students become proficient language users, teachers need to find out what kids are trying to do and then help them do it. Yetta Goodman (1978) added that the way teachers find out what students are trying to do is to become enlightened observers of them; she calls it "kidwatching." For whole language teachers, students are curricular informants (Harste, Woodward & Burke 1984). Based on what they learn about their students and what they know about subject areas, literature, language, and learning, teachers develop curriculum *with* their students. Whole language involves teachers who are classroom researchers, participants, coaches, learners, resource persons, and perhaps most important, listeners. Whole language involves teachers who, even outside their classrooms, are activists and advocates for students, for themselves, and for their curriculum.

It has been said that curriculum is everything that goes on in students' heads; Jerry Harste calls it the learner's "mental trip." Whole language curriculum also includes what *potentially* can go on in students' heads. In keeping with this notion, whole language teachers approach curriculum on a "planning to plan" basis. This important curricular step is taken before teachers meet their students on the first day of school and it is taken every day thereafter. This prelude to curriculum replaces a prescribed and permanent program and is based on all that teachers know about students, subject areas, literature, language, learning, and teaching. It involves generating numerous possibilities for study and being knowledgeable about human resources, suitable inquiry, and materials. In whole language classes, students are at the heart of curriculum planning; nothing is set into classroom motion until it is validated by learners' interests and motivated by their needs.

What Whole Language Is Not

Inappropriate definitions of whole language dismay advocates. Such misconceptions do, however, prompt whole language educators to formulate acceptable definitions in order to clear up the confusion, as well as to think about what causes the misleading and inadequate views.

Up to a point, one can define whole language by saying what it is not. For example, whole language does not mean the whole word (look-say, sight-word) approach to reading, nor is it another name for the language experience approach. Whole language has been defined in terms of a particular strategy or materials: "It is just process writing and big books." It also has been said that whole language means "anything students do is okay, including reading words wrong, spelling any way they want, not caring about proper grammar, and talking a lot in class." These are not whole language, nor is it, as one teacher heard his classroom described, "a place where they spend an awful lot of time cooking and singing, and they hate phonics."

As Altwerger, Edelsky, and Flores (1987) point out, the problem with these definitions/accusations is that there is a grain of truth in some of them. For example, any authentic attempt made by students to communicate is valued in a whole language classroom; language experience is occasionally used in whole language programs; process writing, big books, cooking, and singing are often seen and heard in whole language classrooms; and phonics, as a prescribed skill-and-drill program rather than a cue to be used in concert with all the cues of language, is incompatible with a whole language perspective on reading and therefore is rejected.

Implicit in the above is that whole language is not a program, package, set of materials, method, practice, or technique; rather, it is a perspective on language and learning that *leads to the acceptance* of certain strategies, methods, materials, and techniques, such as using predictable language books, literature discussion groups, acceptance of invented spelling, and so on. Despite the concern for accuracy, I find it easier to talk about "whole language programs" and "whole language practices" (Watson & Crowley 1988) than to work my way around the accurate but awkward "whole language–based programs," or "whole language theory–inspired practices."

From Definition to Description

A single visit in a whole language classroom is worth more than a hundred definitions, for it is in the classroom that the definitions, the theory, and the stated practices come alive. In visiting whole language classes, it becomes evident that no two are exactly alike, but even so there is never any question about the model of literacy instruction that underlies the curriculum. Although whole language classrooms vary and have their own personalities, it is inevitable that within the ebb and flow of the day, certain strategies are included no matter what the age, grade, or label given the students is. These strategies (Gilles et al. 1988; Goodman & Burke 1980; Watson 1987) can be observed daily in self-contained, English as a second language (ESL), special education, speech, Title 1, remedial reading, kindergarten, or adult education classes. The strategies are consistent with whole language teachers' beliefs about language and learning and reflect teachers' respect and regard for story, learner, and community of learners and for the students' lives outside the classroom.

Reading and Telling Stories

Teachers read to their students or tell them stories every day. *Story* refers not only to narrative but also to poetry, songs, rhymes, riddles, jokes, informational pieces, plays, and any other authentic and appropriate text. By daily reading and telling stories to students, teachers make a declaration—story, along with the students, is at the heart of the curriculum. Time devoted to listening to stories indicates something very basic in a whole language classroom. It says that self-understanding is important and that hearing or reading about others can help students know themselves more clearly and completely. It says also that if students are to become authors and readers, story must be bone and marrow to their existence as literate persons.

The content and form of stories heard expand students' experiences with literature and subject areas as well as provide a base for both reading and writing. The sounds of stories provide a story grammar, a frame on which students can create meaning. Literature heard adds to the shared knowledge of the community of learners and sets the stage for listeners to extend a story by linking it with other stories having similar theme, setting, plot, characterization, and content. Listeners may respond to literature through drama, art, and music; by reading more stories by the same author; or even by adding another chapter, verse, or incident to the story heard. When teachers read or tell stories as a natural part of the curriculum, there is no pressure; students are in safe harbors in which they can draw on their own backgrounds in order to create meaning. And, of course, awareness of literature from other cultures promotes understanding of those cultures as well as a deeper regard for one's own.

Students in whole language classrooms read stories of their own choosing every day. Good literature (that to which readers can go back again and again and never "use up") is at the heart of the curriculum. Other reading materials from authentic and suitable sources inside and outside school, however, are found in a whole language program. Through reading quality stories and other real texts, students practice their reading, feel the support provided by the author's language, and become more successful and joyful readers.

Writing

Students and story are celebrated through student writings. Writing in whole language classrooms involves generating ideas, revising, editing when necessary, and celebrating (publishing, presenting, sharing) pieces chosen by the author. After learners have experiences with stories, poems, notes, letters, orders, newspapers, lists, reports, and journals, the invitation to use these forms in their own writing comes through demonstration. For example, students receive the invitation to write a poem by listening to, seeing, and reading a great deal of poetry. In whole language classrooms children learn to write—with conviction and conventions—by writing.

Personal and Social Connections

The whole language curriculum encourages individuals to make personal links to meaning through reading and writing. Students constantly have opportunities for private reading and writing—to work alone if they want, but never in a lonely classroom. Because language is learned collaboratively as well as personally, students in whole language classrooms socialize with each other in ways similar to human socialization outside the classroom: learners talk with each other about what they are writing, the books they are reading, the problems they are solving or not solving, and the experiments they are conducting. Within the community of the classroom there are real reasons to read, write, listen, and speak.

In the context of a classroom that is natural and appropriate for every learner in it, whole language teachers never do for students what students can do for themselves. When help is needed, it is forthcoming, usually from learners who dig deep to answer their own questions, but often from other students. If a spirit of collaboration has been fostered in the classroom, students can help each other when it may be impossible for a teacher to do so. Whole language communities maximize the possibility of learners helping each other through partner and small-group work and through students taking on the role of teacher and resource person.

Students talk with each other not only about the content of the stories they are reading and writing but also about the processes of reading and writing. That is, children and their teachers bring to a conscious awareness what is going on in their heads when they read and write. They talk about what happens when things go right or wrong and about when they do not go at all. Whole language students readily offer each other suggestions for more proficient and efficient reading and writing; the suggestions are given when they are most appropriate and immediately applicable. This attention to the processes of reading and writing takes the place of formalized, direct, and prescribed instruction and happens naturally during group discussions, individual conferences, and partner work and during teacher-initiated strategy lessons.

Planning to Plan

The great authenticity of life outside the school, the experiences and knowledge gained there, and the needs that must be met in order to live in that world provide powerful and immediate motivation for learning. For these reasons, whole language teachers do not finalize curricula before meeting their students. Rather, whole language teachers "plan to plan." Before school starts they explore a variety of units, themes, and lessons. A topic may be *considered* for a variety of reasons: former students have enjoyed the subject; the materials are easily available; the teacher has an abiding interest in the subject; parents encourage the study; the topic is covered on a district-, state-, or province-mandated test; the study is traditional. The topics are *chosen* after the students' larger worlds are brought into the classroom. When students begin to inform teachers about their lives and interests, they can together then weave a curriculum that is meaningful, appropriate, and applicable.

Principles Supporting Whole Language

Whole language is more than a definition and a list of mainstay activities. It is a spirit, an enthusiasm for teaching and learning that is supported by beliefs about teaching and learning. As an authentic and natural curriculum develops within the classroom, whole language teachers refer to these beliefs again and again. There may be no limit to the number of beliefs, but following are some often mentioned by whole language teachers. These and dozens of other theoretical assumptions powerfully influence whole language teachers and support their teaching. No one would ever accuse such teachers of being atheoretical, without intention, or without strong groundings in research and experience.

Ownership Begins with Choice

Choice is the beginning of ownership in both reading and writing. Within the classroom, choice occurs when students are offered curricular invitations. In orchestrating their invitations, whole language teachers use all they know about students, the learning process, language, and subject matter. Interestingly, students usually accept whole language invitations because teachers orchestrate them as carefully as the most gracious host might. It is also interesting that whole language teachers accept their own invitations: they too read books, write stories, and participate in the community of learners. Whole language teachers value the creative and generative powers of students and help them make good choices by offering them good and appropriate invitations.

Students Are Responsible for Learning

Students can take ownership and responsibility for their own learning. To empower learners, whole language teachers do not select all the books to read and the topics to write about, correct students' non-standard forms at the point of production, provide spellings on demand, or revise and edit for students. In other words, teachers do not do things for students that students can do for themselves. They do, however, facilitate a rich environment within which learners are led not into the impossible but into the delightfully difficult. There, learners grasp patterns, see similarities, make connections, take "mental trips," go beyond "minimal competencies," beyond "stated objectives"—often beyond the teachers themselves.

Errors Are Accepted

There is no such thing as perfectibility of the linguistic form (Carey 1985). If students and teachers are not bound to someone else's standards of perfection, they can then become linguistic risk-takers. When the notion of perfection is dispelled, an uptight, must-be-right model of literacy is dispelled and concepts involving "mastery" are replaced by ideas of language learning through natural use.

Language users can learn as much from getting language wrong (producing a nonstandard form) as they can from getting it right, and maybe more. When readers, writers, listeners, and speakers take risks, inevitably there will be mistakes, miscues, misinterpretations, and misconceptions. The personal logic of children as well as their rough drafts in both reading and writing are valued in whole language classrooms. In a healthy learning environment students grow from their mistakes; that is, they grow through the process, through the pursuit of language.

Meaning Is Emphasized

Stopping students at the point at which they are producing meaning (through either oral or written language) in order to make surface-level corrections may result in stopping students in their linguistic and cognitive tracks. When attention is drawn away from the composing process, the construction of meaning can falter and the language user may never regain the moment, the momentum, or the motivation. Attention to conventions and standard forms is a part of whole language programs but is not confused with the construction of meaning through reading, writing, listening, and speaking.

Language Arts Are Integrated

The language arts are integrative and integrated in a whole language program just as they are in life outside the classroom. Within the language arts of writing, reading, listening, and speaking, children learn conventions such as standard grammar, spelling, handwriting, and articulation by using them naturally and in concert with each other.

Content Areas Promote Literacy

The content areas are grist for the literacy mill. Students listen, speak, write, and read about science, art, music, math, social studies, games and sports, cooking, sewing, nutrition—anything that is important in their lives. Whole language teachers understand that the interpretation of concepts basic to content areas precedes or parallels the interpretation of words that are peculiar to a specific knowledge domain. Because of this understanding, teachers value, respect, and make use of the content areas to promote oral and written language as they use the language arts to support the content areas.

Classroom Environment Promotes Learning

The classroom itself is a strategy that promotes learning. Whole language classrooms facilitate learning communities in which students live comfortably and productively. Not only the atmosphere of the classroom but the physical aspects of it indicate to students that this is their home and that it deserves respect and care. There is a working order within the room that allows its occupants to meet with partners and in small groups or to have privacy.

Parental Involvement Is Vital

Children's language and thought have their roots at home and in the community. Teachers make it a point to work with, not without and not for, parents. Whole language teachers do not assume that all students' problems stem from the home. Rather than assigning blame, whole language teachers act positively—they invite mothers and fathers to become whole language parents.

Evaluation Is a Source of Information

Whole language teachers believe that the purpose of evaluation is primarily to inform learners themselves. When this is accomplished, then teachers (and therefore the curriculum), parents, and the public (including legislators) will be informed. When this order is reversed and the primary aim becomes to inform the public, students and teachers are lost in the attempt to boil a learner's efforts down to a single number or grade. As scores become important, students become invisible.

Whole language teachers are cautious about what they accept as evidence of students' abilities and learning. Through student self-evaluation, "kidwatching," and other whole language assessments (Goodman, Goodman, & Hood, 1988), teachers break away from narrowly conceived testing that masks students' achievements and that curricularly leads nowhere. Teachers know that it is difficult to get critics to understand and appreciate the wealth of information available through whole language evaluation; nevertheless, they never stop recommending that the portfolio of written work, pictures, anecdotes, and tapes, along with conferences and written comments, replace letter and numerical grading. Whole language teachers urge learner-referenced evaluation over norm-referenced and criterion-referenced testing.

Is It Worth the Effort? A Student Answers

Many whole language teachers have the respect and encouragement of colleagues and parents. Some, however, have felt strong resistance. When teachers are fortunate enough to belong to a support group such as TAWL (Teachers Applying Whole Language), it is easier to weather the storms. But too often whole language teachers must stand alone. When this is the case, these teachers turn to their own students for confirmation that their efforts are justified, that they are worthy of learners. Children such as Patty renew the spirit and determination of whole language teachers.

Patty was a natural and eager user of language. Her parents could not remember exactly when she began to read and write, but they were sure that her "reading readiness" consisted of being read to every day, watching them read and write, reading (remembering encouraged) favorite stories, reading (guessing encouraged) print in her own world, reading (pretending encouraged) to her dolls, getting and leaving notes on the refrigerator door, and writing stories and letters for her friends and relatives.

In kindergarten, Patty and her language were valued by a teacher who understood child development and enjoyed child logic. Patty grew as a reader and writer who daily experienced the communicative nature of reading and writing and who felt the power that comes naturally to a child who is surrounded by oral and written language. Patty considered herself to be a reader and writer, and during the summer after kindergarten she wrote the following story for her most appreciative audience—her grandmother. (Figure 1 shows Patty's original story as she wrote it.)

Patty's Story

Once upon a time there was a little girl whose name was Jane. And Jane was absolutely a beautiful princess. One day Jane said, "I am so bored that I am going out in the world to find some adventure. I think I'm going in space to catch my adventure." So Jane followed a star beam and went high in outer space. If you want to know more about Jane's adventures read the next chapter in my book.

In almost six years of living in a language-filled world—of hearing literature, paying attention to interesting print, creating oral and written discourse herself—Patty had developed a sense of story. She used a conventional opening (Once upon a time), had a motivation for action (Jane is bored), used a traditional character (an absolutely beautiful princess), utilized an often-used setting (outer space), and employed a continued-next-week ending. Patty categorized speech sounds in her head and invented appropriate spellings. She attended to punctuation. The flowers Patty drew after each of the first two sentences served nicely as periods. One sentence ends with four dashes spaced upward (toward outer space?). Two wavy lines over the *m* in *I'm* indicates that Patty has become aware of the apostrophe. She used writing conventions and she showed a sense of audience and a sense of humor.

Figure 1.
Patty's story.

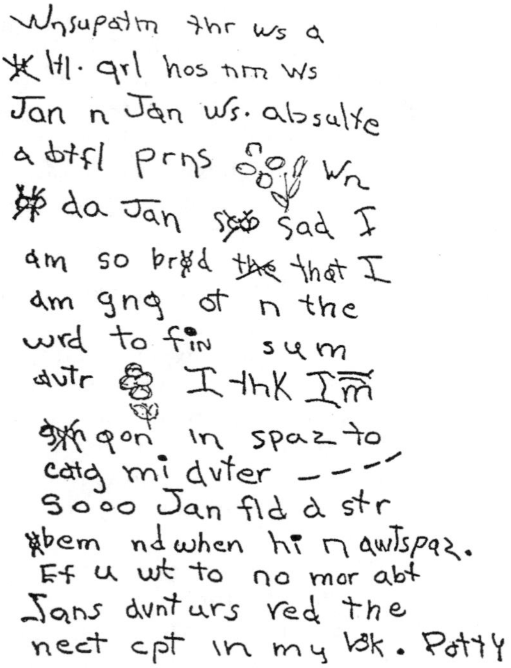

Whsupatm thr ws a
Htl. grl hos nm ws
Jan n Jan ws. absulte
a btfl prns Son Wn
da Jan so sad I
am so brd the that I
am gng ot n the
wrd to fin sum
dutr I thK Im
qon in spaz to
catg mi dvter - - - '
Sooo Jan fld d str
bem nd when hi n awlspaz.
Ef u wt to no mor abt
Jans dvnturs red the
nect cpt in my bk. Patty

Within one month after entering first grade as a natural reader and writer, Patty stopped writing. She moved from a whole language attitude about literacy, both at home and in kindergarten, to a first-grade class in which she was directed to master the smallest units of language before moving on to larger ones and to do it in a setting in which risk taking was discouraged.

In the "eleven basic areas of readiness" in which she was diagnostically tested at the beginning of the year, Patty fell below 80 percent competency on sequencing, recognizing causal relations, and recognizing stylistic devices (humor). She was placed in a "basic prerequisite for reading readiness" program. Some of Patty's "reading and writing activities" were:

1. Visually discriminating between circles, squares, and triangles, and between capital A, B, and C.

Figure 2.
Patty's nonstory.

2. Circling the upside-down apple and the bug without a mouth.
3. Recognizing upper- and lowercase letters.
4. Tracing a path from left to right (left-right progression).
5. Copying step by step the teacher's picture from the board to a piece of paper (eye-hand coordination).
6. Listening for the same sounds at the beginning of words.
7. Drawing rings around pictures whose names began with given sounds.
8. Finding the sound that was the same in a group of three letters.
9. Writing lines of letters.
10. Writing words leaving one finger space between words and two fingers for margins.
11. Copying perfectly a poem from the board.

After two months without receiving a story from her favorite author, Patty's grandmother begged her to try her hand at another story. After telling her parents that she could not write because she could not spell and that she did not know what to write about, Patty tearfully sat down and wrote "Patty's Nonstory" (see Figure 2). An honest critic of her own work, Patty drew an X across the story and pushed it aside.

Patty ended the first grade no longer concerned with the communicative nature of language; she now wanted her text to be error free, which meant using words that she was sure she could spell and spending a great deal of time erasing and forming the letters perfectly. Instead of writing stories and poems and reading self-selected books, Patty read short, controlled-vocabulary stories in basals and worked on endless workbook pages.

Patty's second-grade whole language teacher recognized the fragile condition of this potentially strong language user and on the first day of school firmly moved Patty back into real reading and real writing. Within two weeks Patty:

1. Heard her teacher tell stories, riddles, and jokes.
2. Told a story and made up a riddle.
3. Heard her teacher read Sid Fleischman's *Mr. Mysterious's Secrets of Magic.*
4. Put on a magic show (complete with posters, handbills, and program) with four other children.
5. Wrote "How to Make a Coin Disappear" for *Our Magic Book.*
6. Wrote a text for Margaret Harteliu's wordless picture book, *The Chicken's Child.*
7. Read *Owl at Home,* by Arnold Lobel, and *Strega Nona,* by Tomie de Paola, during silent reading time.
8. Wrote notes to her teacher and friends and a letter to her sixth-grade picture-and-pen pal.
9. Copied the lyrics of a song into her own *Song and Poetry Book.*
10. Wrote in her journal every day.
11. Wrote a letter to the giant telling him how she would spend her gold coin, after hearing *Jim and the Beanstalk,* by Raymond Briggs.
12. Wrote and illustrated a new story for her very happy grandmother.

Whole language. Two words that symbolize a kindergarten teacher's awareness and acceptance of the language abilities and needs of all children who enter her classroom. Two words that represent the rich and supportive program into which a second-grade teacher lovingly invited a fragile language user. Two words that offer hope, not hype or helplessness, to discouraged parents. Two words that identify all the research, theory, and practice that restored the confidence of a little girl named Patty.

Conclusion

Never in the history of literacy education has there been such genuine excitement on the part of educators. Teachers, many discouraged and burned out, are ignited by a new professionalism. Students, many labeled as lost causes, are regaining their strength and finding their way. Parents, many disheartened and desperate, are realizing that their children need not be diminished by a label and a numbing curriculum. An alternative is available. At the heart of this alternative are learners with their teachers—learners inquiring into life and literature by using language fully, teachers taking on the roles of researcher, learner, and educator. This new professionalism, movement, philosophy, spirit is called whole language.

References

Altwerger, Bess, Edelsky, Carole & Flores, Barbara. 1987. Whole language: What's new? *The Reading Teacher, 41*, 144–54.

Anderson, Gordon S. 1984. *A whole language approach to reading.* New York: University Press of America.

Bird, Lois. 1987. What is whole language? *Teachers Networking: The Whole Language Newsletter, 1(1)*, 3.

Carey, Robert. 1985, October. *Toward a new methodology for research in literacy.* Paper presented at the meeting of the Semiotic Society of America, Bloomington, IN.

Gilles, Carol, Bixby, Mary, Crowley, Paul, Crenshaw, Shirley, Henrichs, Margaret, Reynolds, Frances & Pyle, Donelle. 1987. *Whole language strategies for secondary students.* New York: Richard C. Owen.

Goodman, Kenneth S. 1985. *What's whole in whole language.* New York: Scholastic.

Goodman, Kenneth S., Goodman, Yetta M. & Hood, Wendy J. (Eds.). 1988. *The whole language evaluation book.* Portsmouth, NH: Heinemann.

Goodman, Yetta. 1978. Kidwatching: An alternative to testing. *National Elementary Principal, 57*, 41–45.

Goodman, Yetta M. & Burke, Carolyn. 1980. *Reading strategies: Focus on comprehension.* New York: Holt, Rinehart & Winston.

Harste, Jerome C., Woodward, Virginia A. & Burke, Carolyn. 1984. *Language stories and literacy lessons.* Portsmouth, NH: Heinemann.

Newman, Judith (Ed.). 1985. *Whole language: Theory in use.* Portsmouth, NH: Heinemann.

Smith, Frank. (Ed.). 1973. *Psycholinguistics and reading.* New York: Holt, Rinehart & Winston.

Southside Teacher Support Group (Eds.). 1985. *What is the whole language approach? A pamphlet for parents.* (Available from Edmonton Public Schools, Edmonton, Alberta, Canada.)

Watson, Dorothy J. 1982. What is a whole language reading program? *Missouri Reader,* 7, 8–10.

Watson, Dorothy J. (Ed.). 1987. *Ideas and insights: Language arts in the elementary school.* Urbana, IL: National Council of Teachers of English.

Watson, Dorothy J. & Crowley, Paul. 1988. How can we implement a whole language approach? In Constance Weaver, *Reading process and practice: From socio-psycholinguistics to whole language* (pp. 232–79). Portsmouth, NH: Heinemann.

Weaver, Constance. 1988. *Reading process and practice: From socio-psycholinguistics to whole language.* Portsmouth, NH: Heinemann.

Whole Language: Why Bother?

As I reread this piece, I have just returned from the fifth annual Whole Language Umbrella conference. Each of our conferences has been a scary experience: Can we talk hotels and convention centers into booking this fledgling organization for a conference in their city? In Kansas City we had no track record, only our enthusiasm. Would anyone seriously consider going to the second conference—Phoenix in August? Would we have the numbers for Winnipeg and Niagara Falls? Was San Diego too expensive and too far away from home for many of our members? Well, we've made it. We beat the odds. And this year we made it again when teachers across the continent gathered in Windsor, Ontario, for renewal and fellowship. Why bother? Because the adventure is demanding, it brings out the best in us, and it keeps us sane. For me, that's the whole in whole language.

Several years ago at the 1986 International Reading Association convention in Philadelphia, a friend and I overheard a man ask his luncheon companion, "Just what is this whole language movement, anyway?" He may not have captured his partner's attention, but he

Originally published in *The Reading Teacher* 47 (1994), 600–607, as part of that journal's Distinguished Educator Series. Reprinted with permission of the International Reading Association.

immediately seized ours. Before we could hear his answer, the wait-
ress arrived and put an end to our eavesdropping, but not an end to
our speculation on why the question was asked.

My friend and I turned to the conference program for sessions this
questioner might have perceived as indicators of "this whole language
movement." We found something that neither of us recalled seeing
before: sessions that actually used the term *whole language* in their titles. There were two: "It's Never Too Late: Applying Whole Language
Learning Techniques to Secondary Remedial Reading Programs," and
the preconvention institute "A Close Look at What Works: Exemplary
Programs in Whole Language Learning." There were other session titles that used terms often associated with whole language—*process,
ownership, comprehending* and *comprehension, psycholinguistics, miscue
analysis, literature-based,* even *teacher empowerment*; and I had a feeling
that if we had attended "No Basals and No Worksheets: A Literature-
Based Reading and Writing Program," we would have heard about a
whole language literacy program. But do two sessions constitute a
movement?

We speculated on whether or not the questioner had been introduced to the works of Don Holdaway, Don Graves, and Frank Smith,
or been captivated by Ken Goodman's (then) brand-new book *What's
Whole in Whole Language* (1986). Perhaps he had seen over 150 teachers foregoing the Tuesday night publishers' parties to squeeze into a
vacant meeting room to share with each other something more important and heady than free wine and cheese. Perhaps the fellow had
stumbled onto a booth at the outskirts of the exhibition hall (past the
key chains, stickers, and rubber stamps) that had been given (publishers thought this booth was too far off the track to bother with) to a
small group of enthusiastic educators who called themselves whole
language teachers. He may have been drawn in by the comradeship of
the teachers in that booth—teachers willing to spend as long as needed
to talk about children and language and learning as they showed examples of students' work brought directly from their classrooms.
These teachers from across Canada and the United States had found
each other, struck up stimulating friendships, and were writing and
phoning each other when they needed understanding and advice.
This little booth, organized by Peggy Harrison in Ohio and Paulette
Whitman in Nova Scotia, was more than a place to gather with friends
and colleagues; it was a statement, a symbol, a milestone.

The seeds of whole language philosophy had been planted and
nurtured long before 1986, but the shoots were becoming more and
more visible. This attitude toward learning and teaching was a breath
of fresh air, new and exciting. Observers perceived it correctly as a

grass-roots movement. Educators around the world were asking, right along with the fellow my friend and I overheard, Just what is this whole language movement, anyway?

In the years since the Philadelphia convention, teachers have rallied to answer this and hundreds of other questions about whole language. At the 1987 Anaheim IRA conference, dozens of educators presented findings from their whole language classrooms and were swamped with requests from other teachers who sensed the "rightness" and the potential of what had been shared with them. That same year the IRA Whole Language Special Interest Group (SIG) was organized with 175 members. The following year in Toronto, the whole language presentations were so numerous that teachers actually had to make choices, and many of the sessions were filled to capacity. The Whole Language SIG program filled a room for three hundred people and was repeated to accommodate the overflow audience.

A defining moment had come for whole language advocates, time to fish or cut bait. The challenge of survival was articulated by a handful of teachers, and then courageously taken up by fifteen educators who, through the financial help of the Winnipeg CEL (Child-centered Experienced-based Learning) group, met in September 1988 in Tucson to draft a constitution for an organization that would become known as The Whole Language Umbrella (WLU): A Confederation of Whole Language Support Groups and Individuals. In Winnipeg the following February, the constitution of WLU was ratified and a slate of officers accepted. The grass roots were growing deeper and stronger, and they were flourishing in often unexpected terrain—not only with young children in self-contained classes, but in cross-age groupings, special education, inner-city and rural schools, and with academically troubled and academically savvy kids and second language speakers, preschool through adult.

The elected leaders of this fledgling organization made important decisions about its purpose and nature. For starters, teachers needed an immediately accessible way of finding out about each other's work. Networking among the rumored two hundred TAWL (Teachers Applying Whole Language) groups in North America became a major goal. The leaders believed that teacher networking would facilitate another priority of the WLU: to improve the quality of learning and teaching at all levels of education. This improvement was to be accomplished in at least four ways:

1. Encouraging the study of whole language philosophy not only in TAWL groups but in school staff development and in teacher education programs;

2. Promoting research and critiquing whole language curricula and programs;
3. Publicizing and disseminating whole language information to any interested individual and groups; and
4. Facilitating collaboration among teachers, researchers, parents, administrators, and teacher educators in the development of whole language theory and practice.

To make sure that these intentions had backbone, the WLU constitution declared that another goal of the organization was to support and defend educators who might be unfairly attacked in their attempts to promote whole language philosophy.

Whole Language Tenets

Although individuals and groups should never be subjected to a test of conformity as a prerequisite for identifying themselves as whole language teachers or for joining either a TAWL group or WLU, there are tenets thought to be held by all whole language educators. The writers of the WLU constitution articulated that whole language teachers believe in:

1. A holistic perspective to literacy learning and teaching;
2. A positive view of all learners;
3. Language as central to learning;
4. Learning as easiest when it is from whole to part, in authentic contexts, and functional;
5. The empowerment of all learners, including students *and* teachers;
6. Learning as both personal and social, and classrooms as learning communities;
7. Acceptance of whole learners, including their languages, cultures, and experiences; and
8. Learning as both joyous and fulfilling.

Where Are We Today?

Today there are over 450 TAWL groups and 600 individual members, representing some 35,000 teachers in all, affiliated with the Whole Language Umbrella. There may well be countless more whole language educators who are not affiliated with any support group or with WLU. The WLU membership extends to Australia, New Zealand, Guam, Taiwan, Japan, Brazil, Bermuda, Venezuela, and Malaysia as well as Canada and the United States. Despite the fact that whole language teachers are still a minority, at least in U.S. schools, our numbers and locations are multiplying. TAWL groups and WLU membership reflect that growth.

The signs of the movement were not immediately evident in 1986; today they are everywhere. Requests come to my office weekly for names of educators who will lead a district in their whole language professional development or will speak at a whole language conference. It's almost impossible to pick up a literacy education journal without finding references to whole language theory and practice. Even publishing companies, in their zeal to keep up, are publishing materials that range from very useful to ludicrous to bogus—all under the banner of whole language.

Why Bother?

To the question, What do you think of this whole language movement, anyway? we might add, Why did all these nice teachers give up the "comfortable" status quo curriculum for something as politically and professionally "risky" as whole language practices?

In my search for answers to these and other questions, I left my classroom last year to visit whole language educators who are by reputation outstanding teachers. I wanted to get the feel, the essence, of their classrooms. I was eager to fix my attention without interruption on real learners (teachers and students), and, under their watchful guidance, I needed to try my hand at some classroom strategies and then to talk about it all with these teachers whom I trusted and valued. Finally, I wanted to share my experiences with TAWL colleagues and with undergraduate and graduate students; and just as important, I wanted to be directly involved in learning and teaching experiences that would help me grow as a whole language teacher.

During my visits, the teachers and I inevitably addressed a question asked by both the advocates and detractors of whole language philosophy—Why would anyone become a whole language educator? Why bother? Every teacher's story was unique, but there were some common threads and some surprisingly similar experiences. We had been informed, touched, nudged, even irritated by many of the same people, research, and writings. We had been shaped by some of the same powerful experiences and emotions.

When I asked these teachers what it was that caused them to move to whole language, I heard again what teachers have been saying for the past twenty years: that the "comfortable" status quo wasn't comfortable at all. Inquiry into whole language often started with an uneasy feeling about how students were responding when they were—you fill in the blank—struggling with the sting of being in the low reading group, answering irrelevant end-of-the-chapter questions, dreading report cards that masked abilities, being tested on someone else's (a publishing company's or test maker's) spelling words, writing weary book reports, "covering" a prescribed and irrelevant unit of study, and (my favorite), "practicing being quiet."

One teacher told me that she kept getting angrier and more desperate as her years of teaching added up: "I was doing everything I'd been told to do by my supervisors and my college teachers, and my kids were still frustrated and frustrating; unsettled and unsettling; bored and boring. And there was no joy in either their learning or my teaching." Other teachers talked about the disheartening experience of writing the twenty-fifth behavioral objective on the fifteenth IEP. Teachers told of spending precious hours preparing their students for end-of-level basal reader tests and for their district's favored standardized test, only to awaken to the fact that tests had nothing to do with learning how to read and write, but had everything to do with Annie's running home in tears after an afternoon of examination.

I also heard again about the shakiness of not having a well-thought-through theory base—"I didn't know *why* I was doing things that I felt were useless and numbing. I just did them and moved on to the next prescribed activity." Teachers said they felt as if they were walking in someone else's "theoretical boots"—a test maker's, a publisher's, an administrator's, a curriculum designer's, a former college instructor's—and the boots pinched. I learned that there are hundreds of reasons *why* educators turn to whole language. The question then became, *How* did they become whole language teachers? What were the entry points? Is there a formula?

Entries into Whole Language Philosophy

I'm taking the liberty of grouping countless entries to whole language philosophy into three major categories: (1) practice, (2) theory making, and (3) belief formation (see Figure 1). There is no hierarchical "ability grouping" intended in the order of my list, nor is there a formula for mastering and moving from category to category. All beginnings can be professionally and personally rejuvenating, and the

Figure 1.
Developing a whole language philosophy.

journeys following the first steps can be equally exciting, scary, exasperating, enlightening, and fulfilling. The following may help us understand the journeys educators might take as they create their whole language philosophy.

Practice Prepares Us

For longer than I care to admit, I was what Ken Goodman calls a "wholier than thou" whole language advocate. I felt that before attempting any holistic strategy, teachers needed to articulate the underlying theories and the supporting belief system for that particular strategy or experience: don't "do" literature study or writers workshop or big books until you can convince your whole language colleagues that you not only know *what* you are doing, but *why* you are doing it. I've changed my mind. After paying attention to exemplary educators, I've learned that teachers can *begin* to build a whole language philosophy by "doing" whole language strategies that they find appealing and that fit comfortably within their capabilities and expectations. I must add quickly that teachers *begin* at this point but are never willing to stand rooted, filling their curriculum with *borrowed practices*. That is, they can't endlessly just "do" whole language.

Serious whole language practitioners must, in their own good time, edge into the stimulating, but sometimes disquieting, *discomfort zone* of whole language; the practice must become a heuristic that moves teachers along a path that is often risky. Serious educators may begin their journeys with an activity, but they move and grow by asking questions and by collecting evidence. If there is no commitment to inquiry, teachers may find themselves discouraged and ultimately reject whole language in its totality. Even with the best of intentions, this might happen when we sponsor quickie workshops on whole language, offer clever activities, provide formulas for strategies, but fail to emphasize the necessity to study the underlying theories supporting the practices.

Lana, a first-grade teacher, was talked into exchanging pen pal letters with her friend Peggy's fifth-grade class. Peggy explained the procedure, and Lana thought it would fit nicely into her well-established language arts program. She borrowed the activity, having little to lose. If any part of it didn't go well she could easily return to the conventional language arts program that she and her students had followed dutifully for years. Her investment in the pen pal experience was minimal and her commitment to it trifling. At this point Lana was merely *walking the walk* of whole language. The responses of her students to the project made the difference. To Lana's surprise, the children were not only immediately captivated and eager to read and write their letters, but a sense of community was emerging in the room and within the school.

As time went by, Peggy gave Lana a book on pen pal writing, *Someday You Will No All About Me: Young Children's Explorations in the World of Letters* (Robinson, Crawford & Hall 1990) and she took Lana to a TAWL meeting where she heard about kid/learner watching (Goodman 1978; Watson 1992). Then a crucial thing happened—Lana asked her first question: Is the pen pal experience working well because the kids are doing something they think is meaningful and important? If this *is* the reason pen palling is successful, do I need to ask this same question about other activities in my curriculum? Many of the children are choosing topics for their letters. Should I encourage this, or should I tell them what to write about? Related questions emerged: What will happen if I encourage kids to invent their own spellings? Can we substitute authentic spelling instruction for textbook instruction? If I study these letters across time, can I learn about my students' language growth? What will happen if I share these letters with parents as part of their child's evaluation?

Lana's practices prepared her to ask questions, then to actively theorize (hypothesize, guess, have hunches) about those practices. As

Lana collected evidence (data) in answer to her questions, two things happened. First, her *borrowed practice* became her *owned practice*. Ownership meant that Lana had to adjust and modify the pen pal experience so that it more comfortably fit her students and herself; in doing this, letter writing became an authentic and important part of the curriculum. Second, as Lana inquired into the theory that informed the practice, and as she and her students assumed curricular ownership, she began to ask questions about what she valued and believed about working with children; that is, Lana began to examine her own belief system. In turn, Lana's beliefs were tested daily within the pen pal experience itself.

This teacher began her journey by "doing" whole language; she ended (if the journey ever ends) by understanding the *theory* that supports the pen pal experience, by modifying the *practice* for a better fit, and by strengthening her *beliefs* about learning and teaching.

Theory Prepares Us

I'm using *theory* synonymously with *hypothesis, hunch, speculation, assumption,* and even *guess,* as in, I don't know for sure, but I *theorize* that children will be more likely to want to write if they choose their own topics. Theories can be active or inactive, and they can emerge from the work of trusted teachers, theorists, and researchers or from inquiry into our own practices. Happily, the insights into learning and language offered to us by Vygotsky, Dewey, Rosenblatt, Holdaway, K. Goodman, Y. Goodman, Smith, Graves, Harste, Burke, Calkins, Atwell, and countless others have made our heads spin and our lives turn around. Unhappily, we know educators, publishers, and curriculum designers who rattle off tenets of whole language grounded in the works of these thinkers but who only *talk the talk* and never fully activate the theories by inquiring into how they can come alive in real classrooms. For serious teachers, theories are heuristics that fill our heads with questions and move us, sometimes cautiously and sometimes boldly, into inquiry. Through *inquiry* teachers create a theoretically based curriculum. They move into practice, collect *evidence* from the classroom experiences, answer their own queries, and generate more questions and more theories.

Bryan, a first-year teacher, was excited by whole language theories in his undergraduate classes. Everything he heard and read made sense to him and fit comfortably with his beliefs, not only about how children learn but also about how he saw himself as a teacher. Bryan read books and articles, saw videotapes, attended conferences, and even visited whole language classes. He could talk about whole language, but he had not had the opportunity to test out his theories. As Bryan began his first year of teaching, he commenced to activate a previously inactive roster of assumptions. Because he became a TAWL member, he knew he would not be working without a safety net. On the advice of his whole language colleagues, Bryan got to work by articulating his theories and by deciding on the classroom practices that were consistent with them. That is, he brought his theories to life by researching them. Bryan and his colleagues constantly asked questions about both the process and product of his efforts.

Bryan was lucky; he had a support group and he also had an existing belief system that strengthened his theories and practices. He didn't experience an anguishing inner struggle before articulating his belief-supported theories and getting to work. His inquiry reflected both his theory and his beliefs: since I've been taught, and also believe, that choice has a lot to do with motivation, ownership, and independence, I want my students to take over their learning by making choices. What experiences will ensure student choices? Since I've read, and believe, that learning is social as well as personal, I want my students to have supportive experiences. What curriculum will ensure that they have a chance to work independently and within a community of learners?

Bryan's inactive theory became activated because he basically believed that these were hypotheses that could be proved in practice. Bryan answered his own questions as he studied the evidence collected in his own classroom. Just as for Lana, Bryan's evidence helped him make decisions about which practices and theories were consistent, which ones were in contradiction and therefore needed rethinking, and what all this had to do with curriculum. Also like Lana, his belief system was being confirmed, revised, and fine-tuned as he made his round-trip journeys between theories, practices, and beliefs.

This isn't to say there were no bumpy spots along Bryan's journey into whole language philosophy. He was keenly disappointed when students didn't enthusiastically respond to all his invitations to real literature, real writing, real inquiry. He was discouraged if the students were inattentive or not engaged in learning or were downright rude to him and to each other. Without laying blame, his colleagues helped him think about the years in which these fourth graders had been in programs that both underestimated their strengths and misunderstood their needs. TAWL friends poured over videotapes of his class, offering suggestions that came out of their own experiences. They helped Bryan with his inquiry into organization, scheduling, self-evaluation, and reflective teaching.

Belief Prepares Us

I see a distinction between theory and belief. Theory, for me, is panning for gold; we have a hunch something valuable is there, but we have to work at the panning again and again in order to see the nuggets clearly. Beliefs are identified high-quality ore that we have securely in our possession.

Beliefs can be carefully examined or not. We can blindly take on someone else's belief system (fool's gold), or we can bring into existence our own beliefs by examining our values and by studying evidence gained through our own theorizing and practicing.

Beliefs keep us sane. On Monday morning we don't have to reconstruct what it is we trust, what we know is credible, what we accept as true. We are our beliefs. They direct everything that happens in or out of our classrooms. Beliefs, as a heuristic or driving force, must be articulated and held up for ourselves and others to see. When it becomes evident that we can't go public with what we believe (for whatever reason), or when mounting evidence contradicts what we think is trustworthy, we must do something that is tremendously difficult and often very painful—critically scrutinize the credibility of our convictions. An examined belief system is set in theory and practice, not in concrete; only blind beliefs resist examination. Whether or not we discard, alter, or keep a particular belief often depends on the depth and honesty of our reflection, inquiry, and self-evaluation.

Whole Language Communities

What makes the teachers and their classrooms that I visited and continue to visit outstanding? It isn't *where* the journeys begin, it's that the teachers chose the high road, a path that more often than not isn't an easy one. Some educators aren't up to it, and that's okay too. (Once I asked if I thought whole language philosophy was for everyone. My answer remains the same: I have yet to find a learner who could not be supported and helped to grow through whole language theories, beliefs, and practices, but I have met educators for whom whole language philosophy won't fit. That isn't to say that I won't keep inviting them to read, inquire, and most important, study learners. I leave it to their students to convince them.)

When asked what keeps them going on the high road, whole language teachers tend to give credit to two powerful communities, their *classrooms* and their *teacher support groups*. As a visitor to classrooms and to TAWL meetings I see commonalities between the two:

1. Classrooms and teacher support groups exist because of the commitment and dedication of enlightened teachers. The creation and continuance of these dynamic communities take a tremendous amount of effort. There are no teacher's manuals, flowcharts, or kits that can be bought, brought into the classroom or the support group, and followed so that we all turn out looking and acting the same. Just as no two learners are exactly alike, no two classrooms are exactly alike and no two TAWL groups are exactly alike.

2. Both communities have a philosophical base that evolves slowly, personally, and with the help of other learners. That philosophical base includes and supports owned practices, active theories, and examined beliefs.

3. Both communities involve collective reflection. In whole language classrooms, I've seen teachers invite students to take a step back in order to look at what they have done and are doing; they help learners reflect on their actions not only after but during the experience. Such reflection is the substance of the most powerful assessment—self-evaluation. Responsive and helpful communities reflect on their products and their processes *as* they are growing.

4. Both communities encourage inquiry. Ownership of a social studies concept, how to set up an aquarium, how to have a good discussion, or how to help a friend or colleague comes about through asking questions that are personally meaningful and appropriate. Without exception, the teachers I visited had questions about things going on in their classrooms and in their professional lives. One teacher said it well: "If we don't ask questions and encourage our kids to do the same, we will spend our time trying to answer questions asked by people who don't know us, don't know our strengths, and possibly don't care about *our* problems."

5. Within classrooms and support groups, students and teachers see themselves in roles not always rewarded in conventional groupings. First of all, whole language teachers make it clear that they are learners and that their students can be teachers; there is no room for omniscient dispensers of all wisdom. The membership in these communities is made up of inquirers, collaborators, representatives of their groups, apprentices to and for each other, organizers, and friends.

6. It's obvious from the outset that both communities are places of intellectually important and stimulating experiences. In the classroom and at the TAWL meeting, participants are learners who expend their efforts on reading, writing, and talking about matters of importance.

Why Bother?

Good fortune has allowed me to work with many inspired and inspiring teachers. They and their students have patiently taught me the meanings of whole language philosophy. Together we've asked hundreds of questions of ourselves and of the practices and assumptions of other teachers, researchers, and theorists. We've endured the tension of getting our own practices and theories sorted out. We've struggled with beliefs that were rock solid and with those that wobbled. We've endured both the honorable and dishonorable politics of literacy. We've stayed, we've nurtured our roots, and we've grown.

In 1986 when the fellow asked his luncheon companion, "Just what is this whole language movement, anyway?" I interpreted the question, and still do, to be, Why are all these teachers bothering? Through the years educators have answered the question again and again and in many ways, but ultimately, for me, the answer comes down to, This is the way I want the children I know and love to be treated—and it's the way I want to be treated myself.

References

Goodman, Kenneth S. 1986. *What's whole in whole language.* New York: Scholastic.

Goodman, Yetta. 1978. Kidwatching: An alternative to testing. *National Elementary Principal, 57,* 41–45.

Robinson, Anne, Crawford, Leslie & Hall, Nigel. 1990. *Some day you will no all about me: Young children's explorations in the world of letters.* Portsmouth, NH: Heinemann.

Watson, Dorothy J. 1992. What exactly do you mean by the term *kidwatching*? In Orin Cochrane (Ed.), *Questions and answers about whole language* (pp. 98–104). Katonah, NY: Richard C. Owen.

Part Five

Community
(1989–1996)

Teacher Support Groups: Why and How
(with Margaret T. Stevenson)

Just as no two students or two classrooms are alike, no two TAWL groups are alike; groups reflect the strengths and needs of their members. Each TAWL group makes its unique mark, has its unique successes, and makes its unique mistakes. With dedicated membership, each group grows and in the process inevitably stumbles along the way, but like good whole language learners, members learn from problems and begin again—wiser each time.

Support groups help us create meaning and deepen our understanding, and encourage even our most tentative and tenuous efforts. TAWL groups give us strength, but we must provide the passion and the commitment to keep our group alive and lively.

Laura shares:

> Do you remember Jeff? The child I told you about who wouldn't put pen to paper at the beginning of the year? Today he wrote a wonderful two-page story about a dog who had magical powers (MJKL PRS). I was so excited with his story that I showed it to the other

Originally published in *Teachers and Research: Language Learning in the Classroom,* edited by Gay Su Pinnell and Myna Matlin (Newark, DL: International Reading Association, 1989), pp. 118–29. Reprinted with permission of the International Reading Association.

first-grade teacher. Her reaction was, "For gosh sakes, why do we want kids to write when we can't even read what they've written?" I didn't protest, but returned to my desk only to find a memo announcing that the basal reader adoption committee had reached a decision: starting next week there would be a series of inservice workshops to introduce the new materials. Well, there went any chance for the workshop on poetry in children's literature that some of us had petitioned for! The day ended with a telephone message from a parent who wanted to talk about the lack of worksheets, workbooks, and phonics instruction in my class. When was her daughter being taught the basics?

As is typical in a teacher support group, Laura shared the good news first and then poured out the discouraging and disabling problems she was encountering. What Laura received from the twenty nursery school through college teachers who surrounded her that evening was an authentic (I've lived through that one) response to both the good news and the bad. Their comments represent both surface responses (What a pain having a parent react in such a way!) and substantive ideas.

Laura, do you have copies of the children's work so you can show examples to parents when you talk to them?

Sending letters home to parents on a regular basis seems to help me get across the reasons we do some nontraditional things in our classroom. I can give you copies of my letters if you want to see them.

Is there any way you can invite the other first-grade teacher to get involved in a whole language activity that doesn't scare her?

All of Laura's concerns were discussed, and during the break, the teachers/friends continued to offer the kind of support one professional might offer another.

Teacher Support Group Members

In many support groups, the membership is trying to escape from something potentially harmful (drugs, gambling, food). In teacher support groups, the members are trying to move toward or stay with something important—a commitment to a point of view about children and about how they learn language, learn through using language, and learn about language in all its forms.

For more than ten years in Canada and the United States, teachers have been coming together in small and large groups to gain and

give professional support for the development of language arts programs that are often referred to as whole language, student centered,
meaning focused, or literature based. Group members are teachers
who have begun to take notice of students and their work in new and
totally positive ways. They are teachers who have become interested
in the work of educational researchers and theorists who value both
children and their language and who work to support curriculum and
instructional procedures that keep children, their language, and the
curriculum whole. Support groups include teachers who are on the
verge of burnout—dissatisfied with what and how they are asking
their students to learn.

Support group membership cannot be described by conventional
categories such as grades or groups taught, number of years in service,
or whether one works in private or public schools. A group might be
made up of special education teachers, teacher educators, regular
classroom teachers, both public and private school teachers, ESL
teachers, first-year teachers, and teachers nearing retirement. Some
groups include principals, supervisors, directors, and administrators of
special programs, and members in general point out that they are also
parents and taxpayers.

The unifying factor that makes the members a family of professionals is that they hold a holistic view of language and learning. They all
believe that reading and writing are learned through students' active
integration, not disintegration, of the systems of language. Within that
basic belief, the teachers are sure to hold varying degrees of knowledge
about language and language teaching and learning. It also is likely that
some teachers within the group recently moved from a strong, skills-
oriented literacy program and now are seeking guidance from others
who have experience in whole language teaching. Others in the group
feel secure with their practical theory and want to explore, research,
extend, and share their experiences with others.

> Their backgrounds are diverse, but they are all intrigued by the new
> information about how children learn and use language. Many come
> from schools where the curriculum is shadowed by mandated basal
> readers, workbooks, and standardized tests, rather than illuminated
> by the experience and knowledge of teachers, and the strengths and
> needs of children. These teachers see the danger in inappropriate,
> insensitive, expensive, and time-consuming skills and drills, and
> have moved, or are trying to move, toward authentic writing, read-
> ing, speaking, and listening in their classroom. These teachers often
> find themselves in very lonely situations. In attempting to find en-
> couragement for their theoretically better way, they gravitate toward
> other educators who are also reaching out. (Watson & Bixby 1985)

Why Support Groups?

Although many organizations exist that are professionally enhancing, such organizations cannot meet on an immediate and personal level the needs of the teachers described above. Teachers who are going through professional changes (whether the changes are described as moderate or transforming) are also going through personal changes. That seems to be the way it is with teachers. And if such is truly the case, there are few of us who can or want to "go it alone."

Even in Canada, where most teachers have freedom to use materials of their own choosing, where they are encouraged to make the best use of trade books, of environmental print, and of nonprint material—even in these positive settings—educators who are engaging in change need support and encouragement. Implementing whole language programs based on what children know rather than on what they don't know, on real literature rather than on trivialized texts and simulated stories, requires knowledge about the reading and writing processes, the role of talk, and the concept of language across the curriculum. Using these programs means knowing how to observe learners, plan and keep records, continue using new information, turn responsibility over to students, and keep parents involved. In other words, even in the most professional settings, teachers need one another in order to stay informed and to remain on the cutting edge of knowledge and practice.

In varying degrees, those involved in professional change need to *receive* encouragement, approval, advice, and sound information about their new professional adventure. Later in the change process, it seems just as important to *give* encouragement, approval, advice, and sound information about professional adventures. For this reason and many others, teacher support groups such as Child-centered Experience-based Learning (CEL), Teachers Applying Whole Language (TAWL), Children and Whole Language (CAWL), and Support, Maintain, and Implement Language Expression (SMILE) are flourishing and are making vital differences in the lives of educators and their students. Following are reasons why teachers are turning to one another for guidance and growth.

1. In new adventures, teachers must have collegial support—to share successes. Children's marvelous linguistic advances must be shared with someone who will value and celebrate them. Sharing with parents is rewarding, but the acknowledgment of another professional can be even more gratifying.

2. In new adventures, teachers also must have collegial support to share frustrations. It is inevitable that there will be setbacks. At

this time, only someone who is living through or has lived through a similar experience can be of help.

3. A major purpose of the support groups is to educate but not to indoctrinate. Although teachers hold certain convictions about language and learning, they understand that those convictions can be put to the test only in real classrooms. The educational/professional process is ongoing; it is circular. Research, theories, assumptions, and the implications of these for curriculum and instruction are presented for consideration in the support group. Then they are confirmed or disproved in the reality of the classroom. This reality is brought back to the group of professionals to set the stage for more research, theories, and assumptions.

4. By sharing their best classroom practices, teachers can rethink, resee, and relive the principles that underlie their own activities. By offering their best theory, idea, teaching strategy, story, or poem to someone else to consider, teachers are sharing in the truest sense of the word and are reflecting on their own beliefs and practices. Interestingly enough, when teachers share their best, their suggestions often come back to them enhanced, highlighted, and sharpened.

5. Teachers need support for political action. Although most groups are not formed for political purposes, the topic of power inevitably arises. Knowledge translates into power, for as teachers learn about language and the language learning processes, many feel the need to take back control of the curriculum, the classroom, and schooling for themselves and their students. When this happens, teachers need the support and resources of other professionals.

6. Within the support group, there are teachers who are interested in disseminating information about the theory and practice of holistic language arts programs by conducting workshops, by writing materials, or by presenting at conferences. The members of the organization itself become resource persons, presenters, and program developers.

There are other important reasons why educators seek out teacher support groups. And there are less appropriate motivations, also. Teachers who are jumping on the whole language bandwagon usually do not remain in a support group, nor do those who come to a meeting daring someone to convince them to adopt a point of view to which they are basically opposed. Support groups are not for people who need to be talked into a model of language learning of which they basically disapprove. Likewise, members do not come to meetings in order to explain and defend a whole language point of view; they have enough experience doing that day in and day out. As one member put it, "I come to TAWL to keep steady, to get ideas, to enjoy other teachers and their students' work. Don't ask me to spend my evening trying to talk a teacher out of doing skills and drills—not at TAWL!"

Where and How to Organize

At the latest count, approximately 125 support groups exist in Canada and the United States. Often they exist where there is someone active in teacher education at a university.

To give an idea of the purpose and history of two active teacher support groups, a description of the groups in Edmonton, Alberta, and in Columbia, Missouri, follows.

Children and Whole Language
(Edmonton, Alberta) Support Groups

When a two-week summer session attended by thirty elementary teachers was completed in August 1980, the last thing on anyone's mind was the organization of a teacher support group that would be the incentive for eight similar groups. But that is what happened. The thirty Edmonton Public School teachers were excited about the ideas introduced to them by a member of a Winnipeg support group called Child-centered Experienced-based Learning (CEL). New friends were exchanging names of schools and phone numbers, planning to work together to prepare for the year ahead.

But soon questions were raised. How could they give one another the moral support and encouragement they needed once school was under way? How could they explain their program to colleagues, principals, and parents? What if it didn't work? Their knowledge base was shaky. How could they plan for their own professional development? All eyes turned to the workshop organizer, their language arts supervisor. That's how it started. The group began to meet once a month to exchange ideas for professional development and to plan and implement special projects. There are now eight groups meeting in various parts of Edmonton; the two most recent are a second-language group and a junior high group.

What made the CAWL groups catch on? Why has the interest remained so high? Members believe it has to do with the following:

1. Teachers are in charge and see themselves as being their own experts. Teachers chair the sessions, set the agenda, and decide on the projects. When new groups are formed, it is at the specific request of interested teachers.

2. The teachers receive tangible support from the district language arts supervisor and other personnel. A language arts consultant meets regularly with each group. Twice a year, support group chairs meet with the language arts consultants and supervisor to discuss plans and projects. These meetings enable the chairs to meet one another and to see their group as part of a city network. It is important to know that there are other teachers who also are committed to programs that are in the best interest of children. Quality materials developed by teachers are illustrated and printed professionally and made available to all schools in the district. Two notable examples are *We're Still Learning to Read,* a booklet written by two teachers for parents of students in grades four, five, and six, and the booklet *Whole Language,* which explains aspects of the approach.

3. Teachers from the support groups are recognized as leaders and often are asked to make presentations at conferences, at other schools on professional development days, and even to the board of trustees.

4. Professional development is highlighted. Whenever a guest speaker or workshop leader comes to the school district, a supper meeting is arranged for support group members so they may hear and interact with the guest.

5. Support groups limit the number of members to fifteen or twenty so they can meet in their homes. Occasionally, groups meet at a school or in the Centre for Education, but they prefer an informal setting. The small number encourages total participation.

6. The group members are rejuvenated and inspired by being involved in projects and conferences. When teachers feel the need, a summer session is planned. One of the most ambitious projects is the Young Authors Conference held on a Saturday in the spring for two hundred students in grades one through six from the fourteen schools represented by the CAWL group. The children choose from sessions having to do with storytelling, puppetry, and writing and illustrating for the district publication, *Magpie. Magpie* is devoted to children's writing, to interviews, to radio scripts, and to drama activities. Another conference on children's writing was presented for over one hundred parents.

Teachers Applying Whole Language (Columbia, Missouri) Support Group

In the summer of 1977, an elementary teacher and a junior high teacher took a course in which new information was presented about language and about children learning to read and write through all the language arts. For the first time in years, these teachers were professionally excited, and they wanted to put their new knowledge into use. Because they felt they wouldn't be able to go it alone, a group of six teachers met to share their enthusiasm and their problems.

Their first two meetings were spent in venting frustrations—complaining about the insensitivity of others who didn't hold their point of view. The teachers needed this outlet, but they quickly realized that if they were to facilitate their own professional growth, they must do it in the same way they facilitated their students' growth—by beginning with their strengths. Immediately, the six teachers began to share ideas and to discuss their problems constructively. Through the years, two guidelines have been met: share the best, and begin with the positive.

The group has grown from six to one hundred members, with about forty attending each monthly meeting. Because of the size of the group, the meetings are no longer held in homes but in the district's board of education office or in one member's school. For years the group did not have a formalized structure, but several years ago officers were elected and a board of directors formed.

Major projects include writing two books of language arts strategies, starting other TAWL groups, becoming politically active, and holding a renewal conference each fall. At the conference, a resource person speaks to a large general group and then works one day with TAWL members and special guests.

Some Things We've Learned

Talking with members of various teacher support groups, we hear certain ideas about their organizations mentioned regularly. Some of the ideas have to do with forming and maintaining groups in general; others have to do specifically with promoting their own professional change.

1. The organization of a group must be a cooperative effort on the part of all the people who want to be a part of it. Although many groups have been formed by a teacher educator who has the resources of a university available, it is not necessary to have someone in such a position. It is, however, necessary to have at least

one person who will take the initiative for setting up dates and places for meetings and for sending out reminders. A show of life and activity is vital. One person can get things started, but others must assume such responsibilities as preparing a list of names, addresses, and phone numbers; writing a brief newsletter; making telephone calls; or preparing a box of recent publications that are loaned at the meetings. It should be clear what the duties are and who is handling them.

2. Most groups focus around sharing. This activity is most meaningful when it is organized, however loosely. For example, a group might plan to share ideas and materials about a particular theme, which is decided on a month ahead of time. Invite teachers to share an article, a book, a newspaper clipping, or their students' work. Some teachers will share, some won't; some forget; some bring things, but for some reason (which should be investigated), some don't; nevertheless, the constant opportunity to share is powerful.

3. Two or three teachers may present a more formal program. Demonstrations by teachers and role-playing are often very useful when dealing with certain strategies such as conferencing. Teachers who are doing classroom research or graduate students who have conducted research might be invited to present their findings. Time for group discussion should be provided no matter what the program.

4. An evening of small interest groups often is fruitful. Some teachers may want to talk about writing, others about poetry; some may be planning a conference; others may be outlining a book of strategies or compiling a list of concept books for primary children. Another group may be discussing assessment of professional growth.

5. When the group gets large, forming an advisory board that meets prior to the regular monthly meetings is a good move. Members of the board can handle the busywork, report their actions to the entire group, and save valuable time for sharing and study.

6. Ways need to be devised for getting copies of important and informative articles into the hands of members. Money for copying material can be collected and kept for that purpose, or each member might once during the year bring enough copies of an article for all members. Book boxes maintained by one of the members can be checked out for a month.

7. Undertaking major projects that require cooperative planning over a period of time is an excellent way of getting to know one another

and of presenting whole language concepts to other professionals, parents, and legislators. Preparing booklets for parents, writing and publishing instructional strategy books, or presenting a conference provide continuity and a real sense of accomplishment.

8. Socializing is important and some time should be set aside for it at every meeting. A holiday party or an end-of-year celebration provides opportunities to share in an informal way.

9. Concerning professional change, help members realize that:

    • Change is exciting, but it also can be frustrating and discouraging. Internal rather than external resistance may be the most draining and confusing. When teachers are rethinking their beliefs about children, curriculum, teaching, and learning, they need to be as patient with themselves as they are with students and colleagues. Self-doubt, ambiguity, and uncertainty are part of the process of clarification and understanding.

    • Not everyone will appreciate new efforts and new ideas. It is possible for teachers in support groups to unintentionally and inadvertently threaten, antagonize, or even frighten others. Often our enthusiasm and the labels and words we use (*whole language, humanistic, risk free, invented spelling, kidwatching*) act as red flags. Study the effect that ideas, actions, and our language have on others. Avoid being the "in group," excluding those who are not in the know.

    • The lack of an immediate positive response is not outright rejection. Teachers must not be guilty of placing a chip on their shoulder and daring someone to knock it off, nor of jumping to the conclusion that their ideas will never be reviewed objectively or considered fairly.

    • Not all teachers making professional changes have to tread one particular thorny path—the one we took. Teachers must be able to orchestrate their own development. Some teachers will want to plunge intrepidly into a whole language program, while others will move slowly and cautiously—testing, implementing, questioning, and clarifying every move. Teachers must work out their own meanings and moves.

Laura shares again:

It seems years since our last meeting; so many things have happened. I guess the most important thing is that I tried some of the things you suggested. I redid Ann's letter to parents and sent it out. After that, I decided it was time I asked them to come in to talk about some of the things we are doing in the classroom instead of doing worksheets. When the parents arrived, you can be sure the room was "littered with literacy"—the kids' stories and poems everywhere! I talked with the parents about the benefits of their children's reading real literature, and about functional spelling, and I showed them examples of students' stories collected over a year's time. I can't believe how much the parents loved getting solid information. I think Jeff's dad had tears in his eyes when he read his son's three-chapter book *Tiny—The Dog with Magical Powers*. Thanks for your suggestions and encouragement.

And the other first-grade teacher and I are making a collection of poetry that appeals to our students. I've brought our list to share with you tonight.

Reference

Watson, Dorothy J. & Bixby, Mary. 1985. Teachers! A support group needs you. *Georgia Journal of Reading*, 13–17.

Teacher Support Groups: Reaching Out, Bringing In

Since the time the first TAWL groups were formed, the structure and organization of TAWL groups have changed but their overall purpose of support has remained constant. When I think of my own TAWL group and our interests through the years, I am intrigued at how we have developed and defined ourselves professionally. At a recent Mid-Missouri TAWL meeting we celebrated "The Authors Among Us"; the newsletters, articles, chapters, and books written by dozens of our TAWL members were spread out around the room for all to explore. In addition to teaching and writing, our members are conducting workshops and seminars locally, around the state, and nationally.

In the initial version of this article I provided now-outdated information about how to contact the Whole Language Umbrella, and the appropriate names and addresses continue to change periodically. However, WLU and the National Council of Teachers of English now have a joint membership option, so NCTE can serve as a long-term contact for information about WLU. Their toll-free number is 800-369-NCTE.

Reprinted by permission of Dorothy Watson. In *Organizing for Whole Language,* edited by Yetta M. Goodman, Wendy J. Hood & Kenneth S. Goodman (Heinemann, A division of Reed Elsevier Inc., Portsmouth, NH, 1991).

A few months ago I got a letter from a fourth-grade teacher who had just attended a professional conference—her first introduction to whole language theory and practice. What Julie heard and saw in those few conference days shook her beliefs about teaching, especially about how she taught reading and writing. All the new information, presented with great enthusiasm, caused her to do something she had never seriously done before—question what was going on in her own classroom.

Julie left the conference a bit dazed but very excited. She was loaded down with articles and books to read, lists of children's litera- ture, ideas for thematic curricula, and innovative suggestions on how to encourage and celebrate children's reading and writing. What she didn't leave the conference with was someone to talk to about the storm of ideas buzzing in her head.

In Julie's letter, she told of the exhaustion and discouragement built up over ten years of teaching, and then in contrast she told of the excitement and enthusiasm generated during the three-day confer- ence. And now that she was committed to further whole language study and was seriously planning curriculum revisions, she was scared. The excitement of the conference was gone, the discussion groups were over, the confident whole language teachers were miles away, the keynote speaker's tape had been played a dozen times, and the message was no longer enough—she felt terribly alone.

In response to her letter, Julie received two letters: one from a fourth-grade teacher in our TAWL group and one from me. We stuffed our envelopes with articles, bibliographies, and encouragement. We offered invitations, advice, and suggestions. We told Julie how hard it was to go it alone, and each of us told her that she needed a support group.

Yesterday Julie phoned. She had taken our advice and was en- couraged when she found two other teachers in her school district who were eager to study whole language and to share their ideas and concerns with her. The teachers decided to meet after school every other Friday. Julie's telephone conversation was filled with reports of her students' growth and love of language, and filled with questions about the care and keeping of her teacher support group that, accord- ing to Julie, "amazed us by growing so fast we can barely fit into my front room."

Like Julie, other whole language teachers from across Canada and the United States are asking for information about forming groups of teachers who are practicing whole language theory. The following ideas from members of support groups in Canada and the United States might be of help not only to Julie, who teaches in a small rural community, but also to teachers who are members of larger, well-established groups in urban settings.

What's in a Name?

Teacher support groups are known by a variety of names. TAWL (Teachers Applying Whole Language) is an often used acronym, but there is also CEL (Child-centered Experience-based Learning), SMILE (Support, Maintain, and Implement Language Expression), and a dozen or so others. Any group calling itself TAWL should be prepared to hear a few jokes about TAWL teachers who are short and TAWL teachers who are tall; we endure. The *A* in *TAWL* has caused some confusion. The Bloomington, Indiana, group calls itself "Teachers Attempting Whole Language"; it seems that Jerry Harste, one of the founders of the group, heard *Attempting* for *Applying,* and the name stuck. The members think that it not only distinguishes them but also describes their efforts, especially when the going gets tough.

The groups in Edmonton, Alberta, are CAWL, not Canadians Applying . . . , but Children and Whole Language. Mid-Missouri TAWL is faced with the problem of a location name; happily, we are no longer the only group in the middle of Missouri. In fact, the other mid-Missouri group has grown so rapidly that our TAWL may soon be eclipsed.

The name is up to the members. Politically, it's a good idea to let the name reflect your purpose and what you stand for.

Yet Another Organization?

Over the years I've heard teachers tell stories about what it was that brought their group together. For the most part, the histories are similar: teachers unite because they need to be with others who are experiencing similar professional concerns. Whole language educators have issues and problems that simply are not addressed by other professional organizations. There is an eagerness to learn more about the theory and practice of a "new" and exciting way of teaching and learning. Add to that urgency a burning need to break out of professional isolation, and you have the makings of a whole language support group.

In addition to growing professionally by studying and sharing with each other, many teachers also want to share their own research and practices with potential whole language educators. TAWL is an organization through which they can offer whole language conferences and inservice workshops and seminars.

Whatever the reasons for starting a whole language support group, those reasons need to be clear to the membership and be reviewed regularly. Such an inquiry provides the criteria on which evaluation of the organization can be based.

Who Is Invited to Join?

In most cases, the answer to this question is, any teacher applying or attempting whole language. For a time, our members considered inviting teachers who were riding the fence or who needed to be convinced of the merits of whole language. One member commented that she needed help and that she didn't want to spend TAWL time talking someone out of doing phonics and into holistic and authentic teaching and learning. TAWL, she said, was a place where she knew her beliefs would be accepted and strengthened. We decided that this teacher was right; we spent a lot of time, day in and day out, defending our practices, and we didn't need that at TAWL, too. Our group opened membership to all professionals who were trying to understand the theory and practices of whole language; potential members needn't have all the problems worked out, but they must have a commitment. The "fence riders," we decided, would be invited to our annual conference or any special meeting more suitable for "interested skeptics."

We have in our group both private and public school teachers, including a substantial number of special education teachers and teacher educators. A few administrators and state department of education people attend meetings on an irregular basis; we're encouraging greater participation. Many of our members are in graduate school, some full-time. Many members are parents; their children are often placed in skills-based classrooms. As yet we have no librarians; we need to work on that. We are contemplating starting a "small TAWL" within our group for preservice undergraduate students.

The diversity of professionals in our group adds to its richness. You may choose to identify your group membership more precisely (e.g., teachers who work in junior high, ESL, primary, and so forth).

How Are Groups Structured?

Many groups start small; ours began with six members, a comfortable fit for a living room. A year later, when membership rose to twenty-five, we moved out of our homes and into an elementary school room that holds fifty or sixty. After thirteen years, our membership is one hundred, with about forty attending each meeting. We continue to meet in Stephens College's elementary school, where we often spill out into the halls and other rooms for small discussion groups. This year our meetings will be held in different members' classrooms to see various whole language environments firsthand.

We have an advisory board of thirteen members. Officers are elected for two years; a one-year term is inadequate for our needs. We meet monthly in the evening. The advisory board convenes at 6:00 P.M.; between 6:30 and 7:00, the members check out books, look at new materials, and talk with each other; the program starts at 7:00 and runs to around 9:00. We can't meet immediately after school, as many groups do, because of the long distances some of our members travel.

Some groups attempt to hold their numbers constant, say twenty-five, primarily so they can truly get to know and help each other but also to have the luxury of meeting in homes. When groups are kept small, there is often the understanding that once the membership grows to thirty, the group will split, forming two smaller groups. Dividing a group that has been together for a long period of time is often so difficult that the members decide to stay together and move to larger quarters or they meet together as a large group every other month.

Some groups have a core group of thirty or so members. This group organizes programs, inservices, and conferences for a much larger group of whole language teachers. Although such an organizational structure appears to work well, it's important that this inner group not become, or be perceived to be, elitist and controlling.

When there is a close relationship with the local International Reading Association, a whole language special-interest group is sometimes formed within the IRA chapter. In such an arrangement members of the interest group meet with the entire chapter but also meet regularly on their own. Such special-interest groups within the local IRA add a great deal to the spirit and enthusiasm of the total organization.

Some school districts help with the organization of support groups. Often an administrator, a language arts supervisor, and a teacher will cooperatively start a group. Such an arrangement facilitates good communication between classrooms and middle- and upper-level administrators. Some whole language schools have an active support group within their own faculty.

Size of the group is not the primary concern. Julie started her group with two teachers who met after school every other Friday. Some teachers begin with just one other person whom they phone once a week in order to share successes and struggles. The organizational structure of your group may or may not be similar to the ones described here. Not to worry. The point is to get started; the form will work out naturally.

The Terrible Twos and Other Problems

When in the course of human events it becomes evident that things are not going well, do what you do in your whole language classrooms: stop and reflect. Our second year presented pesky problems: the sharing took too long, and people were stifling yawns; three members were doing the majority of the organizational work, while others felt left out; we were losing our sense of history and purpose; we needed some finances and didn't have a penny; other annoyances plagued us. Midway through the second year, we looked at the rut we'd gotten ourselves into and decided that TAWL was worth the effort needed to understand and solve the problems. It became evident that, despite our "we are all leaders" attitude, we did need officers and an advisory board to organize ourselves in a reasonable way and to spread the work around. We also decided to collect dues (mainly for duplicating and mailing notices). We began to rethink our program of sharing and decided to expand (sharing will always be a part of our meetings) to include focused topics.

Your group's problems may not come as they did for us, but if they do, don't ignore them. Give them the attention they deserve. Experiment with new programs, logistics, organizational structures. With foresight, major problems may never arise, but don't be discouraged if they do. When members are consulted, informed, and have representation, and when there is ongoing evaluation, the problems are surmountable; they may even make the group stronger.

Programs

Groups that have a small number of members seem to have very little trouble planning meetings. The members share—classroom strategies, language stories, research, literature, students' accomplishments, their own writings, gains, and losses. Members study together. They are renewed by each other.

When groups get large, programs need to be rethought. Even the backbone of many support groups—sharing—undergoes changes. Seven members sharing successes and problems is not the same as thirty teachers doing so. Such sharing may be informative and confirming, but it can also get tiresome. Guidelines are needed. Most groups don't want to give up sharing but have found it to be a richer experience if "volunteers" are designated prior to each meeting. Time, of course, is available for those who have something that just can't wait. Some large groups divide into interest or grade levels for sharing.

Many groups plan their programs two or three months in advance, and a few try to schedule a full year. Typically, members volunteer to present something they are particularly interested in: dramatization, literature study, student as researcher, whole language evaluation, reading and writing across the curriculum, parental involvement, conferencing procedures—anything immediately important and compelling. To enrich these programs, the presenters give members appropriate articles to read prior to the presentation and ask teachers to bring examples from their own classes that illustrate the points being made.

Opportunities to piggyback on the visit of an author, illustrator, publisher, or teacher are explored. Sometimes local resource people, such as an administrator, a member of another support group, or a parent, are asked to speak. One of our most memorable meetings was when a seventh-grade poet presented her work to us. Many of us will never forget her lovely poetry and her last piece of advice to teachers: "Don't give kids topics. They can think of wonderful things to write about on their own, with just a little help from you or from a friend."

Some groups have small TAWLs (we got the name from the Tucson TAWL) within their large organization. Our Political Action Small TAWL leads us in our political education and awareness. This group planned a meeting in which all the candidates for the board of education gave answers to five predetermined questions concerning literacy. All nine board candidates took their responses (two minutes for each question) very seriously. The meeting closed with a brief presentation of the TAWL point of view. Another meeting planned by this subgroup involved the study of the governor's advisory committee report on literacy education. After gathering suggestions from the entire membership, the subgroup met on the following Saturday morning to draft recommendations. They then sent TAWL members to the six state meetings in which the literacy report was deliberated. In the Phoenix area, a group was organized for the purpose of orchestrating district-wide change in the curriculum.

Many groups spend some part of every meeting in study sessions discussing something they have read. Professional articles and books are usually studied, but literature for children and youth is also explored. Members receive the books and articles prior to the meeting in order to prepare for the discussions. In Tucson, Small TAWL members share their own writings with each other.

Whole language teachers are great at adopting and adapting good ideas, but be careful of focusing too long or too intensely on a single age group or a specific subject. Most important, consider the interests of all members—the high school teachers, the elementary school principal, the nursery school aide. Explore all potential resources, and keep the meetings lively.

Finances and Projects

During our first two years, we resisted collecting dues. After awakening to the realities of printing and postage costs, our dues rose gradually over the years to $20. This may seem like a big investment, but members get their money's worth. New members receive a folder of "classic" whole language articles and a copy of Ken Goodman's *What's Whole in Whole Language* (1986). Those renewing their membership get new articles and a copy of a newly published whole language book. Dues defray the cost of the monthly newsletter and a booklet of members' addresses and school affiliations.

Our first money-making project involved writing and selling a little book of strategy lessons that had been used successfully by TAWL teachers. That book evolved into *Whole Language Strategies for Secondary Students* (Gilles et al. 1988) and is now published by Richard C. Owen. The prepublication copies of the strategy book not only provided good suggestions for teachers but also financed our first renewal conference. The topic for that first conference was chosen just as we choose themes today, ten years later. At that time, because we felt a need for information about the writing process, we invited Ben and Beth Nelms to talk about writing theory and practice. We were delighted when a whopping forty people showed up for the conference. We were also relieved to learn that we actually covered our expenses and made a little money, and, just as important, we were delighted to know that we had established a reputation for having a substantive conference. The following year 350 attended, and this year 675.

TAWL kids are a part of TAWL. At the renewal conference, children sell copies of books they have written and illustrated. The money received from the sales goes toward buying books for Rainbow House, a local shelter for abused children. TAWL kids also write book reviews for our newsletter.

- Baby-sitting at our meetings is provided if needed. Parents and TAWL share the cost.
- Support groups invest in their members. An amount is set in the Mid-Missouri TAWL budget to help finance two or three members to attend a conference. We have a growing library of professional literature to lend to our members. Two years ago we began buying sets of children's and young adult literature. These sets consist

of seven or eight copies of a single title; these can be checked out
for classroom use. We also have a few big books.

- We order large quantities of professional literature and some children's books to sell to our members at a slightly reduced rate. This
  is also a money-maker for the organization.
- When members travel to appear before the state legislature or
  represent our group at a political meeting, we pay their expenses,
  including hiring a substitute teacher.

Growing

Along the way, it became apparent to our members that we needed to
elect officers, establish an advisory board, circulate a monthly newsletter, conduct a conference, enliven our programs, and become more
politically active. When we realized we had a substantial treasury, we
needed to establish our tax-free status. These are all benchmarks.
Your group will have its own major moments.

Some groups have grown to such an extent that help in exceed-
ing what active members can accomplish is required. In such cases, a
group may employ one of its own members as a part-time director. It
is vital to plan and to think carefully about this person's role. The executive director is needed, not to take over the duties and chores that
should be handled by the membership at large, but rather to enhance
the organization and facilitate members in their professional development through their membership in TAWL. An executive director
works closely with the president, offering assistance when and where
needed. Activities such as planning workshops and visitations to outstanding classes and organizing a newsletter might be coordinated by the
executive director.

Perhaps one of the most important tasks of a director is to be a constant source of information to the board about membership. Occasionally teachers attend TAWL a few times and are never heard from again;
they may even continue to pay dues but don't attend meetings. Appar-
ently, TAWL isn't meeting their needs. Why aren't they returning?

The Whole Language Umbrella

On February 18, 1989, the constitution of the Whole Language Umbrella (WLU) was ratified in Winnipeg, Manitoba. There is now an international network that makes communication between individuals
and groups possible. The WLU provides a mechanism for whole lan-

guage advocates to get in touch with each other; a way to share across states, provinces, and countries; a way to break out of our isolation. WLU, in its first year, has organized conferences (as well as meetings at IRA and NCTE), sent our articles and bibliographies to members, established a newsletter, provided information to whole language educators concerning sociopsycholinguistic theory and practices, and organized for political awareness.

Local, state, and regional support groups are encouraged not only to join WLU but also to contribute to its operation through creative ideas, work, and finances. CEL in Winnipeg almost single-handedly financed WLU's birth. It did so by adding a $5 fee to its annual conference registration; this surcharge is donated to WLU. Other groups have promised to support WLU in a similar way. Members of TAWL in Detroit have taken over the writing and production of the WLU newsletter. Members of the Whole Language Teachers Association in Massachusetts answer the stream of letters that come in asking how to start support groups. Members of the Mid-Missouri TAWL try to keep up with letters from teachers such as Julie, from those who ask, Can you help me? I'm trying to become a whole language teacher.

The Beginning

Nothing happens by itself. If a support group is organized and flourishes, it will be because of your commitment and through your effort.

References

Gilles, Carol, Bixby, Mary, Crowley, Paul, Crenshaw, Shirley, Henrichs, Margaret, Reynolds, Frances & Pyle, Donelle. 1987. *Whole language strategies for secondary students*. New York: Richard C. Owen.

Goodman, Kenneth S. 1986. *What's whole in whole language*. New York: Scholastic.

Community Meaning: Personal Knowing Within a Social Place

*Last week I was listening to fifteen young men and women who
are deeply involved in a semester-long internship. Linda brought
up the topic of talk in the classroom. She gave examples of her students' exploring ideas by reading, writing, drawing, and most of
all, talk: "I know my kids never really understood the problem until they began to discuss it. I think I helped by being quiet and letting them talk it through. It took a long time, but it was worth every minute!" Others in the group contributed stories of using talk,
one of the most powerful and accessible tools available to learners.*

*After a few minutes, three of the teachers, who were interning
in the (as they later called it) "You-Better-Be-Quiet School," told
us of their silent classrooms, of a sign on one bulletin board—Silence Is Golden and Restful and I Need My Rest!—and of the kindergarten children who stood in the hall for ten minutes until all
the children "zipped their lips" and clasped their hands behind
their backs. To support their description of the school, they pulled
out their assessment forms in which a teacher noted their need for
"more work on keeping the children quiet, in their seats, and on
task." I gave my copy of* Cycles of Meaning *to the three students.*

Used by permission of Dorothy Watson. From *Cycles of Meaning: Exploring the Potential of
Talk in Learning Communities,* edited by Kathryn M. Pierce & Carol J. Gilles (Heinemann,
A division of Reed Elsevier Inc., Portsmouth, NH, 1993), pp. 3–15.

Family gatherings, courtrooms, clubhouses, even coffee shops and playing fields are places where real people come together to create meaning. But of all the settings in the world, school is where people are *expected* to think, to explore, and in the process, to create meaning. *Talk is fundamentally connected to that creation.* It follows, therefore, that the classroom is, or should be, the most conducive and inviting setting in which to promote the human act of talking.

As learners journey together, they "cycle" (sometimes cautiously, sometimes with abandon) into experiences in which they share their meaningful personal knowing and take on the responsibility for creating new, but just as meaningful, understanding.

How does talk that leads to understanding emerge? What contributes to it outside school and what facilitates it within the classroom? The paths that lead to classroom "talking places" are as varied and unique as the school talkers themselves. It's along diverse paths that children absorb language, accept values, and take on the rules of their culture and of their many societies. It's along these paths, smooth or bumpy, that the form and substance of their utterances emerge. It's along the twists and turns that the creative minds of others contribute to the creative mind of the learner. The journey of a six-year-old may be filled with family jokes and rejoinders, "really real" questions, lengthy speeches from adults, big and little stories—in other words, with talk. Given an understanding of learners' diverse roots, the question now becomes, will they be allowed to bring their personal knowledge and personal ways of knowing (including the powerful, meaning-making tool called talk) into the classroom, or will they be expected to check the depth and breadth of their lives and their power of communication at the door? If students are welcomed whole and intact, what then constitutes the school talking places in which they can genuinely use the fullness of their language, the metaphors and stories of their lives, and the questions in their heads to cycle once more (this time in school) into the creation of meaning? Finally, how do we as teachers interpret and encourage such phenomena?

Oracy

When teachers refer to the power of language in the creation of meaning, their focus is often on visual language—reading and writing. Literacy demands a major part of the curriculum. Oral language—listening and speaking—is often relegated to the "assumed curriculum," which may never be actualized. This problem is not a new one. Almost thirty years ago, Andrew Wilkinson (1965) wrote that in our preoccupation with literacy, the study of oral language, whether spoken or heard, had been neglected. To help prove his point, he reminded educators that there was no term for the ability to use the oral skills of speaking and listening. There is a term to relate persons to books (*literacy*), at least one term to relate persons to things (*numeracy*), but not a term to relate persons to persons (one of the major functions of talk). Wilkinson found only one word, *euphasia,* coined by T. H. Pear in 1930, that might be used to label the phenomena of speaking and listening. But Wilkinson discarded the term because it described only half of oral language and because "despite its impeccable Greek ancestry it sounds like some terrible disease" (p. 14). Instead, Wilkinson proposed the term *oracy* to describe the neglected half of language education. He gave the phenomenon a name and challenged teachers to define it "in terms of particular skills and attainments, for different ages, groups, circumstances; to discover the best methods of teaching it; and to bring it into synthesis with other work, especially that designed to promote literacy" (p. 14).

In the early 1960s another researcher, Douglas Barnes, became interested in talk and the systematic way in which teachers could observe, record, and analyze their students' learning through oracy. His work with Britton and Rosen (1969) and Britton and Torbe (1991) as well as his research over a professional lifetime (Barnes 1992) have established a substantial and rich theoretical base that supports the practices of teachers who espouse a whole language philosophy and who create a whole language curriculum.

Oracy and Literacy in a New Light

In *Philosophy in a New Key* (1957), Susanne Langer tells us that new ideas and insights are the result of a metaphorical light that illuminates presences that did not have form for us before the light fell on them. She argues that the truly great ideas that help us generate knowledge are born not of new answers but of new questions.

When we read Douglas Barnes's accounts of classroom discussions, we are drawn into the richness and potential of the phenomenon of oracy. Barnes calls our attention to instances of students' and teachers' creativity and courage as they work to make sense of a situation or a text. Just as important, he points out opportunities for creating meaning that, painfully, were missed by both teachers and students. Through it all, Barnes asks questions of us as critical and creative teachers and as caring humans. In so doing, he helps us "discover things that were always there." Barnes invites us to use our own classrooms as talking places in which to ask our students and ourselves new questions. He asks us to investigate the realities of our classrooms by using inquiry in order to illuminate classroom experiences.

Theorists such as Britton (1982), Goodman (1985), Goodman, Smith, Meredith, and Goodman (1987), Graves (1983), Emig (1971), Shaughnessey (1977), Smith (1979), and others have helped us illuminate literacy education. They have done so by turning from the static product paradigms of reading and writing to process paradigms that value the dynamic relationship of thought and language that results in inquiry. And they have done so without abandoning the information provided by the products of authentic literacy experiences.

Douglas Barnes's investigation of oracy paralleled the shift in literacy research. He moved us from a production/performance view of oracy to one of active process. In so doing, he has not dichotomized product and process, but instead has drawn our attention to the dialectic between speaker and speakers, speaker and the speaker's past, and speaker and text or artifact. Just as we have come to understand that teaching the sounds of letters is not teaching reading and that teaching grammar rules is not teaching writing, we now know that focusing only on production/performance speech is not promoting oracy. Barnes, his colleagues, the theorists mentioned above, and others shed light on the *realities* of communication in the classroom. This new light, if focused, will illuminate a new philosophy that includes owned practices, active theories, and tested beliefs about the learning and teaching of literacy and oracy.

Personal Knowing and Social Learning Through Talk

The quality of creative, expectant, and probing discussion about the phenomenon of talk, especially what Barnes refers to as *exploratory talk,* should not be diminished because of the presence of typical hesitancies and silences or the use of nonstandard language forms. Utterances may be tentative, searching, and often fragmented because speakers don't always know the outcome when they speak, although they may be able to predict the responses to their talk because they have memories of previous dialogues and experiences. This remembrance of past experience is part of each learner's personal knowing.

Exploratory talk is an acceptable, even necessary way for speakers to bring their tacit knowing, or "personal knowledge" (Polanyi 1958), to a talking place where, through socialization, they can construct new meanings. Personal knowing *and* social learning are essential to our understanding of talk within a classroom community. Michael Polanyi, whose training in chemistry gave him firsthand experience of scientific discovery, viewed personal or tacit knowledge as the dimension that allows learners to integrate the particulars of their lives with the wholes that are meaningful and important to them. "In the structure of tacit knowing, we have found a mechanism which can produce discoveries by *steps we cannot specify*" (p. 140, emphasis mine).

Polanyi's discussion of scientific discovery enlightens our investigation of all discovery through talk, yet we can only speculate on what he means by the "steps" of tacit knowing that "we cannot specify." Could these steps help us understand the powers of the active mind that are evident in exploratory talk? I propose that such steps might include the inquiry, imagination, and creativity that precede (or accompany) understanding. I am convinced that personal knowing[1] is more than an idiosyncratic store of facts. Personal knowing must include the processes through which learners create meaning, processes that are more valuable to learners than their personal "data banks."

The *personal knowing* any learner brings to a talking place is constructed not in isolation but with others. In order to understand the *social* construction of knowledge, we must look at the concept in a new light. The Russian psychologist Lev Vygotsky's (1962) beliefs about the emergence of thought and language in children help to explain the personal and the social nature of meaning and talk. Vygotsky defined very young children's spontaneous talk as egocentric speech. Such speech not only provides a release of tension, but also facilitates what children are trying to do. This personal or egocentric speech helps children understand their surroundings, including all the people in it. Gradually, egocentric speech becomes a guide that determines and dominates children's actions: it directs the plans they have already conceived but have not yet acted out. As much as it may sound like a chicken-and-egg argument, it appears that personal speech becomes a base for social speech, just as social speech is a base for personal speech—a complex cycle of meaning making.

Vygotsky (1978) also helps us understand the phenomenon of social learning. By observing a child, we can identify when the child is able to solve problems on his or her own, without outside help. Vygotsky theorized that prior to this point there is a broad indicator of learning, called the *potential* development level. At this time the child can solve problems in collaboration with "a more capable peer or with adult guidance." The distance between a child's actual accomplishments and his or her potential accomplishments is called the "zone of

---

[1] In order to move Polanyi's concept of personal knowledge to a more active meaning-making view (a new key), I will use an alternative term, *personal knowing*.

proximal (next/near) development." Frank Smith provides an appealing metaphor for Vygotsky's "more capable peers." He talks about
"joining the club" (1986, p. 37). He believes that "we learn from the
company we keep . . . and that children grow to be like the company
they keep. . . . In other words, learning is social and developmental.
We grow to be like the people we see ourselves as being like" (1992,
p. 434). The "club" and the "zone" must be places in which a community of learners, both capable and less capable, can use talk in order to
advance all the members' learning and knowing.

Community Meaning

Blurring the distinction between personal knowing and social learning, inextricably combining them, leads to the concept of *community*
(or *communal*) *meaning*. Community meaning is generated by and be-
longs to the *individual* in ways that make sense to that individual, and
it is generated by and belongs to the *community* in ways that are meaningful to that special collection of learners. To understand and promote community meanings, it is essential to value personal knowing,
while at the same time accepting that the base of learning is social. In
large part, community meanings involve the same processes required
of personal knowing: inquiry, imagination, and creativity.

Mikhail Bakhtin (1981, 1984, 1986), considered by some to be
Russia's greatest literary and cultural theorist, provides yet another
view of *personal knowing, social learning,* and *community meaning.* Bakhtin redefines the relationship of individuals to *themselves* and to *others.*
For Bakhtin, self and others cannot be divided or separated, they can
only be distinguished or pointed out, and even then only with great
difficulty, because they are so intertwined within a community. Bakhtin refers to the personal as the "inside" voice and the social as the
"outside" voice(s). Both exist because of each other. Each exists within
the other. Bakhtin believed that we respond to both "the others *without*," and "the others *embedded within.*"

For Bakhtin, it is the tension between the personal and the social
that stimulates the talk necessary for intellectual growth. It is in the
tension that we hear Bakhtin's "symphony of voices." He explains the
communal nature of discourse and the notion of multivoices:

> We come into consciousness speaking a language already permeated
> with many voices—a social, not a private language. From the begin-
> ning, we are "polyglot," already in process of mastering a variety of
> special dialects derived from parents, clan, class, religion, country.
> We grow in consciousness by taking in more voices as "authorita-

tively persuasive" and then by learning which to accept as "internally persuasive." Finally we achieve, if we are lucky, a kind of individuality, but it is never a private or autonomous individuality in the western sense; except when we maim ourselves arbitrarily to a monologue, we always speak a chorus of languages. Anyone who has not been maimed by some imposed "ideology in the narrow sense," anyone who is not an "ideologue," respects the fact that each of us is a "we," not an "I." (Quoted in Booth 1984, p. xxi)

Creating Talking Places Within the Classroom Community

If the personalization of knowing and the socialization of learning are to become a way of life, it falls on teachers to create with their students a community in which meaning making is their intention, and it can't be done without talk. In a fifth-grade class, for example, six children are discussing the book *Tarantulas on the Brain* (Singer 1982). John asks, "Are tarantulas spiders?" Without feeling any need to ask permission, Judy and Rachael go to the class resource center and choose three books on spiders. As the group explores the references chosen by the girls, Tim begins to talk about a tarantula he and his uncle found. After almost a minute in which the children are absorbed in his hesitant, but detailed information, Tim ends with, "I didn't know I knew all that!"

As Judy, Rachael, and Tim set the scene for creating meaning, the children related the new information gained from reference books, their common book, and Tim to their awakened personal information, whether it was accurate or not. It was not a matter of adding new bits of information to old; rather, it was the hesitant but dynamic process of bringing forth personal knowing in a social place. Within this setting, talk:

- *Encouraged real questions* (John: "Are tarantulas spiders?").
- *Was informative and hesitant* (Tim: "Me and my uncle—we—uh found this spider—a tarantula. It was—remember when I went to Florida? G—it was—um, about this big—like maybe—at least two inches—yeah. Have you ever seen one? They're neat, real hairy and—uh—two big parts and see, we don't have 'em 'round here. I think in hot places, wet maybe . . . the tropics. If you get bit I think you get real sick, maybe die. I didn't know I knew all that!").
- *Was natural* (Tina: "Tarantulas are creepy.").
- *Was a way of connecting with other texts* (Lisa: "Charlotte was a spider, she wasn't no . . .").

- *Expanded knowledge* (Judy: "Tarantulas are poisonous.").
- *Allowed a learner to emerge as a resource* (Tim: "Yeah, you're right.").
- *Expanded knowing* (John: "Tarantulas are spiders, but Charlotte was a spider that wasn't a tarantula. Right?").

As these students worked, it became evident that talk in this social place was fundamental to their journey into meaning and to the strengthening of their sense of community.

Inquiring into Community Meanings

Perhaps the only way we can understand the complexity of the children's discussion during twenty minutes of talk is to study talking and thinking not simply as a relationship between two speakers but as a semiotic that involves the personal knowing of Tim and of all the participants, as well as how each child creates meanings within a social place. In other words, as teachers and researchers, we need to study oracy just as Berthoff (1991) suggested we study multiple literacies, "by supporting . . . ethnographic approaches to reading and writing, learning with them [colleagues] what it means to begin with meaning" (p. 281). In our investigation of multiple oracies we must describe, as ethnographers do, the origins and characteristics of learners' attitudes, customs, values, and experiences. In order to understand the theoretical interpretations of Douglas Barnes and other whole language theorists and teachers, we must attend to our own classroom histories and record and reflect on the multiple voices of our students within the talking places—the social settings—of the classroom. Histories that richly portray learners come about through the study of authentic talking experiences.

Berthoff (1991) also tells us that if we are to have a theory of the way we interpret what we see (for example, learners talking about a book they have all read), we must also have a theory about what we accept as experiences that are truly representative of learners engaged in making meaning. That is, a *theory of interpretation* requires a *theory of representation*.

An acceptable theory of representation supports wholeness and process. If students are not to be misrepresented and therefore underestimated, it is important to keep the learner whole, that is, to shun single, one-dimensional labeling, such as "learning disabled" or "in the low reading group" or "the nontalker." If students are not to be misrepresented, we must understand how learners mediate (process) the symbols of their lives; that is, how, through socialization, they have come to be the people they are. One of the most trustworthy ways of determining the multidimensions of personal knowing is not through conventional testing procedures but through experiences of talk. *Authentic representation* sets the stage for *authentic interpretation.*

In order to understand the concept of authentic interpretation I want to return to the concept of community meaning, the creation of meaning through both personal knowing and social learning. Community meanings come about when students are encouraged to "be alone with their own thoughts," and to bring their lives to the lives of others through talk. Then, within the community of learners, we can interpret the inquiry, imagination, and creativity involved in making meaning.

Suzanne Davis's fifth graders accepted me as a regular visitor in their classroom as I observed their literature study groups. They all generously shared their stories and projects with me. All, that is, except Gary, who, to my knowledge, had never recognized my presence, much less struck up a conversation.

I was surprised when Gary abandoned his routine of sitting through entire literature study sessions without saying more than a couple of words; one morning he arrived first at the table, spread his hands over his book, and before anyone could comment said, "I wish I could write as good as Paula Fox." His quiet statement didn't go unnoticed by the other students. Without a moment's hesitation, Alon replied, "Gary, you do write as good as Paula Fox." For the next five minutes, Gary's peers recounted, in surprising detail, pieces he had written. Cory ended the discussion with, "And Gary, you draw good, too!" At the end of the day, as I was leaving, Gary spoke to me for the first time. "Here's a story I just finished writing and illustrating. Alon thinks you might like to read it." Through talk, these learners encouraged a friend, strengthened their community, and made each other feel a head taller.

In that same session Mynett, one of the least proficient readers in the class, got the group's attention by jabbing at the word *gargoyle* in her book, demanding, "What did you do when you came to this word?" The students immediately turned to their own books and began, sometimes hesitantly, to offer advice:

Tom: Well, that's really, uh—just look—and say it the best way you can. It's *garc-gol-ee* I think. That's what I did.

Alon: And you know it means something bad because it's talking about—describing the housekeeper and you know how bad she . . .

Chris: Yeah, really mean. Just say, um, um, just say "ugLEE old dog" and go on. [Nods and smiles from the group.]

Cory: Or, Mynett, it was at a really exciting place and I just, just, skipped the word and went on.

Rhona: Yeah, the author never says it again—if she don't say it again, well
. . . well . . .

Chris: Can't be too important.

Rhona: Yeah, that.

Billy: I didn't even *see* the word.

Alon: Mynett, do you want to know what it means, like . . . or what . . .
how the enounce . . . *pro*nounce it?

Mynett: Well . . .

Cory: Mynett, if you want to you could look it up in the dictionary now. If
you think it's an . . . an . . . interesting word.

Mynett: I think I get it.

How do we interpret this oracy experience? First of all, it may come
as a surprise to learn that the teacher, Suzanne Davis, was seated with
the group. One of her contributions to the discussion was that she re-
frained from directing or taking over; instead, she was an interested
listener. Suzanne did what I find few adults are able to do—she kept
quiet. She did not do for students what they were quite capable of
doing for themselves—creating meaning within their community.
This teacher understood that children learned not so much when she
was talking but when they themselves were talking. She therefore
made it possible for children to do what Barnes calls "shaping" the discussion. It was not that Suzanne withheld information when it could
not be provided by other members but that she refused to ask all the
questions (especially at the beginning of the discussion period). Paulo
Freire (1973) tells us that until learners ask their own questions about
things of importance to them, there will never be any genuine ownership of learning. Ownership has a great deal to do with developing
a social consciousness, whether with the peasants in Freire's Brazil or
with this handful of eleven-year-old boys and girls. The students in
this group did not think of their teacher as the only source of information, nor did they view her as the one responsible for their learning.

But how else can we interpret these two talking events?

Through talk, an authentic representation of these students' lives
has been established. We can now explore, describe, and interpret
communal meaning, that is, we can investigate the inquiry, imagination,
and creativity that came about through students' talk.

Together the learners inquired into the work of another student
(Gary), and they responded honestly and kindly to him when he
made the genuine comment, "I wish I could write as good as Paula
Fox." This is not conventional inquiry, but it indicates that the children had not only learned "content" from their experiences within

their community, they had also learned how to respond truthfully and helpfully to their peers. In the second discussion, Mynett's inquiry, "What did you do when you came to this word?" was a three-tiered question: (1) How do you pronounce this word? (2) What does this word mean? and (3) What strategy did you use when you met this word? The students responded to real "problemization" (Freire 1972) by taking the question seriously. By activating their imaginations they were able to see the similarities between Mynett's problem and those they had in their own reading. Finally, they were able to create not just one but a collection of relevant strategies that allowed Mynett to take control of her own reading.

Teachers' Responsibilities

In all his work, Barnes opens up the possibility of talk-in-the-community-of-learners as he closes down teachers' controlling routines (such as question-and-answer Ping-Pong). In the concluding chapter of *From Communication to Curriculum* (1992), Barnes specifically addresses the responsibilities of teachers for learners' creation of meaning, particularly when teachers are not present in a group setting. He suggests five ways teachers can support communal learning:

1. Provide learners with a feeling of competence. Instead of trying to guess what is in the teacher's head, students need to feel confident of their own understanding of possible solutions to real problems. Teachers must show that they value students' contributions and the language with which these contributions are made. It is equally important that the teacher "educate his pupils' sense of relevance by encouraging them to make connections between new knowledge and old" (p. 192).

2. Facilitate "common ground." Barnes suggests that shared experiences, such as investigating tangible artifacts, can provide this common currency. These artifacts set the stage for children's imaginations. In Barnes's words, children "can set up hypothetical ways of organizing or explaining whatever has been put before them" (p. 193).

3. Facilitate a focus for learning. Barnes cautions teachers, "it is all too easy to do the learning for our pupils, to try to bypass the struggle to recode by dictating the adult version ready-made" (p. 194). There is the risk that teachers will focus learning too narrowly, so that students see no room for their own interests. There is also the

risk that their focus will be too wide, so that the students haven't a clue about their own role in the learning experience. Barnes suggests that it is the teacher's responsibility to direct pupils' attention, while emphasizing how learners can take control of their learning by asking their own questions. Questioning is "all the more powerful as a means of learning in that it has been set up by the children themselves in a leap of imagination" (p. 194).

4. Provide suitable pacing. Pacing has to do with time—an essential element in learning. As Barnes cautions, "if the teacher thinks of pupils' language in terms of *performance* instead of in terms of *learning*, he will not give them time for the reorganization of thought to take place" (p. 195).

5. Help learners fulfill their need for a public audience. When exploratory talk is emphasized, learners are encouraged by their social setting to inquire, imagine, and create in whatever messy, convoluted, or logical ways group members encourage or tolerate. According to Barnes, however, learners also need "a more public discussion of the same topic." This presentational talk provides "new demands for explicitness and organization" (p. 197).

Conclusion

Just as individual learners can't create meaning without others, neither can a social context exist without individual learners. When students walk into our classrooms we can make diverse assumptions, from "here are empty heads for me to fill with *my knowledge*" to "here are children filled with ways of knowing that can enlighten us all." If we make the first assumption, we allow only a fraction of the learner into the classroom. We spend time and energy on "covering" a prescribed, often irrelevant, curriculum, which keeps the student standing alone at arm's distance, busy with controlled oracy and literacy activities. If we make the second assumption, we invite learners to bring their lives, their stories, their experiences, and their personal ways of knowing into the classroom. The curriculum that emerges from such invitations embraces learners, valuing and encouraging their individual and communal voices.

Watching learners engrossed in a conversation fills us with questions: How have they learned to talk and behave this way? What was the teacher's role in all this? We must learn to see relationships within the complex process of talk, to understand and value both personal knowing and social learning, to make a commitment to community meanings. A starting place may be what Douglas Barnes calls "working on understanding" through the phenomenon of talk.

References

Bakhtin, Mikhail M. 1981. *The dialogic imagination: Four essays*. Austin: University of Texas Press.

Bakhtin, Mikhail M. 1984. *Problems of Doestoevsky's poetics*. Minneapolis: University of Minnesota Press.

Bakhtin, Mikhail M. 1986. *Speech genres and other late essays*. Austin: University of Texas Press.

Barnes, Douglas. 1992. *From communication to curriculum* (2nd ed.). Portsmouth, NH: Heinemann.

Barnes, Douglas, Britton, James & Rosen, Harold. 1969. *Language, the learner, and the school*. New York: Penguin.

Barnes, Douglas, Britton, James & Torbe, M. 1991. *Language, the learner, and the school* (4th ed.). Portsmouth, NH: Boynton/Cook.

Berthoff, Ann E. 1991. Rhetoric as hermeneutic. *College Composition and Communication, 42,* 279–87.

Booth, Wayne C. 1984. Introduction. In M. Bakhtin, *The problems of Dostoevsky's poetics,* Caryl Emerson (Ed.). Austin: University of Texas Press.

Britton, James. 1982. *Prospect and retrospect: Selected essays of James Britton*. Portsmouth, NH: Boynton/Cook.

Emig, Janet. 1971. *The composing process of twelfth graders*. (Research Report B). Urbana, IL: National Council of Teachers of English.

Freire, Paulo. 1972. *Pedagogy of the oppressed*. New York: Continuum.

Freire, Paulo. 1973. *Education for critical consciousness*. New York: Seabury.

Goodman, Kenneth S., Smith, E. Brooks, Meredith, Robert & Goodman, Yetta M. 1987. *Language and thinking in school: A whole language curriculum* (3rd ed.). New York: Richard C. Owen.

Goodman, Yetta M. 1985. Kidwatching: Observing children in the classroom. In Angela Jaggar & M. Trika Smith-Burke (Eds.), *Observing the language learner* (pp. 9–18). Urbana, IL & Newark, DE: National Council of Teachers of English & International Reading Association.

Graves, Donald H. 1983. *Writing: Teachers and children at work*. Portsmouth, NH: Heinemann.

Langer, Susanne. 1956. *Philosophy in a new key*. New York: Mentor.

Polanyi, Michael. 1958. *Personal knowledge: Towards a post-critical philosophy*. Chicago: University of Chicago Press.

Shaughnessy, Mina. 1977. *Errors and expectations: A guide for the teacher of basic writing*. New York: Oxford.

Singer, Marilyn. 1982. *Tarantulas on the brain*. New York: Harper & Row.

Smith, Frank. 1979. *Reading without nonsense*. New York: Teachers College Press.

Smith, Frank. 1986. *Insult to intelligence: The bureaucratic invasion of our classrooms*. New York: Arbor House.

Smith, Frank. 1992. Learning to read: The never-ending debate. *Phi Delta Kappan, 73*, 432–41.

Vygotsky, Lev. 1962. *Thought and language*. Cambridge: MIT Press.

Vygotsky, Lev S. 1978. *Mind in society: The development of higher psychological processes*. Cambridge, MA: Harvard University Press.

Wilkinson, Andrew M. (Ed.). 1965. Spoken English. *Educational Review, 17* (Occasional Publications No. 2, supplement) (Birmingham, England: University of Birmingham).

Many Cultures, Many Voices

The strength of the whole language community lies in the richness that is created from the interests and talents of all learners. The whole language community invites and embraces every one of us to join in the exploration of joyful learning and teaching. In the whole language community we are never ignored because of any label we may have been given; we are not one-dimensional. Our differences are not obstacles to be removed but rather assets to be explored and valued. Not only do we strive to recognize our assets and diversity, we strive to hear from the members of all circles of learners, from all culture circles. Under the whole language umbrella every one of us is invited to lift our voice and be heard.

When I was asked to address the opening session of the second Whole Language Umbrella Conference, I was pleased but nervous about the responsibility. At one point worry took over, and my solitary attempts to write stopped dead in their tracks. It was time to practice my unwavering belief in collaboration. I needed friends. My first call for help was to Ken Goodman. I chatted with Ken about his presentation at our

Originally presented as a presidential address at the second annual Whole Language Umbrella conference, held in 1990 in Phoenix, Arizona. Previously published in *Under the Whole Language Umbrella: Many Cultures, Many Voices* (Urbana, IL & Bloomington, IN: National Council of Teachers of English and Whole Language Umbrella, 1994), pp. 27–41. Copyright 1994 by the National Council of Teachers of English and the Whole Language Umbrella. Reprinted with permission.

first WLU Conference. I suggested that because it was such a moving speech and because there were a lot of people who had not heard it, it deserved repetition. And, I said with hesitation, would he mind if I just read it again at the Phoenix conference? After what seemed to be an unnecessarily long silence, Ken replied, "No, Dorothy, that would be a sin." I controlled my disappointment but could not resist telling Ken that as far as his work was concerned, a lot of us had sinned.

I was dismayed that Ken was not demonstrating the whole language spirit of sharing, but, undaunted, I sidled up to another friend. Years of experience have taught me that if I sounded pitiful enough, Rudine Sims Bishop would always come to my rescue. I reminded Rudine of a perfect talk that she had given several years ago—a presentation that we always referred to as "the vitamin speech." "How about it, Rudine, that talk is just right for 'Many Cultures, Many Voices' . . . for old time's sake?" After what seemed to be another unnecessarily long silence, she caved in. But I could tell (I am sensitive to these things) that she really did not think it was a good idea. Something in her voice made me reconsider the value, no matter what the struggle, of raising my own voice.

Under the Umbrella—Together

Whole language. What is this force? What is this collection of thought and action that has brought us together from classrooms around the world? What are the substance and essence of this philosophy of learning and teaching that has inspired educators from diverse societies and cultures to raise their voices—to tell their stories? Perhaps whole language cannot be described or defined any better than to say, *it is our stories:*

- Stories that have their roots in the works and messages of countless researchers and theorists who help us see that children, when given a chance, are smart, and that teachers are the professionals who can best tap children's intelligence, energy, and imagination.
- Stories that are written by a community of teachers who, with the help of their students, have dared to create new classrooms and important curricula.
- Stories that are told through the work of a growing number of educators who are represented by us—teachers, administrators, librarians, authors, publishers, and parents gathered under the Whole Language Umbrella tonight.

- Stories—often including pesky ones that keep getting us into trouble as we create their plots and themes—that reside so deep within us that they capture our learning, our teaching, and our imagination; and once we have those pesky stories in our heads, it seems that nothing can shake them out of us—and no one can scare them out of us.

Welcome

Welcome to the second Whole Language Umbrella conference. Welcome to a festival of learners and of language. Welcome to a celebration in which we can experience the beauty and achievements of many cultures, where we can listen to the stories told and songs sung by many voices, and perhaps, to use Paulo Freire's term, where we can create a cultural circle of our own, one in which no voice is lost.

To all those who have artfully designed this conference with such great dedication, we are indebted for helping us take another step along the whole language path. To reach our greatest potential and to distinguish our support groups from all the other organizations available to us, we know that we must do more than recognize cultures other than our own; we must give voice to those whose lives place them on the fringes of society and schooling. We must accept this invitation to become more sensitive and more caring, and to find the courage to pull down the barriers that wall out knowledge and understanding.

What can we expect of this conference? After our first WLU conference, the experience that remained with everyone was the opportunity we had for *talk*—talk with other professionals who shared our interests and concerns. Through our talk we sorted things out so that we could inquire more deeply into our important questions and concerns, and through our talk we could more fully celebrate our successes. This year the conversations will continue—again there will be talk, inquiry, and celebrations.

And if, through our talk, our beliefs are confirmed by a teacher's practices or if a teacher nods in agreement with our ideas (and even takes notes on a suggestion that we make), we can expect to feel gratified that the work in our classrooms, in our schools, and in our libraries is confirmed and valued by people whom we trust. But in addition to the confirmation of our familiar practices, through our talk we can expect to experience the unfamiliar—a tentative theory with which someone is wrestling, a classroom strategy, a poem, a picture—an idea that makes our pulses beat faster and that causes us to draw fourth-grade stars and exclamation marks in the margins of our notebooks to remind us, when we return home, to reflect on these important ideas.

We can also expect to have our blind spots revealed, to be nudged into that discomfort zone of whole language where we must make our intentions as teachers much clearer and our agendas as educators more explicit. At this conference we may make some tough decisions, maybe some that we have been putting off—decisions about how our students are evaluated or what materials are allowed in our classrooms; we may make decisions about what really should take up our students' and our own time and energy—what is so right and good that it can be called our curriculum; and we may make decisions about those students who are overtly or covertly denied because they bring their nonstandardized minds, bodies, ages, interests, and needs to a standardized classroom and curriculum.

During this conference, we, as individuals and as groups, may make some "policy decisions"—decisions that require all our political wisdom in order to conduct ourselves productively with both those who support us and those who do not—colleagues, parents, administrators, publishers, and people who write about us in newspapers, magazines, and professional journals. No one at this conference will presume to make decisions for us, but here we can decide to do more than just wring our hands over thorny problems—whether those problems involve mandated tests that mask our students' abilities and worth, or how to exist ulcer-free with the skills-based eclectic next door who fills the curricular cauldron halfway with obligatory texts and tests, adds a numbing amount of workbooks and worksheets, stirs in large quantities of direct "banking model" instruction, and, just to add a bit of flavor to this tasteless ferment, sprinkles some whole language on top. (And if that teacher does not understand whole language practices and principles, she might just put anything in and *call* it whole language.)

At this conference, we are educators doing our homework. Here we will talk about, study, mull over, reason with, reflect on, and reject some of what we see and hear. But here is our chance to become *enabled,* which in turn gives us the anchor needed for becoming *empowered.*

At this conference, we will be doing what we invite our students to do. We will take ownership of our own professionalism by making choices and taking risks. Choices and risks. If we have chosen whole language, it necessarily involves both. I am reminded of the message that Beverly Greeson wrote on the board one evening in our graduate class called Whole Language Curriculum. The message was advice from that wise philosopher Bert to his friend Ernie: "If you want to learn to play the saxophone, you've got to lay down the ducky and pick up the saxophone." Choices and risks. If we have chosen to play the saxophone, at this conference we will get to talk about how rewarding but how scary it is to let go of the ducky. Here we can experience with friends the theory and practice of playing the saxophone, as well as the rewards and frustrations of learning to do so.

At this conference, we, as educators and as members of our support groups, can expect to plan our next steps, even if they are shaky and tentative ones. As members of an umbrella organization, we must decide where we will place our next efforts as leaders in the whole language movement. WLU is organized by an enthusiastic advisory board. Our network of active interest groups has grown stronger, but we need to move ahead in our responsibility to our profession and to our membership. This is a working conference. We can expect to get very tired this week, but we will not get sick and tired. *For this is our work, and it ignites us rather than burns us out.*

Our Stories

This week we will eagerly listen to voices of authors, theorists, and learners, all emerging from a kaleidoscope of societies, ages, genders, experiences, politics, and cultures and resulting in the heartbeat of the whole language movement, the heartbeat that gives life and meaning to our whole language culture circle. But first we must recognize our own worth, reflect on our own history, and realize our own strength that rises from the bedrock of our own culture.

To help us with our inquiry, I am going to take the liberty of defining *culture* as a powerful collective of all the qualities that define us as human beings. Some of those qualities are expressed in the art of Diego Rivera, R. C. Gorman, and Norman Rockwell; the music of Mozart, mariachis, and the Grateful Dead; the dance of Maria Tallchief, Gregory Hines, and Mikhail Baryshnikov; the architecture of the Navajo hogan, the high-rise apartment, and the row house; the poetry of Nikki Giovanni, Lucy Tapahonso, and Langston Hughes; the literature of Isaac Bashevis Singer, Margaret Laurence, and Toni Morrison.

Culture is the nuances, the looks, the sayings, the lessons, the jokes, the quirkiness, the rituals, the rules, the connectors, the contexts, the designs of our lives that we as members of groups have in some way allowed to emerge, not only from our past but from what is being created right here and now in the circles of our families, our classrooms, our support groups—our lives.

In order to respect the lives of those outside our own groups, we first need to understand the qualities within ourselves that have contributed to the sum total of who we are and what we consider of value and importance. Even though we may have consciously or unconsciously rejected some attributes of our cultures, we are inextricably shaped by people, language, and experiences that were, and are, so pervasive and powerful that they help identify us as human beings, just as they help identify our culture circle: I know that I am FDR, the New Deal, and Bible stories for Presbyterian boys and girls; I am Saturday matinees, Shirley Temple, and Gary Cooper; I am also Woody Guthrie, Patsy Cline, and Station KVOO in Tulsa. I am all those side-splitting wisecracks from family and friends, stories that I absorbed while sitting on the fender of our old Ford V-8 as it moved around the town square on magical Saturday nights. I am "Idle hands are the devil's workshop" and "Fish or cut bait." (I rejected "Pretty is as pretty does.") I am friendship rings and Girl Scout camp songs. I am a lot of penny candy, home-canned peaches, and Chubbette dresses.

We are *all* so many precious things of quality that we could make E. D. Hirsch look culturally deprived. Through our cultures we make sense of our lives. But through *culture shared,* we are informed and enabled; through culture shared, we make sense of the world.

We know that lasting and deep appreciation of diversity is not gained by shaking hands and talking with someone at a conference for a few minutes. It is also not gained through the February Brotherhood Assembly and the Ethnic Food Festival. We cannot even be sure that it will be achieved when learners of diverse backgrounds come together in a classroom. These "tokens," however, should not be belittled; rather, they should be assessed for what they are—beginnings, or perhaps even better, little celebrations along the way toward more-genuine recognition of the richness of many cultures and the beauty of many voices.

Authors' Stories

Whole language educators know that literature shared can be an invitation to culture shared, and we depend on authors to let us see and feel the lives and hear the voices of others. I have chosen one author to represent all those writers who have spoken so eloquently to our students and to us.

Perhaps all of Katherine Paterson's books are celebrations of people and their relationships with others, but in her collection of essays *Gates of Excellence: On Reading and Writing Books for Children* (1981) Paterson directly shares her life with us. In the following passage, she makes us feel the helplessness of not being seen or heard for who we are. As you experience Paterson's story, I invite you to think about those students whose lives are shaped by rich traditions and language that clash with or in some way are not comfortably and conveniently matched with the larger society, which includes organized schooling:

> I can remember clearly how it feels not to have any words. In those months after I went to Japan in 1957, I would often find myself being taken somewhere by Japanese friends, not knowing where I was going or whom I was going to see. When I got to wherever I had been taken, I would find myself surrounded by people who were talking and laughing away, but because I did not know their words, I was totally shut out. As I began to learn a few words, people would try with infinite, exaggerated patience to talk with me. And because my speech was so halting and miserable, they would try to help me, try to put words into my mouth, try to guess what on earth it was I was trying to convey. When I was finally able to get out a sentence near enough to Japanese so that my listeners could grasp what I was driving at, they felt sure I'd appreciate knowing how I *should* have expressed that particular thought, and they would gently, firmly, and ever so politely, take my pitiful little sentence apart and correct it for me.
>
> I'm sorry to report that I was not grateful. I wanted to yell, cry, throw a tantrum. I *am not a fool!* I wanted to scream. If only you could know me in *English,* you would see at once what a clever, delightful person I am. But, of course, I didn't say it. I couldn't say it. I didn't have the minimum daily requirement in either vocabulary or syntax. The first time I saw the play *The Miracle Worker,* I knew what had been happening to me in those days. It was the rage of those starving for words.
>
> In 1961, after four years in Japan, I boarded a jet in Tokyo and landed about twenty hours later in Baltimore. I was met by my parents and one of my sisters and taken home to Virginia. Every night for many weeks I would get out of the soft bed, which was killing my back, and lie sleepless on the floor. I was utterly miserable. "These people," I would say to myself, meaning my own family, "these people don't even know me." The reason I thought my family didn't know me was that they didn't know me in Japanese. (pp. 7–8)

Real appreciation of someone else's identity comes from long-term experiences in which all the learners can, as Katherine Paterson put it, see themselves and others in their own language, in their own achievements and successes, displaying their own trophies.

But if learners cannot come together face to face over time, we must seek out the literature of others, explore their accomplishments, and build communities in which respect for widely diverse cultures becomes a way of life. And that way of life has no room for a killer culture in which those in power have an inflated sense of their own language and traditions.

Researchers' and Theorists' Stories

As whole language educators, we listen to the voices of researchers and theorists whom we trust. I am convinced that never has a group of educators taken their profession so seriously, felt so responsible, or studied so hard. Witness a TAWL (Teachers Applying Whole Language) meeting where teachers are critically investigating the theories and research of another educator, asking what all this has to do with them and their students and how the assumptions and suggestions stack up with what they know to be true about learners and learning.

Of all the researchers and theorists to whom we have paid attention in understanding whole language principles and practices, I have selected one to represent them all. I have chosen Paulo Freire because of his influence on the lives of three friends, teachers who have experienced such hurtful and shabby treatment from colleagues that one of them seriously considered resigning from a successful ten-year teaching career, three teachers who have virtually withdrawn to the saneness of their classrooms and closed their doors. These teachers came together in an attempt to cope with some of the torment that they have faced for almost two years. I would like to share an excerpt from Shor and Freire's *A Pedagogy for Liberation* (1987) that touched these teachers, and then tell you about their reactions.

> This is a great discovery, education is politics! When a teacher discovers that he or she is a politician, too, the teacher has to ask, "What kind of politics am I doing in the classroom? That is, in favor of whom am I being a teacher?" The teacher works in favor of something and against something. Because of that he or she will have another great question, "How to be consistent in my teaching practice with my political choice? I cannot proclaim my liberating dream and in the next day be authoritarian in my relationship with the students."

Freire's words gave these three beleaguered teachers courage and perspective. They had learned some hard lessons from the almost daily gut-wrenching experiences that included being denied and ignored by former colleagues. After a great deal of sorting out and struggling with Freire's words, they came to a *realization* and a *question*. They realized that their decision to live a whole language curriculum was a political act. They did not set out to be political, but it happened. Although this was scary, the realization and the fear it brought gave them an opportunity to be courageous. They were also led to consider these questions: While we're proclaiming *our* need for freedom and liberation, are we hearing all the voices within our own classroom? Are some students' beliefs, traditions, efforts, and abilities valued over others, just as others' opinions and practices are prioritized over ours?

Figure 1.
A science entry in William's learning log.

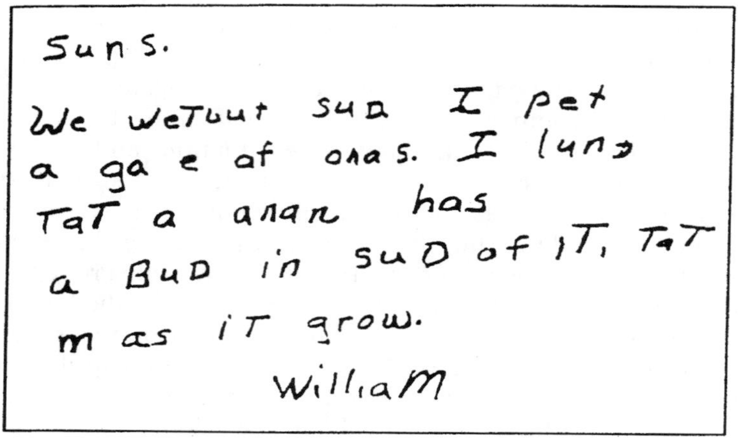

```
Suns.
We weTout sua  I pet
a ga e of onas. I lung
TaT a anan  has
a BuD in suO of iT, TaT
m as iT grow.
              William
```

Through asking liberating questions about the unquestioned obedience that was expected of them, these teachers began to investigate choice and voice and ownership in their own classrooms. This is grassroots whole language politicalization.

These teachers began to heal when they realized that Freire was right: education *is* politics (at least for them it was), and they had to move politically both outside and inside the classroom. But curiously, it was primarily their actions *within* the classroom that enabled and empowered them. As one of the teachers said, "I'm not so scared now, because I'm a teacher again, and one of the things I am teaching my students is how to be heard."

Learners' Stories

And it is time that we heard from students. While listening to authors, to theorists, and to ourselves, we urge learners to raise their inquiring voices. I have chosen three examples of students' voices to share with you. I have selected these examples because they are quiet but powerful examples of kids becoming informed, speaking up for themselves, and speaking out for beliefs that are worthy of their time and energy.

First, in a collaborative study, Kittye Copeland and Kathryn Mitchell Pierce invited Copeland's students to reflect on their science

Figure 2.
A science entry in Chip's learning log.

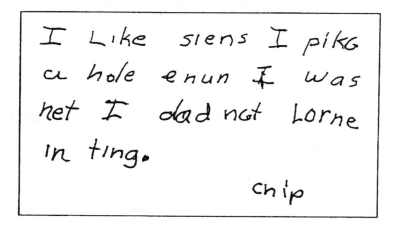

I Like siens I pikG a hole enun I was net I dad nat Lorne in ting.

chip

experience. William's learning log entry is typical of the children's re-flections: "Science. We went outside. I picked a group of onions. I learned that an onion has a bud inside of it that makes it grow." (See Figure 1.) Classmate Chip, however, knew that his teacher encourages and expects children to be candid about their learning and that they are not expected to play at schooling, so he was forthright in his com-ments: "I like science. I picked a whole onion. It was neat. I did not learn anything." (See Figure 2.)

Second, Grace T. (who has asked to use a pseudonym here) was told that school board members would be visiting her classroom be-cause there had been a complaint about, among other things, her lack of textbook use. The principal was supportive of Grace's curric-ulum and suggested that she tell her students that they would be having visitors and that they might want to welcome the visitors and to explain what went on in the classroom. Grace told her fifth grad-ers about the visitors, and the kids talked about how they could make their visitors welcome. Then one of the students suggested that guests to the classroom could not possibly understand in one visit everything going on there. On the student's suggestion, a com-mittee of five children worked hard for a week making a guest book and composing the following letter to be given to everyone who vis-ited their room:

Dear Visitor,

Thank you for coming to our classroom. We think you will understand us better if we tell you a bit about our room and offer a few
suggestions.

First of all, please take a walk around the room. Although we try
to run a tidy ship, this is a working classroom, so you will find unfinished projects, work in progress, and OUR STUFF. WE do the bulletin boards (not Mrs. T by herself), we write our assignments on the
board, we arrange the books and try to keep the files orderly. We *live*
here.

We also have a say in what we want to study through our special
expert projects, and we choose our own books to read. We would be
glad to answer your questions about any of the fifty topics we have
learned about this year.

Please read some of our completed stories. If you want to talk to
an author or if you want our autograph, just ask. If you look at some
of our unfinished stories or research reports you might find different
spelling or funny grammar. We call this our rough draft spelling and
writing. Don't worry, we get better as we go along. No, we don't
have spelling tests and grammar sheets. We just write stories, poems,
do research, and draw pictures to illustrate our work.

We also talk a lot to each other. If you think we are wasting time,
just listen in. But we can be quiet, too. If we are having silent reading time, please join us by getting a book. You might want to read
some we've written.

Since we write a lot in this room, we hope you will, too. Please
sign our guest book. You'll notice that there is lots of room in the
book to write your comments and questions. If there is something
you like about us, please say so. If there is something you think we
should be doing differently, we are all ears.

Sincerely yours,
Grade Five and Mrs. T.

Finally, in a second-grade classroom at Columbia Catholic Elementary School, Gary Shaw encouraged his students to speak up for
themselves or for others when they felt the cause was a worthy one.
When Kristen and Alexis noticed that only the boys got to be servers
during the communion services, they felt slighted and decided to talk
with their teacher. Shaw explained that he thought the priest chose
boys as servers in order to get to know them and to bond with them;
letting them participate in the services might result in their growing
up to become priests.

The two girls did not accept this argument, so their teacher suggested that they write to Father Flanagan (see Figure 3). Kristen and
Alexis did not sign their letter initially, but then Shaw reminded them
that the priest would not retaliate, and that when people feel strongly

Figure 3.
Alexis and Kristen's letter.

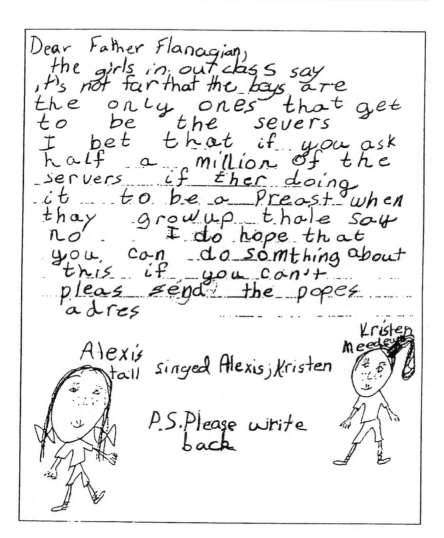

about an issue, they usually strengthen their position by signing their names. Not only did the girls sign their names, but they drew pictures of themselves and provided a little description (Alexis is tall, Kristen medium).

Our Colleagues' Voices

We respond to *all* our colleagues' voices, not just the select group of teachers who are as informed as we are. We encourage dialogue with those who, in our eyes, are making a muddle of whole language principles and practices, those who are merely manipulating the "stuff" of whole language. We also listen carefully and are sensitive to the hopes and potential of the enthusiastic but scared whole language novices. We remember that perhaps the reason we know better than they or that we are more successful in our practices is that we started before these teachers did; we have had a chance to get it wrong and then get it right; we self-correct; we have colleagues and students to help us grow. And now it is up to us to issue the invitation that moves less informed learners from simply talking the talk of whole language to singing the songs and dancing the dances of whole language—that is, to practicing whole language principles not as a mimic but as an artist, as a teacher. It is easy to fall into a "stage theory" of whole language when we are working with less experienced educators. When this happens, we expect all teachers to walk the same thorny path that we walked and to have the same conversations that we had. We think that if they read the right books and if they attend the right meetings they will "develop" into us. Educators with fewer experiences in whole language are not necessarily less capable than we are. Some of their experiences will be similar to ours, but they and their students will also have unique and extraordinary experiences, some that will be richer and more informative than ours, and some that will be tenuous and confusing. In any case, their voices must be heard.

We must hear the voices of the cautious skeptics and must attempt to understand and respond thoughtfully to their questions. We must never avoid the questions of the skeptics just to keep an uneasy peace. Such discussions can help us grow in our understanding, leading us to important inquiry.

We also must hear the voices of the dissenters—those who ask us questions and then will not listen to our answers or do not like the answers that we give. They dismiss us by saying that we are not responsive or intellectual enough to talk with them. They are the ones who say, Those teachers can't even define whole language. We need to point out to these detractors that we have defined whole language linguistically, historically, pedagogically, curricularly, and politically. Whole language is the most defined and redefined concept in education today. We invite them to listen. I believe, however, that there comes a time when we need to let the detractors, those who would minimize our efforts and our answers, know that we have had enough. We can find ourselves emotionally and physically drained from the struggle of defending our principles and practices. Our time, energy, and hope must be available to those who will enter into a real dialogue.

Sometimes people ask me if I believe whole language is for all learners. I have no trouble answering that one: yes, all learners. I am also asked, Is whole language for all educators? My answer to that one is maybe not. If that educator is not looking to learn, our efforts to inform may be futile, and we may want to direct our efforts toward those who are more receptive learners. Depending on how much energy, patience, and time we have, we can continue to invite, to highlight articles and put them in mailboxes, even to get resisters to attend conferences and classes, but we cannot feel responsible or guilty or even angry when the invitations are ignored and our messages fall on closed minds.

The Whole Language Umbrella

The Whole Language Umbrella is a network of whole language teachers, an umbrella under which we can invite all educators, researchers, theorists, parents, publishers, and learners to gather. Under the umbrella we can sing the songs and dance the dances of all cultures. We can search out the very best in us all, and we can create our own culture circle.

Under the umbrella and in our TAWL groups, there is even room for some whom we might never have expected to find there. A miracle sometimes happens. One did in our area when a parent complained to the school board about a teacher practicing whole language. This parent caused a great deal of pain and undermined two years of building a whole language curriculum. The miracle is that, eleven years later, that parent called a local tutorial service to ask about having her second child tutored—in whole language. Miracle or hard work?

I suppose that we have to let it rest for some. There are those Dicks and Janes who are always going to think that we are strange. But don't underestimate the funny Baby Sallys of this world—Sally just might join us under the umbrella.

References

Paterson, Katherine. 1981. *Gates of excellence: On reading and writing books for children*. New York: Elsevier/Nelson.

Shor, Ira & Freire, Paulo. 1987. *A pedagogy for liberation: Dialogues on transforming education*. South Hadley, MA: Bergin & Garvey.

Welcome to Our Wonderful School: Creating a Community of Learners

If my memory serves, when most of the earlier pieces in this volume were written there was no talk about creating communities of scholars in our classrooms and schools. Now, teachers are intrigued with the idea; our support group meetings and conference programs reflect that persistent interest. Community is perhaps the concept that is most thoroughly whole language in nature and practice.

Despite the feeling that "Community Is Us," teachers caution us not to let a good idea get distorted or wither from lack of wisdom on our part. While describing their classrooms, teachers remind us to build community on the strengths of the learners in our own classes. They tell us that no two classrooms will look alike, and they refuse to provide any prescriptions that attempt to standardize nonstandardizable groups of human beings. Just as important, these experienced community members urge us to do our homework by exploring the theory that supports the concept of living and learning through a very special and thoughtful socialization of learners.

A first grader tells his college pen pal, "This is my room. I feel good here."

A second-grade committee makes a poster for open house, "WEL-COME TO OUR WONDERFUL SCHOOL."

You walk into Room 16 and are struck by the exhilarating atmosphere: there are important things going on here! The spirit of whole language is everywhere, although the sources are not easy to pin down. It isn't just the learners' stories and pictures covering the walls or their other handiwork and brain work evident everywhere you turn. It isn't just that when you listen to any of the many conversations, you hear people talking about matters of genuine interest and importance. It's not just the literature study, the author's chair, the big books, the puppet play, the conferences, or even the comfortable humor. Room 16 isn't special because of the abundance of whole language stuff found there. It is special because of the spirit of whole language that pervades the room. Many teachers believe that this spirit or essence or chemistry stems from a sense of community created by all the learners who share not only space and time but themselves as scholars and friends in democratic "fields of meaning" (Peterson 1992). To understand the kind of community that flourishes in this room, we need to investigate some of the many facets of building community.

Why a community, rather than some other social organization? Perhaps we need at the outset to distinguish between a community of learners and a collection of people. The passengers on an airplane, the teachers at a faculty meeting, even students in a classroom are collections or groups of people until they share their lives—that is, their meanings, their intentions, their stories—with each other. If the airline passengers are headed for the Brazilian rain forest with the intention of gathering facts and planning an ecological course of action to help save our planet, they make up a potential community. This community might be temporary or it could flourish into a network of dedicated members of a "global village." Informed teachers at a faculty meeting who feel the responsibility and authority for developing an invitational, constructivist-based curriculum for their school and who know that their task is meaningful could develop into a cohesive and long-lasting community of dedicated educators. Likewise, fifth graders reading Elizabeth Spear's *Sign of the Beaver* (1983) who share their lives through talk about Matt and Attean's uneasy relationship, and consequently experience the rewards that come from having their ideas heard and their opinions valued, have a good chance of creating a gratifying, authentic community of learners.

Learners' Stories, Meanings, and Intentions

Through stories, learners organize and tell about their lives and make known both the meaning and the intentions that lie deep within them. Meaning arises out of learners' memories of past experiences (their histories) and the sense they are making out of what is happening in their lives here and now. Today's stories grow out of learners' reflections on what things mean and in turn create the potential for tomorrow's stories. Likewise, intentions grow out of history and current experiences. Intentions move the learner into the next thought, next question, next experience—into the future. Intentions differ from conventional goals in two important ways. First, intentions must be created by learners in search of something that they believe to be meaningful; goals can be set by someone else and often prove to be inappropriate or useless. Second, intentions are always in process; as intentions are met, new anticipation and new intentions emerge. Goals, once met, frequently require no more attention and action.

When individual stories become public, the potential for common meanings and common intentions emerge. When students make known their loves and hates, when they share their knowledge and the things they value, the spirit necessary for a community of learners can emerge. Community is created as individuals realize that their stories are valued by the group and as the group makes its own unique story. Sensitive teachers are open to unexpected and unusual meanings and intentions, never limiting learners' interests and aims only to those valued by the powerful kids (such as those who are academically or socially savvy); this is crucial to building community.

Winkelmann (1991) reminds us that when the meanings and intentions of one student are not valued and lie in opposition to the meanings and intentions of the other class members, there can be trouble ahead for an emerging community. Yet she warns that it would be problematic at this point for teachers simply to reduce the idea of community to a metaphor in which we dream up some idealistic notion, where we attempt to "neutralize the inherent violence . . . in the interest of seeking the consensus" (p. 23). Winkelmann suggests, however, that the "properly managed" community helps members handle this kind of problem by addressing such questions as:

- What is the relationship of each individual to the community?
- How are the criteria that shape the classroom community determined?
- How and why are individual alternatives preserved?

When these important questions are not addressed, an actual community never emerges, or if a community exists and then the voice of even one learner is denied, the community weakens; it either dissolves or continues as a sham.

When meanings are made public and are valued within the classroom, learners realize they have helped build a safe place in which they can invent, create, learn, teach, make mistakes, and create meaning. At the same time they begin to understand the limitations and the conventions that guide, restrict, and support their inventions, creations, learning, and teaching. The balance between invention and convention parallels the fragile balance between the needs of the individual and the needs of the group. This phenomenon of social convention controlling individual invention keeps the classroom a sane place to live and therefore allows and invites renewed individuality and creativity. Democratic communities allow teachers to recognize and ease tensions that might exist between each student and the group.

Learners are encouraged to tell their countless stories in countless ways: through conversations, group discussions, writing, dance, and other artistic and expressive forms. Through stories, students and teachers present not only their values but also their knowledge, their culture, their successes and failures—their lives. Over time and through great effort, classroom communities develop an ongoing narrative quality that reflects the unique lives of all the members. Teachers come to realize that every community has its own special narrative; no two stories are ever alike.

These narratives focus on all that is important, whether the text was created in the past or in the present, whether it propels learners to the next minute or the next year. Winkelmann's concern about using the term *community* as a metaphor to help conceptualize the classroom forces us to become specific about fostering a classroom organization that doesn't sacrifice, scapegoat, or stifle any learner. In a democratic community, learners can be safe, and their stories can be heard and valued.

Why a Democratic Course of Human Events Within the Classroom?

A class has a good chance of flourishing into a community of learners if its social organization and its philosophy of learning are compatible. Of all the befitting forms of governance and of all the pedagogical philosophies available, a democratic structure and a whole language curriculum appear to be compatible and mutually supportive. Their practices reflect similar principles such as freedom with responsibility, respect for all learners, the need to hear all voices, choice, self-regulation, and attention to process.

All these democratic notions may sound scary when we think about what they mean for us as teachers within the classroom, especially if we or the students have a history of control from the top. But if we are hesitant, we might be encouraged by no less a statesman than Thomas Jefferson. When asked about the wisdom of letting "the people" gain power over their own society, Jefferson replied that if we think citizens are not enlightened enough to exercise control over themselves, the remedy for the dilemma is not to take power from the people but to educate them in the use of such a privilege. If we accept this point of view, it follows that creating such a society within our classroom takes a tremendous amount of thought and effort; and it makes sense that a democratic community must be carefully planned and constructed by everyone it touches. It's the responsibility and challenge of the informed teacher to open the door and invite the citizen-learners to raise their voices, exercise their rights, and create shared stories within a classroom community that is honestly their own.

The narrative of classrooms evolves in part from the stories of individual learners within the community. If a group is to become a joyful and cohesive community, the shared stories must form the community narrative and must be composed by all members.

Both teacher and students are invited to ask, Who are we? This question can be answered only in collaboration between teacher and students. The answer tells the story of a community and its members. This self-discovery is part of the process of changing from a group to a fellowship; it involves discovery of me, of others, of us. How a community understands itself is part of its common meaning and shared intentions, and therefore part of what it is.

From One Teacher and Twenty-five Kids to a Community of Learners

A classroom can be a collection of one adult and twenty-five students in which the individuals meet to give and follow directions, sometimes cooperating and sometimes competing, or it can become a community whose members share their lives as they plan for and engage in learning. To engage in learning means much more than being a spectator who is engaged in observing classroom activities; it assumes active involvement on the part of all learners.

If it is the teacher's intention to facilitate a democratic community, there is no better starting point than to take an inventory of personal, group, and environmental assets and resources and then to ask: Given our strengths, how can our classroom become a very special place to live and learn? What can make it a vibrant human community of eager learners? Many teachers who have been successful in facilitating a community agree that learners (teacher and students) can create their own democratic community when teachers:

1. Make a commitment to create the best social structure available for all learners.
2. Build on compatible beliefs and theoretical frameworks.
3. Invite and create a genuine fellowship of learners, rather than impose a structure with rules and regulations that is a community in name only.
4. Are willing to take risks.

Further, learners (students and teacher) are more likely to create a democratic community when they:

1. Know, accept, and trust themselves and each other.
2. Create their own rules, routines, responsibilities and celebrations.
3. Take on roles not always valued in conventional classrooms.
4. Engage in intellectually important and stimulating experiences.
5. See that learners' meanings and intentions are not limited to the classroom.

Communities and What Teachers Have to Do with Them

Although more and more educators are talking about classroom communities, there seems to be a need for a deeper understanding of both the spirit and the process of building community. Classroom community isn't a commodity; it won't materialize just by wishing we had this "product" in place in our classes. But what Carolyn Burke calls curricular wishing is powerful and can help teachers take a step toward a classroom community. Curricular wishes arise out of a teacher's burning desire to make some important changes in what is going on in the lives of learners. Let's look at how the first group of suggestions above helps teachers facilitate their curricular wishes.

Make a Commitment to Create the Best Social Structure Available for All Learners

Genuine commitment on the part of the teacher is an absolute necessity. Such intention involves a great deal of time and effort, beginning with doing our homework: scrutinizing our own classroom and visiting others; talking with teachers, administrators, and parents; and most important, talking with students. In addition, we must read, read, read! One of the most valuable books directly related to the issue of classroom community is Ralph Peterson's *Life in a Crowded Place* (1992). Peterson helps us understand the complexity of living in a crowded but very special "field of meaning." He tells about making what he considers his most important discovery about learning: *"community in itself is more important to learning than any method or technique.* When community exists, learning is strengthened—everyone is smarter, more ambitious, and productive. Well-formed ideas and intentions amount to little without a community to bring them to life" (p. 2).

In his short book, Peterson elucidates the concepts of ceremony, ritual, and rite within the classroom. Ceremony helps learners make transitions between life outside the school to living within and between classroom activities. Ceremonies include classroom opening and closing events and activities such as a song or stretching exercises that help kids move their bodies and minds from one experience to another. Ritual involves little acts that bring order to our lives and include both individual and community experiences. Individual rituals are played out; for example, as Bobby settles into his writing: he builds his nest by sharpening pencils, selecting special paper, and placing his desk in its special writing place. The class enacts its ritual as the children bring out the candle and pillows and get comfortable on the rug ready to hear a story. Peterson defines and describes rites as those enactments that mark times and places of passage: culminating activities, activities that pull the class together. Peterson makes us think about the organizing structures that help learners live harmoniously in a crowded place called school.

Build on Compatible Beliefs and Theoretical Frameworks

Because our beliefs are so closely related to what we deeply value, it is critical that the theories and practices we accept be in harmony with them. If there is no compatibility, teachers report consequences ranging from discomfort to burnout. Recognizing distinctions between theories and beliefs may help teachers feel comfortable about venturing into community building without insisting that all their questions be answered before they take the first step.

Through reflection on theories, practices, and beliefs, teachers sort out which assumptions hold water, which practices pay off, and which beliefs are confirmed. When practices are examined, theories get examined as well; some are rejected and some are so powerful that they become the trustworthy foundation of a belief system. Having a solid belief system keeps us sane; we don't have to reinvent the wheel each time we use it. A belief system that emerges from inquiry into theory and practice in a real classroom allows us to move on into further inquiry and into more clearly articulated practice. A belief system must never spring up on blind faith, nor should it be set in stone. Belief systems can, with continued inquiry, undergo growth and change.

The concept of teacher as inquirer may help us understand the relationship of theory, practice, and belief. Inquiry may start with exploring theoretical assumptions, examining classroom practices, or probing beliefs. Inquiry entails collecting, categorizing, and analyzing evidence. Both the beginner and the experienced teacher can mentally view some aspect of curriculum and community when they ask questions, generate hunches, and gather information that provides insights into their inquiry. Teachers who theorize about their practice reflect and ask questions about their past and current experiences and speculate about changes or modifications in their practice. For example, a question about the appropriateness or success of basal readers could lead to trying an alternative reading program that is more compatible with the teacher's existing beliefs about learning. Such an alternative program might include having students engage in personal reading, literature study, and strategy lessons. Inquiry experiences provide the basis for researched practice that is supported by existing beliefs and by the values that strongly influence those beliefs.

Some areas of inquiry that have helped teachers understand community are:

1. Grouping:
   - How can we replace "ability groups" with study groups and "interest/action groups"?
   - What is the best make-up of an interest/action group?
2. Management:
   - Who and what control behavior and curriculum in this classroom?
   - Who and what are being controlled?
   - What are the processes and outcomes of rule making by and for learners?
   - Can we organize our classroom around task committees?
   - What about a classroom court, including trial by a jury of peers?
   - How do children assume responsibility for resolving conflicts?
3. Space and time:
   - How and by whom are space and time organized?

4. Teaching:
   - Can I move from transmission teaching (transmitting information from my head to students' heads) to reflective teaching (learners as thinkers and inquirers)?
   - How do we all become inquirers?
5. Media:
   - How can we add to the spirit, organization, and scholarship of our classroom through experiences with music, drama, art, dance, photography, and electronic media and tools?
   - How can technology support learning?
6. Evaluation:
   - How can we use self-evaluation?
   - How can families become involved in assessment and evaluation?

The questions above allow us to cast our nets rather wide, but once an area of concern is determined, more specific inquiry questions can be addressed:

7. Choice:
   - What happens if I invite kids to select their own books to read and their own topics for writing?
8. Rules:
   - How can the citizens of this classroom generate and evaluate their own rules about discussion groups, attendance, general behavior, etc.?
9. Environment:
   - What happens if we move our desks out of rows into flexible small groups?
   - What happens if we get rid of desks?
10. Beyond the classroom:
    - Can we set up pen pals and reading buddies with other classes, or can we write to senior citizens?
    - How can we address the issues of homelessness, pollution, drugs, and other undeniable problems?

Hunches about theories, practices, and beliefs get examined in our classrooms as we ask questions and collect evidence. Theoretical memos, practice memos, and belief memos are tentative conclusions or current (for right now) understandings that are composed as we reflect on tentative answers and on any additional questions emerging from these reflections. Teachers and administrators have said that once they become researchers in their classrooms and schools, they are never again without an ongoing inquiry project. Inquiry becomes a necessary part of their professional lives. In effect, they find themselves doing what they invite their students to do—inquiring.

It is possible to work toward building community whether the teacher is making tentative hunches about whole language communities or has already moved into a strong belief system that is well articulated and experientially rich. All of us are novices in some respects, experienced in others. Since there is no one developmental path that all teachers must follow and since there is no end to this journey called learning, both the experienced educator and the newcomer are invited to let the questions begin.

Invite and Create a Genuine Fellowship of Learners, Rather Than Impose a Structure with Rules and Regulations That Is a Community in Name Only

There is a growing realization that learning is not only a personal experience but also a social one, and that it thrives best in a social setting described as a democratic community of scholars. Despite this, many teachers say that it's very difficult to let go, relinquish total control, take the risks involved in sharing power with learners—all necessary steps if a community is to emerge. Ironically, by letting go, teachers can get a real grasp on insights about behavior, learning, and teaching, as well as discover the strengths and needs of their students and themselves. The rewards outweigh the risks.

At the outset, even before the commitment is made, we need to ask:

- Do I really want a democratic community?
- What if we get into this and can't make it work right away?
- Am I willing to give up my total control for a partnership arrangement?
- What do I see as milestones along the way to a democratic community of learners?

Such questions may create enough interest to warrant discussion at a teacher support group or a faculty meeting. Teachers may want to focus a professional development inservice program on the issues. Others may visit with teachers whose classrooms are exciting places where students are happy, confident, and in control of themselves both academically and behaviorally. Teachers taking a college course can research the issues and then present their findings to their colleagues and classmates.

Be Willing to Take Risks

Educators involved in building community are necessarily vulnerable: "Vulnerability lies at the foundation of genuine human community" (Watson, Burke & Harste 1989). The stakes are high; our students, our curriculum, and we ourselves are open to criticism and attack. Such vulnerability is a powerful incentive to become inquiring professionals—scholars and researchers—and, ultimately, enlightened teachers. Theories are articulated, practices are evaluated, we link what we are learning to familiar and accepted patterns, our eyes are opened to weaknesses in our curriculum, and our resolve to become the best we can becomes stronger. Teacher support groups often arise out of a sense of vulnerability, formed not only to share successes and information but to share our fears.

Students and Teachers Create Their Community of Learners

What makes a group of children and one adult more than just a social phenomenon? What brings a sense of wholeness into a classroom? There is a good chance of its happening when a number of conditions are present.

Learners Know, Accept, and Trust Themselves and Each Other

Community members must know one another. Learning names is a good place to start. In March, a fifth grader talks about her classmates as "what's-his-name" or "the girl who sits in the fourth row." Compare that to a sixth-grade narrator who in September introduces the seven members of a class play by both their first and last names, names that are Spanish, Portuguese, Hindustani, and Thai. Knowing the names of classmates doesn't constitute a community, but it is a beginning. We all feel more at home when others call us by our name.

How do we learn names? We learn them naturally, by using them in our conversations. When Timothy kept pointing to a girl in his third-grade class, referring to Shana as "her" and "she," his teacher, Kathy Cummings, asked who he was talking about and suggested that Shana would like it if Timothy used her name. Although this may seem a small thing, Kathy made it clear that in our "class family" we let people know they are important and that one way of showing respect is by learning names.

In some classes, students begin their day by signing in for lunch count, committee work, conferences, or special assignments. Both first and last names are used, especially in classes in which there are multiple ethnic groups. Another class plays name bingo during the first week of school. A committee makes bingo cards, making sure all names (first and last) are on several cards. Winners read names for the next game.

Giving each student two lists of their classmates' names, one list to take home and one for school, allows students and their families easy access to others in the class. If families agree, phone numbers and addresses might be included. The point is that the pupils see the names, perhaps even talk about their derivations, but most important, establish a rudimentary sense of belonging to "our class."

Of course it isn't enough just to know a name. Students define or redefine themselves as members of a community when they can present not just their names but themselves as unique. Through their stories, individuals see that they also have much in common with classmates. Both the uniqueness and the sameness are significant. Individually crafted name tags and collages can present the makers' personalities and interests. Shirley Russell uses information from name tags and personal collages to chart similar and different interests in pets, books, games, teams, foods, songs, movies, and so on.

Through "Who in the World Are We?" experiences, students have a chance to present themselves as multidimensional: I'm not just a kid labeled LD or academically talented or just a fifth grader with a hearing problem or just an ESL speaker. When we label students one-dimensionally, something strange happens, not only to the curriculum, but also to the spirit of community—it shrinks before our eyes. We must have experiences that help us tell stories in which we are multifaceted, interesting, intelligent, and lovable.

Here are some experiences that have helped students get to know and accept each other as citizens and learners within the community.

1. An old favorite: "What's in the Sack?" With flourish, display a paper bag for all to see; then read Shel Silverstein's poem, "What's in the Sack?" from *Where the Sidewalk Ends* (1974). After reading the poem, pull out of the sack, one at a time, three objects that tell something about your life and interests. Let the objects help you tell a story about yourself. Invite questions and stories. Ask volunteers to bring a "this is me" sack to share, or invite "birthday kids" or the "friend of the week" to share their lives. If Silverstein's poem is written on a chart, the class might read it (soon they'll have it memorized) before each sharing.

2. Some teachers encourage students to bring in photographs of their families. If photos aren't available, draw pictures. The students write a bit about a favorite family activity or a special holiday time or write a story about one particular member of the family (pets included). These pictures and stories might become part of a class yearbook. Important happenings in the lives of students in and out of school and special experiences in the life of the class community are added to the book as the year progresses. Class members take turns taking the album home to share with their families.

3. Interviews present possibilities for learners to know each other. Most of us need help in forming good interview questions and in developing interviewing techniques. With the teacher or an older student as resource, a class committee pulls together interview suggestions and demonstrates an interesting interview. The interviewers tell about their interviewees not only through writing but through pictures, songs, collages, and perhaps even a guessing game. To determine interview partners, match up halves of pictures or shapes or draw names.

4. Designating a learner (or scholar) of the week is a good way to showcase every student in the classroom. A special bulletin board or mobile filled with pictures, photos, letters from the principal or another adult, the honored student's work, titles of favorite books, and so on help everyone see the talent and trophies of these unique learners. Students are often honored during their birthday week; students with summer birthdays might choose weeks in which there are no birthday celebrations.

Learners within a classroom community can't be strangers; on the other hand, they can't be expected immediately to become fast friends. Some children actually need help understanding how friendships work. Some may need to talk about the art of friendship. The theme of friendship is explicit in many books for children and youth. Teachers have reported success in using such literature as a basis for class discussions on the challenges of friendship.

Learners Create Their Own Rules, Routines, Responsibilities, and Celebrations

Traditionally the school year begins with paying very close attention to THE RULES. Last year's failed attempts to make the teacher-generated regulations work are forgotten; the rules chart is dug out and once again displayed at the front of the room for all to absorb. Supposedly these words-to-live-by will be embraced cheerfully and will govern smoothly everyone's behavior for the entire year. Slim chance.

In Denys Cazet's picture book *Never Spit on Your Shoes* (1990), students and their teacher, on the first day of first grade, make their rules for the year. The teacher demonstrates by writing a rule that is important to her, "Don't run in the hall." She then invites the children, represented by animal characters, to contribute to the class list. "Waste not, want not." "Always keep your tools dry!' "Just say no to catnip." And Raymond's memorable, "Never spit on your shoes." When Arnie tells his mom about helping the teacher make rules, it is the children's rules, especially Raymond's, that stick in his mind. We can be sure Arnie will never spit on his shoes. Mom promises not to either.

In the story, Cazet shows us that Arnie's teacher values what her students value and understands the power of inviting students to take ownership of their behavior. On the very first day of first grade she trusts the members of this would-be community to the extent that she invests them with the responsibility of making their own rules to live by. Granted, children in real classrooms are not charming little animal characters who suggest kitten rules like "Just say no to catnip." But students are individuals who come together with a history of rule making and breaking, and with a sense of how people ought to work together to get things done and to enjoy the experience.

Tina McVay and her fifth graders offer an alternative to the rules-and-regulations-first approach to the new year. Class meetings during the first week focus on freedoms and rights by introducing the students to the U.S. Constitution and the Bill of Rights. After the children consider their own rights, and after Tina suggests other freedoms that are possible within a democratic community, it then makes sense to think about the rules that allow for privileges. Learners talk first about the responsibilities of citizens and then about the limitations that make freedoms possible. They talk about family rules and about rules that work in other classes and other organizations such as Scouts and sports clubs. They consider the fairness and appropriateness of each potential regulation, and then they begin the work of taking control of their own lives by creating the rules, routines, responsibilities, and celebrations of their community.

Tina learns a lot about what her students value through this experience. Last year her fifth graders categorized their beginning-of-the-year rules under two headings: (1) safety and health and (2) property loss and damage. Later in the year, one more category was added, a category that resulted from experiences within the learning community: (3) care for others. This new category included "Show authors that you are listening and are interested in their stories" and "Don't disturb a group when they are working unless it's an emergency." This fifth-grade group was not just a class with a set of rules, but rather a community with a conscience.

Figure 1.
Joel's reminder.

Sometimes additional reminders and rules especially for the occasion are necessary. In Lynn Moore's class, after a botched science experiment, Joel wrote the piece shown in Figure 1 for his group. It's a firm message, but written with feeling. (Notice the hearts.)

In addition to making their own rules, many children want to talk about the consequences of breaking them. Kittye Copeland and her multiage class address this issue by setting up procedures in which offenders appear before a class court.

In rule making, as in all aspects of a democratic community, all students' views must be heard if the complete strength and spirit of the community is to be realized. No one student or group of students can receive priority over their classmates. Many children, through custom or culture, are more familiar with the traditional operation of schools. It's usually easy for these kids to "play the school game." Often they are rewarded by being made leaders, ensuring that their voices are heard. But there are too many other students who are silenced because they bring their "nonstandard" lives to a standardized school. Classrooms in which all learners govern themselves through democratic processes and procedures can become safe places in which children are invited to let their customs and cultures influence their point of view, including their notions about rule making and breaking.

Students who have experienced only conventional classes are sometimes baffled by the rights and routines of whole language communities. When this is the case, the need to talk and talk and talk about democratic governance must be met. In addition to incidental discussions, there need to be regularly planned times in which the responsibilities of rights and the consequences of rules are thoroughly explored. Building community takes time and talk.

Teachers and administrators who are wary of whole language curricula and democratic classrooms may not know where to begin, fearing there will be no organizational structure to provide everyone with needed security. Many experienced teachers believe that a good starting place is to create a daily schedule that accommodates all learners' intentions. Fortunately, whole language educators are willing to share their very best ideas, strategies, even suggestions about classroom routines. For example, in *Joyful Learning: A Whole Language Kindergarten* (1991), Bobbi Fisher presents a world of information about comfortable routines that lead to wonderful celebrations of joyful learning without becoming relentless ruts.

In *Creating the Child-Centered Classroom* (1990), Susan Schwartz and Mindy Pollishuke's advice includes examples of flexible timetables for setting up comfortable routines. Susan and Mindy suggest that input sessions (for group discussions, explanations, and directions) and sharing times (for the celebration of progress and accomplishments) be built into the daily schedule. Scheduling facilitates learning and living, and in doing so makes it easier to be flexible.

We never cease to be amazed at how eagerly students take on responsibilities when they know that their work will be valued and that it isn't an exercise in futility. Pat Miller's primary class and Kittye Copeland's multiage class are organized around committee work. The committees arise as needed, their tasks are taken seriously by the entire community, and they disband when their work is done. Possible committee responsibilities include the writing corner, portfolios (what goes in, where they are kept, etc.), pen pal procedures, field trips, beginning and ending daily routines, and the organization of library and resource centers.

What gets celebrated is an important issue in any community. Many teachers invite students to talk about the amount of time and effort devoted to popular holidays such as Halloween, Valentine's Day, Christmas, and Hanukkah. They discuss the appropriateness of celebrations in light of today's diverse classrooms. They consider nonreligious celebrations that help them share larger cultural connections, such as Kwanzaa, an elegant African holiday of affirmation. Kwanzaa, which means "the first fruits of the harvest," draws on common themes found in many African societies. The celebration starts on December 26 and ends on January 1. Each of the seven days represents a symbol for daily living: unity, self-determination, collective work and responsibility, cooperative economics, purpose, creativity, and faith. *Kwanzaa: Everything You Always Wanted to Know but Didn't Know Where to Ask,* by Cedric McClester (1985), provides extensive information about this nonreligious, noncommercial celebration.

Are things that merit celebration happening within the school, the neighborhood, or the world? Can special events at home, such as the birth of a baby, be honored? Perhaps even more important than the well-known holidays are the experiences that merit recognition and that arise directly from the classroom. Are there worthy accomplishments of the scholars within the classroom that are being overlooked?

The process of establishing rules, routines, responsibilities, and celebrations is complex and difficult. If, however, this component of community is not in place, teachers often use Band-Aid-like measures to solve problems and end up with an even more frustrating and often chaotic classroom. Self-generated and reasonable rules and routines provide a sense of stability and saneness. Within any community there are responsibilities that are shared by all who have a vested interest in this special place. Celebrations need to be so meaningful, justifiable, and needed that they become magic moments all learners remember.

Learners Take on Roles Not Always Valued in Conventional Classrooms

In whole language communities, students become inquirers (researchers), teachers (resources), collaborators, apprentices, representatives, and friends.

The role of inquirer or researcher may be a difficult one for some students and teachers to grasp; it isn't prevalent, much less rewarded, in many school experiences. In conventional settings, the information pupils are expected to learn is usually identified by those who construct textbooks, curriculum guides, and tests—seldom by the learner. Once a body of knowledge is identified, it is likely to be directly taught to kids who are "ability" ranked according to achievement test scores. These rankings are important in traditional classes because they dictate both what is to be learned by those in each group and by what methods the information is to be taught. Students quickly understand that they are expected to be relatively passive and that they are on the receiving end of the teacher-learner relationship. They are neither designers of the curriculum nor researchers of information, nor do they ever take on the role of teacher.

To develop a community within a whole language classroom, passive students must change into active researchers who inquire into subject matter because they are consumed with curiosity and because they choose to pitch into the exciting work of researching and learning. In this new role, the students' first task is to ask questions. John Dewey told us that until children ask their own questions, the curriculum will be trivial and unimportant to them; if learning is to be authentic and important, learners must pose problems. Similarly, Paulo Freire's "problematizing" refers not to answering someone else's questions, such as those found at the end of each chapter in the social studies text, but to asking the truly intriguing questions that constantly bombard the minds of learners living in interesting and inviting environments, such as whole language classrooms. Learners ask their own important questions not to collect a bunch of facts and to do well on a test but rather to outgrow themselves and to engage in the delightfully difficult tasks of searching, finding, and reflecting—researching—and then teaching others and moving on to new inquiry.

The teacher has at least two major roles in helping students ask important questions. Frank Smith (1973) made the first role clear when he said that teachers must find out what kids are trying to do and then help them do it. Why would we want to do otherwise? Why would we make life dreary, perhaps miserable, by forcing students to spend their valuable time, energy, and potential working on something perceived as tedious and trivial? Students learn little except that you don't learn anything interesting or valuable in school. So teachers facilitate, within the supportive classroom community, authentic student inquiry. They schedule time for research, they take inquiry seriously, they make sure that learners know they can count on support for their questions from the community of scholars, and they help students learn how to be teachers and resources.

The second role teachers assume is exactly the same one we want students to take on—that of inquirer. Just as pupils are asking important questions, so too are teachers. This doesn't mean being an interrogator or asking questions for which the one right answer is already known. Rather, such inquiry involves teachers' digging into interesting and important matters right along with their students. Teachers question their own intentions; they inquire about their students, about the curriculum, about everything that relates to the community of learners. Such research renews teachers. You can always tell when kids and teachers are grappling with real inquiry: they want to talk about it, they want to show you their data, they want to ask your opinion, they want to tell you what they've learned, and they want to be a resource for others.

Within the community, students who are inquirers and who have firsthand knowledge that might enrich another student's research are encouraged to share that information. They may pass on information directly by offering references for texts and other media resources, ranging from newspaper clippings to songs to photos and other appropriate artifacts. When Kittye Copeland and her students decide on inquiry topics in their multiage classroom, they make a list of the topics and researchers on a large chart. A copy of the list is sent home with an invitation for families to get involved in the students' projects by sharing any expertise, information, or artifacts they might have. The family is not only a resource for their own child but for all researchers in the classroom community.

Classmates help each other as resources for coproducing meaning. By talking, they present tentative information about the topic or theme, and they begin to sort out the substantive from the trivial. Through their talk, they learn to organize information so that they and others can add to it, ask questions about it, make it mean something. Inquirers need each other—kids helping kids—to clarify what they know, don't know, and need to know. A fifth grader, after a long, involved answer to his partner's question, exclaimed in amazement, "I didn't know I knew that!" Learners make each other look a head taller because they have been the supportive resource—someone who asked the right question or made a needed comment at the right time.

Inquirers are also evaluators, critics of their work and of other learners' work. Within a community of scholars the purpose of such evaluation is not to find fault but to help one another build on strengths, to keep momentum going and motivation alive. Sincere learners want sincere criticism. Teachers must help students understand the very sensitive nature of criticism, help them see that constructive evaluations can be powerful learning experiences.

In Kittye's classroom, as the researchers present their inquiry to classmates, the listeners take notes and write suggestions for the researcher. These notes are passed on to the researcher following his or her presentation. The researcher may or may not choose to use these comments to modify the final written report.

Bobbi Fisher (1991) invites her kindergartners to take on the role of teacher during special "child as teacher" days. Since she wants families to get involved in the activity and because the planning is done at home, Bobbi sends the parents a letter explaining the event and listing each child's special day. This is not the run-of-the-mill show and tell; Bobbi and the children talk about their role as resource people. When all the learners gather in a circle to hear the "child as teacher," the presenter tells why and how she selected the topic, tells about the topic, and answers questions. At the beginning of the year,

Bobbi acts as scribe, but later the children take on that responsibility. Often the children illustrate their reports, and everything is displayed on a sharing table or bulletin board. Students bring in special books, artwork, cultural artifacts, collections and hobbies, science experiments, poems, and songs; the possibilities are limitless.

To some extent, the role of collaborator overlaps the roles of inquirer and of resource person. There is, however, a distinction that needs to be made between students' cooperation and their collaboration. The term *cooperation* is often used to describe a process of stating a goal and then figuring out who is going to take on the chores needed to achieve that goal. Usually there is a schedule and there are certain behaviors expected of all participants. For example, a group might work cooperatively on a science project. They decide on or are given the goal of the project by the teacher or the textbook. The children meet to talk about how the task can best be completed. There may be a prescribed series of steps the learners are to take to accomplish the goal. Assignments and due dates are made, and the kids set to work. At the appointed time, they meet and put the pieces together. All students are expected to learn approximately the same things from the experience; they may be tested on "material covered." Their finished product is submitted to someone outside their group to judge and they receive a grade. Unfortunately, students usually leave the experience relatively unchanged, even uninformed.

On the other hand, a group working collaboratively generates its own topic for study and sets its own goals. There is never the assumption that everyone involved in the project will emerge with exactly the same knowledge or feelings about the experience. While students are supporting others in the group, they maintain their own interests and have the right to diverge in order to pursue any aspect of the experience they find significant. It's understood and acceptable that some learners may never reach a major group goal, while others may go far beyond it. Collaboration involves active, shared learning. All learners leave the experience changed.

When three of Carolyn Dye's first graders came together to read an unfamiliar story, the collaborative effort of all three enabled them to construct meaning; that is, to read. The learners pored over the text, hypothesized strategies, negotiated meaning, and "worked" the text for the purpose of understanding. Their intention was to comprehend, and through collaboration, they did exactly that. Nevertheless, they didn't exit the experience as identical triplets; they parted as three learners who shared an event, who gave to it and took away from it different understandings.

The roles of apprentice and of resource/teacher are two sides of the same coin. As resource person to an apprentice, students become teachers in the most caring and giving sense. Apprenticing is natural and expected within the family and in many settings outside the school. In a whole language community it becomes instinctively the right thing to do, as in New Zealand when children arrive in kindergarten at staggered times immediately after their fifth birthday. These newcomers are welcomed by children who are familiar with routines and who have certain information and strategies that the younger students have not yet acquired. These experienced youngsters feel responsible for showing newcomers the ropes. In Kittye Copeland's multiage classroom, we see the same social phenomenon. When Tina helps newcomer Conrad sign up for morning meetings, it is with uncritical acceptance of Conrad's lack of experience. One of the reasons apprenticeships within the classroom community are effective is not because one child is labeled strong and the other weak; rather, it is because the resource student, who may be either younger or older than the apprentice, offers an implicit invitation: *I've been here longer than you, I know how this works, and I'd like to help you* or *I have knowledge and experience that I am expected and happy to share with you.*

The role of representative is fascinating and can best be explained through example. A visitor walked into a fifth-grade classroom that was empty except for two students. Thinking she couldn't get the information she wanted without the teacher, she turned to leave. The two boys stopped her with, "Hi, this is the fifth grade and Mrs. Riley's room. Everyone will be back in about twenty minutes. Are you going to visit us?" The students then proceeded to show the visitor around the room, explaining the projects of various "action groups" and pointing out examples of other kids' work as well as some of their own. All this was done with the confidence of hosts who are proud of and comfortable in their own home. The visitor was so impressed that she later asked the teacher if the boys had been instructed to greet her. The teacher said that at the beginning of the year they had talked about how guests were to be treated, but that as the year progressed, the students felt such ownership of their classroom that the graciousness and confidence had emerged naturally. These boys were representatives of and for their community. They knew what was going on in their room, and perhaps even more important, they knew why these things were happening. They were eager to share their work with the visitor, but just as willing and able to talk about the projects their classmates were involved in. When learners create their own community, they assume responsibility for it and quite naturally take on the role of representative spokesperson for it.

Throughout this discussion of community, we have only briefly mentioned the concept of friendship, even though it is often one of the first words teachers use when they wish for a classroom community: *I wish the kids were kinder to each other. If only they could be friends.* Ironically when the teacher's primary goal is to get the kids to become friends, the relationship may be very slow in coming, or friendship may never exist at all. Such a relationship comes through truly knowing one another, authentically sharing needs as well as strengths, and genuinely investing in the lives of others. Within the community, learners begin to know, trust, and value one other. Some relationships blossom into deep and lasting friendships; many will involve acceptance and respect. Even a natural unfolding of friendship needs a supportive environment and invitations along the way. Without pushing, many teachers invite their students to inquire into the concept of friendship through special stories and even a theme cycle.

Learners Engage in Intellectually Important and Stimulating Experiences

Some teachers see building community and learning as a hierarchy, thinking either, *Once I get my classroom organization in place I'll start on the subject matter* or *I'll get the curriculum going and then we'll work on community building.* But other teachers contend that both content and community are stronger and more natural if they emerge together. Attempting to get math or social studies underway without also trying to develop the spirit of community is to hold off on the socialization of learning. To institute community without the richness of content leads to dry-run exercises in "group work" that kids may perceive as pointless. The reason any classroom exists is to provide a safe and comfortable place to learn. So, from the first day—or even earlier, if the children receive a summer letter from their new teacher—students need to know that important things are going to happen in a secure and supportive classroom that they will help create.

In *Schools of Thought* (1991), Rexford Brown makes a case for creating "thoughtful" learning environments that help students think critically and creatively, solve important problems, and exercise good judgment. He argues that it isn't enough that students master "basic skills." Brown advocates that students must engage in intellectually important and stimulating experiences. He believes that all learners know how to develop an attitude of thoughtfulness. Brown describes what can take place in a community of scholars:

> If you want young people to think, you ask them hard questions and let them wrestle with the answers. If you want them to analyze

something or interpret it or evaluate it, you ask them to do so and show them how to do it with increasing skill. If you want them to know how to approach interesting or difficult problems, you give them interesting or difficult problems and help them develop a conscious repertoire of problem-solving strategies. If you want them to think the way scientists or historians or mathematicians do, you show them how scientists and historians and mathematicians think, and you provide opportunities for them to practice and compare those ways of thinking. (pp. 232–33)

The first thing that needs to be put to students is, What are your questions? Once those questions are asked, teachers and other students help each other engage in the processes of immersion, inquiry, and reflection. They talk about problem-solving strategies; they bring the process of learning to conscious awareness. They talk and they act, unlike in many conventional classrooms where students spend a great deal of unrecoverable time in inactivity, waiting for a directive from the teacher, the textbook, the test—from someone or something outside themselves. In a community of scholars, time is considered a precious commodity. Students are not asked to engage in time-consuming tasks that are little more than a pretense at learning.

When you walk into a classroom, it doesn't take long to determine whether or not kids are thinking, learning, and creating knowledge. If you find students passively enduring a teacher's lecture or filling out endless and pointless worksheets, or you spot two or three kids who have no voice or interest in the topic under consideration, it's likely that what they are learning is that school equals boredom and self-denial. On the other hand, if the classroom is filled with students who are talking about matters of real interest, who are head-over-heels involved in projects that help them create knowledge and make sense of their world, and who are constantly invited to engage in a variety of intellectual endeavors, you can be sure those students are learning that thinking and creating are exciting and worth their attention. Kids will even choose to spend their time involved in these compelling experiences. Teachers like to tell about the first time their students worked right past the dismissal bell or begged to stay in from play time to finish writing a story or to practice a puppet play. For scholarly experiences to be this compelling, learners need the support of the teacher, other students, and the curriculum—they need a community of scholars.

No two whole language classrooms are alike. They all have their own personalities and idiosyncrasies, but as part of the ebb and flow of the life within each classroom we find that there is always a commitment to thinking, learning, and scholarship. This is true because whole language teachers believe that all students can learn—all of them, not just the rich ones or the tidy ones or those with high IQ scores or the ones fluent in English or those with no physical problems. These teachers know that in a nourishing environment, children's intellect and creativity are boundless. Once motivated, the sky's the limit.

Without a doubt, knowing that a teacher believes that you are an intelligent and lovable person is powerful motivation. You even begin to believe it yourself. But what else in a classroom community motivates students to be scholars? There is an untold number of motivating factors that contribute to an intellectually stimulating and rewarding environment, but one is particularly central: a sense of wholeness, a lack of fragmentation. The schedule, the content of study, the learning-teaching strategies and methods, and the learners themselves must be kept intact. Let's consider each of these.

The schedule intrudes and controls the classroom if it is a strict inflexible timetable rather than an aid to organizing for learning and living. Schedules must be part of a routine that helps by suggesting a way of handling time. Are we managing time in the most efficient and productive way or is time (the calendar, the schedule, the clock) managing us? Do we need to get rid of, modify, or combine certain tasks and activities? Should we rethink how we decide which experiences merit more time? When a discussion is going well, can we adjust our schedule in order to extend this thinking time? Are there things that could be done as homework that would free up school time? Perhaps a class committee might conduct a "time audit" and "time interview," wherein they examine how time is spent individually and as a group.

When the content of study, or areas of knowledge, are thought of as Science, Math, Social Studies, Language (all capitalized!) that can be disembodied from the curriculum and neatly mastered in relative isolation, the climate for intellectual pursuit becomes burdensome and the amount of material to be "covered" becomes overwhelming. Brown (1991) says that when the curriculum becomes fractional it

> become[s] too broad for anyone to master all of it, and too shallow for anyone to know anything in depth. This is an inevitable result of the goals-and-objectives, scope-and-sequence approach to organizing knowledge, which breaks any item into dozens of subitems and subsystems. It is what happens when you apply an administrative rationality to a knowledge base that is conceived as a collection of facts and to a teaching technology that is conceived as a means of transmitting facts: you get this huge pile of unrelated, decontextualized facts. Test after test of factual recall reveals that this curriculum does not work. Students cannot remember much, and what

they do recall is superficial and useless. We have long since reached the limits of what we can "shoehorn" into such a curriculum and what we can get out of it. (pp. 237–38)

The learning/teaching strategies and methods must engage and motivate learners so that students exercise a large degree of choice, are encouraged to take intellectual risks, and are constantly invited to research and reflect. The instructional focus is on students' strengths rather than their weaknesses, and "reflective" teaching and learning replace the outmoded concepts of "direct" or "indirect" teaching and learning.

Learners themselves are kept intact; that is, they are not considered one-dimensional. When students are thought of as learning disabled, hearing impaired, poor readers, or nonwriters, they are immediately relegated to a restrictive environment that diminishes not only their abilities and motivations but their curricular opportunities. While teachers need to be aware of information such as right-brain/left-brain theory and learning modality theory, such information must not hinder the intellectual growth of the entire child by failing to consider the learner as a whole human. Students are whole and they use both sides of their brains and all learning modalities; they have many accomplishments and talents, just as they have many needs. When all these factors (schedule, content of study, strategies, the learners themselves) are thought of as a cohesive whole, students are supported in their intellectual and creative pursuits.

Learners' Meanings and Intentions Are Not Limited to the Classroom

A robust classroom community is politically and socially aware. This involves looking both inward at what is happening politically and socially in our own room and outward at what is happening politically and socially in the school, neighborhood, and world—no small task. Because learners' meanings and intentions are influenced by these larger communities, such influences must not be set aside when children enter the classroom. Harris (1989) suggests:

The task facing our students . . . is not to leave one community in order to enter another, but to reposition themselves in relation to several continuous and conflicting discourses. Similarly, our goals as teachers need not be to initiate our students into the values and practices of some new community, but to offer them the chance to reflect critically on those discourses—of home, school, work, the media, and the like—to which they already belong. (p. 19)

Freire (1985) tells us that learners must be able to "situate" what they've learned in school to the outside world and that they must be able to situate knowledge gained outside of school to the classroom. Looking beyond the doors of our classroom doesn't distract from the work of students; rather, it adds purpose and authenticity. This great transcending of knowledge, information, and wisdom is a check on reality that assures genuine learning. A two-way flow of influence between the classroom and the culture and politics of the outside world helps learners experience life as an unfragmented whole. It's a way of making sense of the world and letting the world make sense of the curriculum and the classroom.

Transcending classroom boundaries involves accepting all learners—their language, their culture, and their stories. Members of the student's family are the greatest partners we have in bringing the reality of life outside school into the classroom. In the past we have often been guilty of a one-way information flow to parents; we talked at them, explained procedures to them, and closely directed any input they might offer. We now know two important things: first, not only parents but brothers and sisters, extended family members, even friends and neighbors, can make life and learning richer for our students, thus broadening our resource base; and second, that the relationship between school and home must be mutually supportive, with information flowing in both directions.

Even before the history-making changes in South Africa, Eastern Europe, China, and the former Soviet Union, we have known that our classrooms needed to respond sensitively and humanely to world events. But these life-shaking experiences have caused us to realize that inattention to world affairs is as irresponsible as inattention to classroom affairs. Tearing down the Berlin Wall must mean something to our students, the homeless and destitute in our own country must mean something to our students, the many acts of kindness and selflessness on the part of caring people must mean something to our students. These experiences merit our attention through "morning messages," reading of newspaper accounts, and most of all, discussion and action.

Eighth- and ninth-grade African American students in Holmes County, Mississippi, transcended their classroom boundaries when they conducted a series of interviews with relatives and older friends who had struggled to gain the civil rights that these students took for granted. The students' work resulted in the publication of *Minds Stayed on Freedom: The Civil Rights Struggle in the Rural South* (Youth of the Rural Organizing and Culture Center 1991). Even though the students knew many of those they interviewed, they were unaware before the project of the courage and commitment made by their neighbors and relatives. The dialogue between generations was positive for both groups. The students were awed at the sacrifices of these older friends, and the former activists were gratified that the young people were awakening to the importance of the civil rights movement. The students learned not only about the key figures and events of the struggle, such as bus boycotts, freedom rides, sit-ins, and marches, but they also learned about the history of their own county. They learned that even under slavery, during their community's first settlement in 1833, African Americans began a tradition of resisting domination. By the time the students published the book, they knew a great deal about the economic and political advances and development of their race that were crucial to the success of the civil rights movement, but they had also found out about themselves—about their own stories through their own history and their own future.

The Courage to Try

As more teachers and students share their stories about building classroom communities, we get a sense of the enormous amount of courage needed to create such an extraordinary place. A teacher recently commented that when she began to accept a whole language philosophy, she thought it was exciting but very frightening. Now that she is committed to building a democratic community of learners, life in the classroom is even more exciting and, as you might suspect, even scarier. But a growing number of teachers who have summoned the courage to try, tell us that despite the inevitable mishaps along the way, the journey is one that no teacher or student should forgo.

References

Brown, Rexford G. 1991. *Schools of thought: How the politics of literacy shape thinking in the classroom.* San Francisco: Jossey-Bass.

Cazet, Denys. 1990. *Never spit on your shoes.* New York: Orchard.

Fisher, Bobbi. 1991. *Joyful learning: A whole language kindergarten.* Portsmouth, NH: Heinemann.

Freire, Paulo. 1972. *Pedagogy of the oppressed.* New York: Continuum.

Harris, Joseph. 1989. The idea of community in the study of writing. *College Composition and Communication, 40,* 11–22.

McClester, Cedric. 1985. *Kwanzaa: Everything you always wanted to know but didn't know where to ask.* New York: Gumbs & Thomas.

Peterson, Ralph. 1992. *Life in a crowded place: Making a learning community.* Portsmouth, NH: Heinemann.

Schwartz, Susan & Pollishuke, Mindy. 1991. *Creating the child-centered classroom.* Katonah, NY: Richard C. Owen.

Silverstein, Shel. 1974. *Where the sidewalk ends.* New York: Harper & Row.

Smith, Frank. 1973. Twelve easy ways to make reading difficult. In Frank Smith (Ed.), *Psycholinguistics and reading* (pp. 183–196). New York: Holt, Rinehart & Winston.

Speare, Elizabeth G. 1983. *The sign of the beaver.* Boston: Houghton Mifflin.

Watson, Dorothy, Burke, Carolyn & Harste, Jerome. 1989. *Whole language: Inquiring voices.* New York: Scholastic.

Winkelmann, Carol L. 1991. Social acts and social systems: Community as metaphor. *Linguistics and Education, 3,* 1–29.

Youth of the Rural Organizing and Culture Center. 1991. *Minds stayed on freedom: The civil rights struggle in the rural South.* Boulder, CO: Westview Press.

Afterword

Helping to compile this book has been one of the most humbling experiences of my life. How could I risk being so presumptuous as to offer these pieces, descriptions, vignettes, definitions, and stories to other teachers who are quite possibly far more advanced in their thinking about learning and teaching than I am? Perhaps the answer lies in one word within the question: *risk.* I'm a risk taker and a learner.

I'm willing to take risks because through the years I've come to trust other learners. I'm willing to take risks because I'm confident that my thoughts, as made public through my writing, will be received in the same spirit in which they are offered—with a desire to grow. I'm willing to take risks because I never write alone; there were dozens of you in my head as we collaboratively composed all the pieces found here.

I have on occasion throughout my career turned some fast corners, made shifts and changes that I consider breathtaking and exciting; at other times my movements and growth have been painstaking and tedious. But lightning quick or frustratingly slow, the journey is always in the company of others; it is far more interesting to go adventuring with students, friends, and colleagues.

So it is with writing; if the stories in this volume are told well or if the messages don't make it, I share the credit and blame with my collaborators. I'm comfortable making that statement because whole language teachers are so good at taking threads from their own experiences and weaving together the thin spots for others. I know I'll have help from the heads and hearts of smart colleagues as our work is read.

This book has not been compiled to dazzle; nothing could be further from my ability or intention. Rather, it is an invitation given with great respect and admiration for other learners. This teacher holds no greater hope than that ideas from these pages will encourage other teachers to continue the story. As in most artifacts that emerge from the influence of a whole language philosophy, this afterword can be another beginning.

Dorothy J. Watson:
A Brief Curriculum Vitae

Experience in Teacher Education

University of Missouri-Columbia, Department of Curriculum and Instruction, 1977–present. Professor. 1995–1996, Chair.

University of Houston-Victoria, College of Education, 1973–1977. Associate Professor.

Wayne State University (Detroit), 1970–1973. Instructor and Reading Research Assistant.

Kansas City Public Schools and University of Missouri-Kansas City, 1968–1970. Director, National Teacher Corps Program.

Kansas City Public Schools, 1955–1968. Teacher and language arts coordinator.

Education

Wayne State University. Ph.D. (Curriculum and Instruction) 1973.

University of Missouri-Kansas City. M.A. (Education) 1964.

Park College (Missouri). B.A. (Psychology) 1952.

Honors and Awards (selected)

The College of Education, University of Missouri–Columbia, Citation of Merit Award, 1996.

University of Missouri, William T. Kemper Fellowship for Teaching Excellence, 1995.

International Reading Association, Invited Author, Distinguished Reading Educator, 1994.

Whole Language Umbrella, Lifetime Membership Award, 1994; Scholarship and Leadership Award, 1993.

International Reading Association, Alpha Upsilon Honor Scholar Award, 1993 (given for scholarship and for personal and professional leadership in the field of language arts).

International Reading Association, Teacher Educator Award, 1988.

Books Published (selected)

Allen, P. David & Watson, Dorothy (Eds.). 1976. *Findings of research in miscue analysis*. Urbana, IL: National Council of Teachers of English.

Goodman, Yetta M., Watson, Dorothy J. & Burke, Carolyn L. 1987. *Reading miscue inventory: Alternative procedures*. New York: Richard C. Owen.

Watson, Dorothy (Ed.). 1987. *Ideas and insights: Language arts in the elementary school*. Urbana, IL: National Council of Teachers of English.

Watson, Dorothy, Burke, Carolyn & Harste, Jerome. 1989. *Whole language: Inquiring voices*. New York: Scholastic.

Goodman, Yetta M. & Watson, Dorothy. 1980. *Reading strategies: Focus on comprehension*. New York: Holt, Rinehart, & Winston.

Offices In Professional Organizations

International Whole Language Umbrella: President, 1989–1991.

Center for Expansion of Language and Thinking: President, 1980–1983: Board of Directors, 1972–1990.

National Council of Teachers of English, Commission on Reading: Director, 1985–1987.

Consultant and Speaker

Dorothy Watson has spoken at conferences and universities, conducted workshops, and provided consultation to school districts and departments of education in dozens of states of the United States and several provinces of Canada, as well as several other countries, including Australia, Greece, Hong Kong, Sierra Leone, Kenya, Brazil, and Sweden.